Make
EVERY
day
CREATIVE

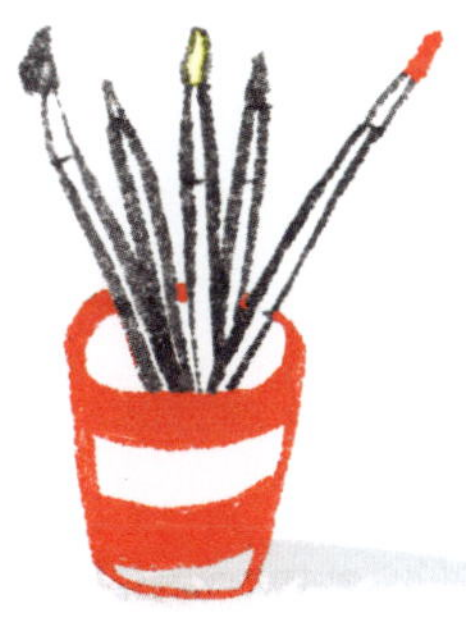

ABOUT THE AUTHOR

Author of the best-selling *Let's Make Some Great Art* series of books, Marion Deuchars is a Scottish-born award-winning illustrator with a globally recognizable style. Her influential hand lettering and illustration work has been used in campaigns from Samsung and HP to posters for Formula 1 and stamps for the Royal Mail. Her books have won six international awards for design and illustration. She is a member of the Alliance Graphique International and A Royal Designer for Industry. Deuchars lives in North London with her husband and two children.

www.mariondeuchars.com

THANK YOU

I could not have written this book without acknowledging some of the great teachers who have helped me along the way. I hope I've mentioned many of these teachers and artists in this book. Special recognition goes to my tutors at the Royal College of Art, including Quentin Blake and Dan Fern. The philosophy of that course, which emphasized finding your own voice and nurturing curiosity, has been very influential. I'd also like to thank Angus Hyland, my husband and guiding light, and also Zara Larcombe, Roly Allen, Sara Goldsmith, Felicity Awdry, Vanessa Green at the Urban Ant Ltd, Elizabeth Sheinkman PFD, and Henrik Kubel of A2/SW/HK for the use of Typewriter font.

MARION DEUCHARS

MAKE EVERY DAY CREATIVE

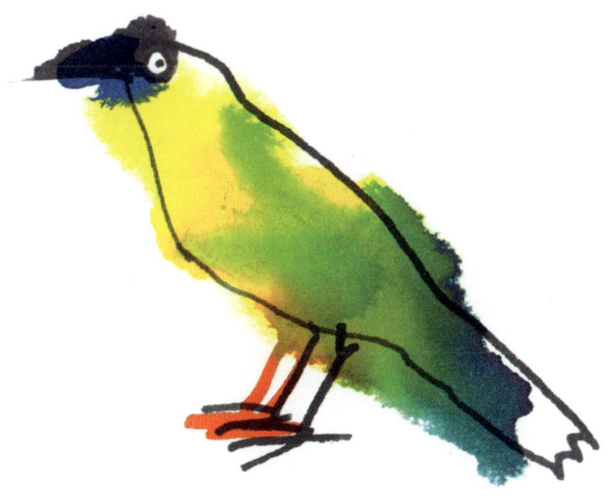

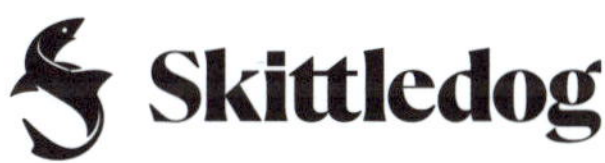

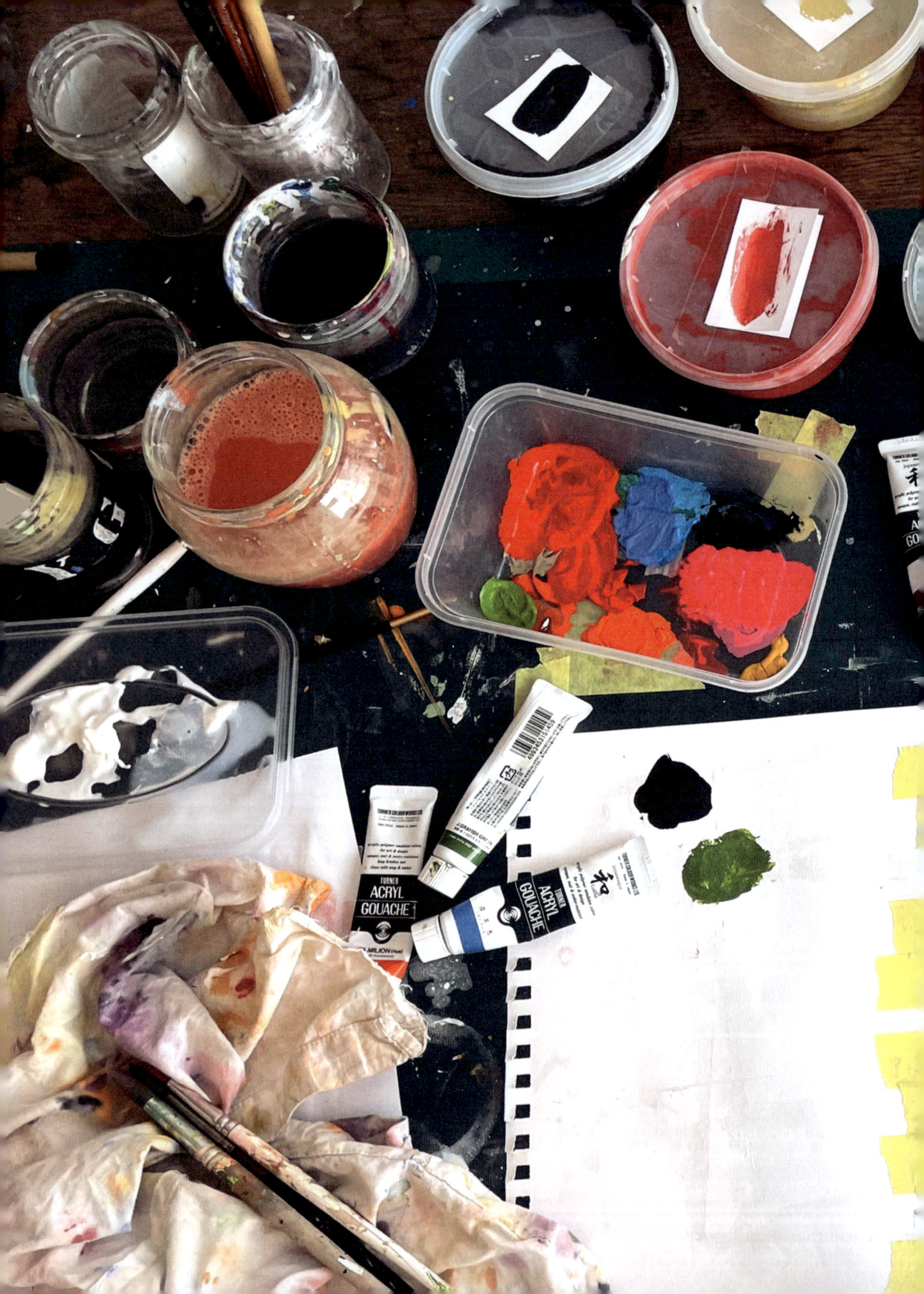

TURNER
ACRYL
GOUACHE
TURNER
ACRYL
GOUACHE

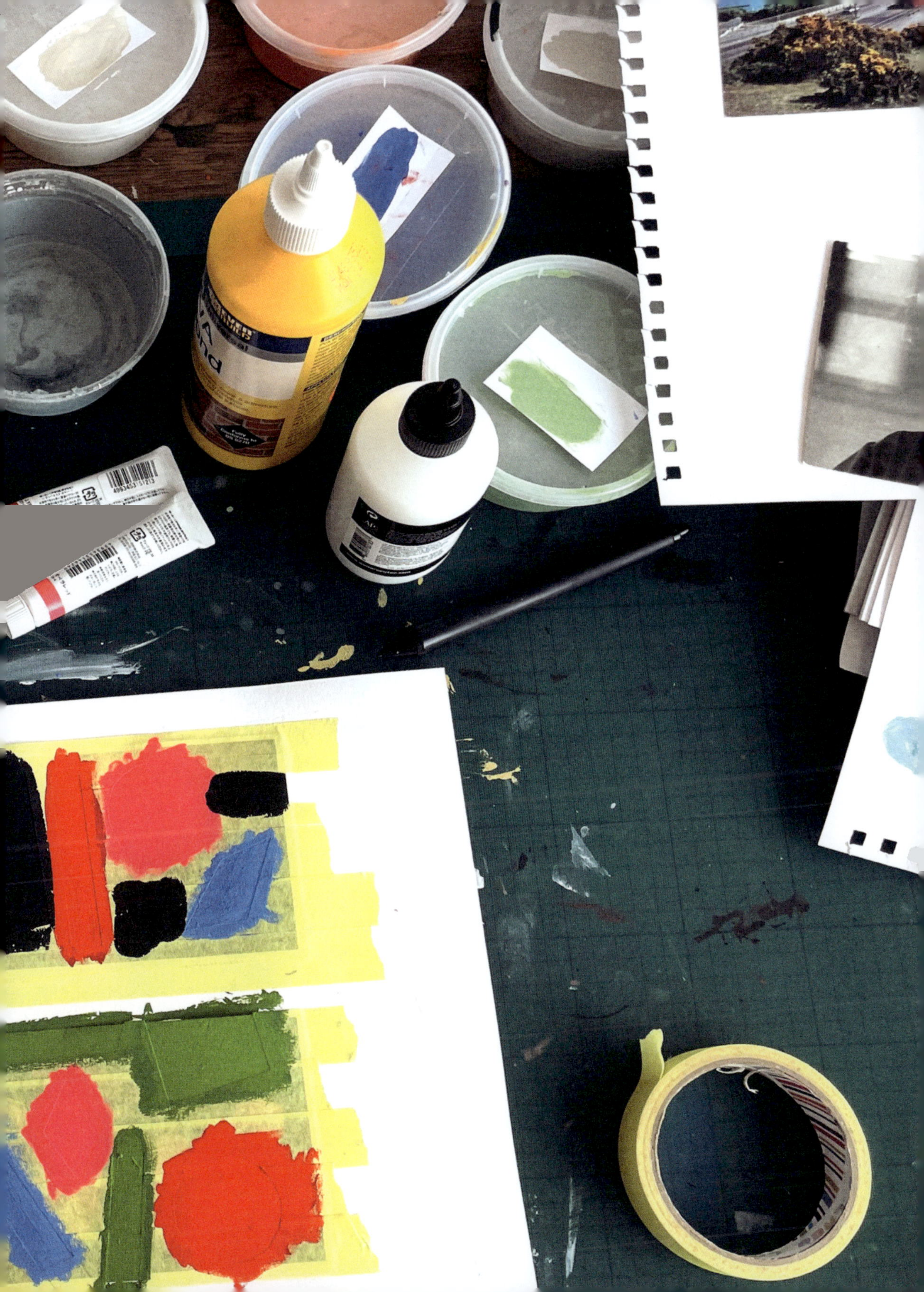

CONTENTS

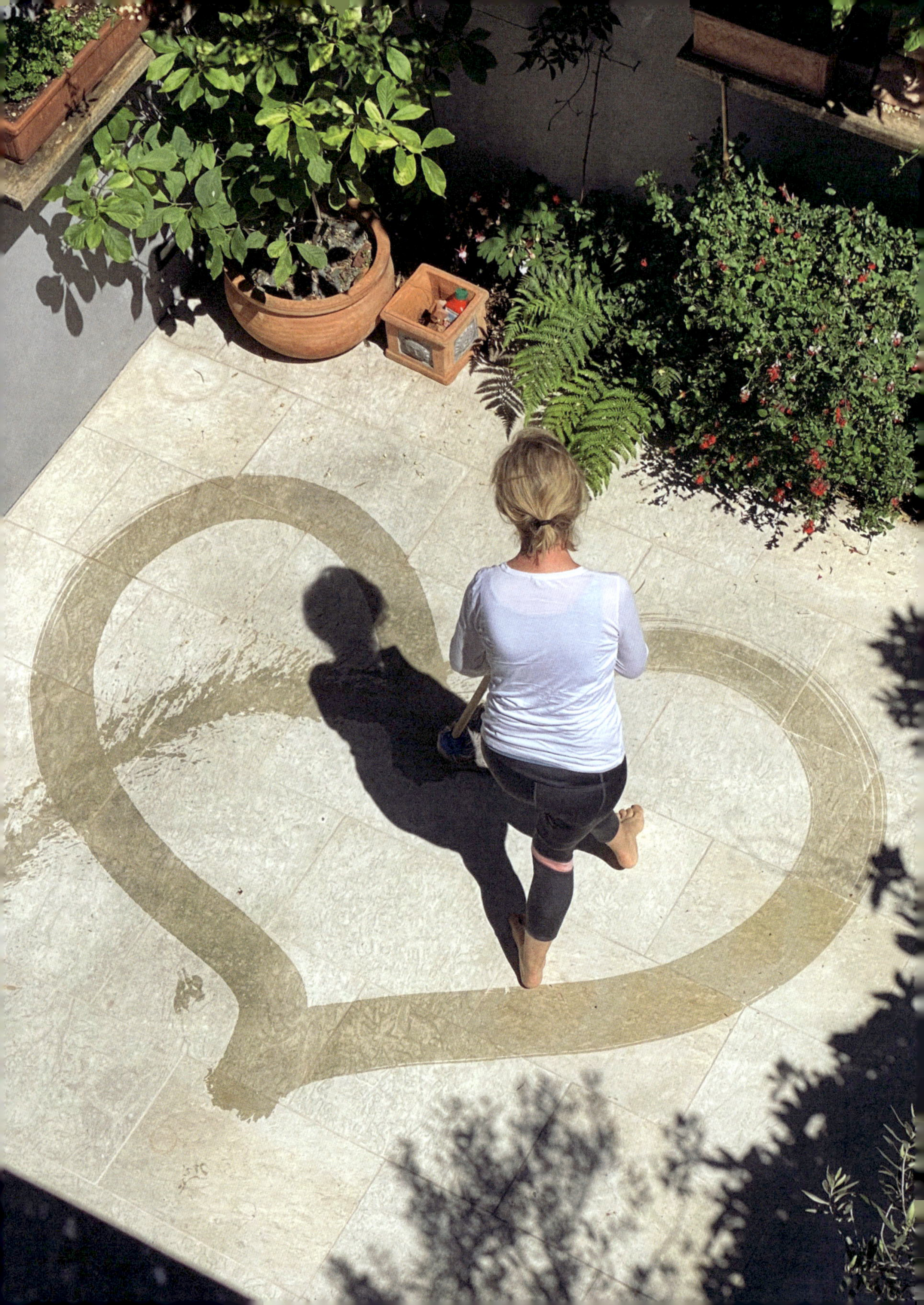

ART ANYONE CAN DO

Everyone is born creative, but it's easy to doubt our abilities. The following pages can help awaken and nurture the artist in you. In my own artistic journey over the last 25 years, I've come to realize that there are three things at the core of my creative process: curiosity, observation and play.

Curiosity is the spark that ignites creativity. It is the process of opening yourself up to new ideas, perspectives and ways of thinking. It lays the groundwork for experimentation. Observation is the art of truly seeing, not just looking. Pay closer attention to the world around you, especially the everyday, and you can uncover the extraordinary hidden in the ordinary. Play is exploring without the constraints of fear or the burden of expectations. It's about wholeheartedly embracing mistakes and reconnecting to your inner child's sense of wonder.

The most challenging part is taking the first step, but it's also the simplest. The artist Jasper Johns expressed this idea as 'Take an object / Do something to it / Do something else to it.' Think of this book as your guide. Flick through the pages, find an image or idea that catches your attention, and start from there. You can do this daily, weekly or at your own pace.

The first four exercises in the book require only paper and pencil, making them an easy place to begin. And once you've started, keep going. Take a daily walk and focus on a single colour or look up at cloud patterns. Keep a small notebook and pencil handy to capture snippets of conversation, captivating faces or unusual sounds. These habits will help fuel your creative journey. When you find yourself stuck or blocked, look for the yellow pages – they're your creative coach, offering a helping hand. You can make every day creative. Start with this one.

PENCIL WARM-UP

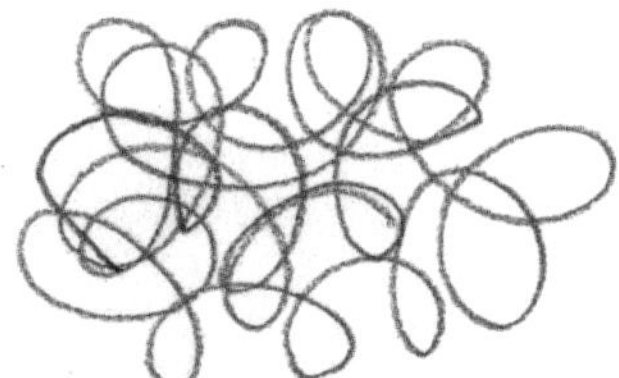

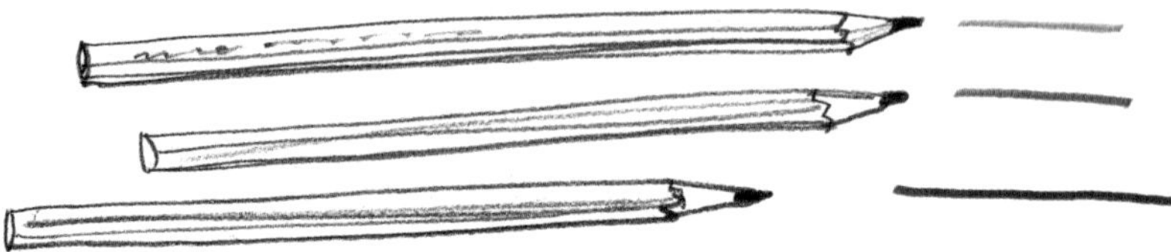

THE BASIC TOOL

Sometimes all you need is a pencil and a piece of paper and you can create an entire world! However, this can also be a daunting starting point, so it's good to start with a warm-up instead. Grab some pencils with different levels of hardness: HB is regular, H is hard, B is soft, 6B is very soft. Don't aim to draw anything specific – just doodle and enjoy it. Take a moment to appreciate the versatility of the humble pencil.

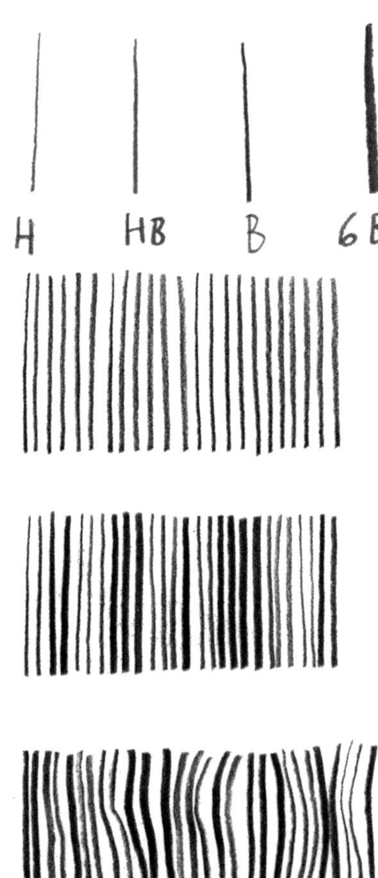

Creative exercise

Try these:

1. Draw close straight lines, then vary the tone and add wobbly ones.
2. Crosshatch for tone: overlap vertical, horizontal and diagonal lines.
3. Shade dark to light.
4. Fill a page with doodles and line play.

Creative inspiration

The line drawings of Paul Klee and Julie Mehretu.

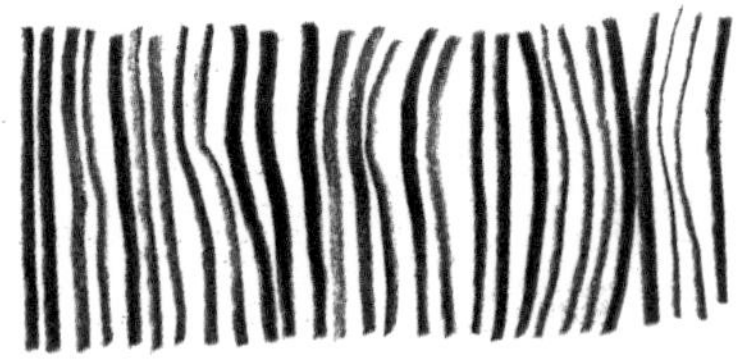

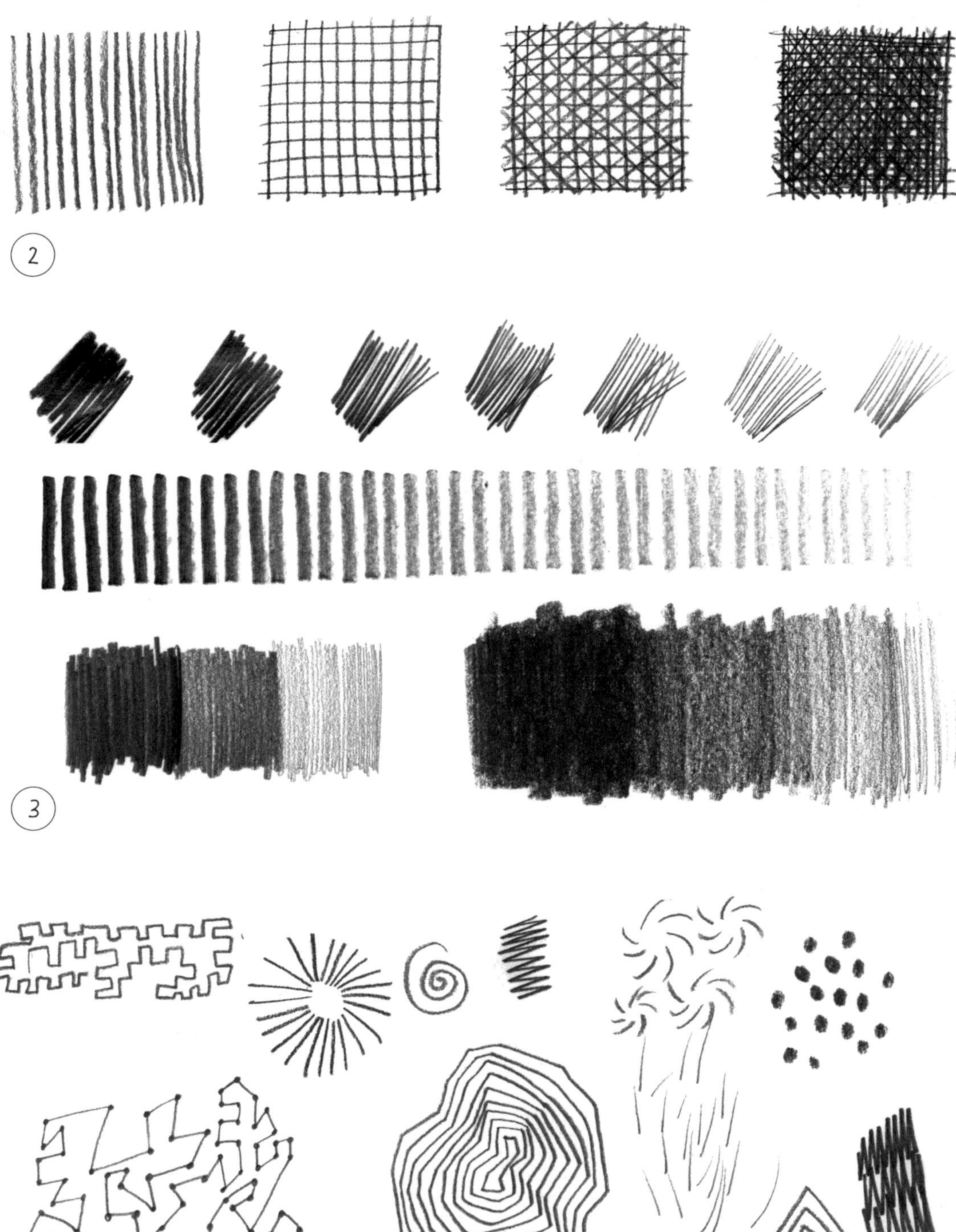

2

3

4

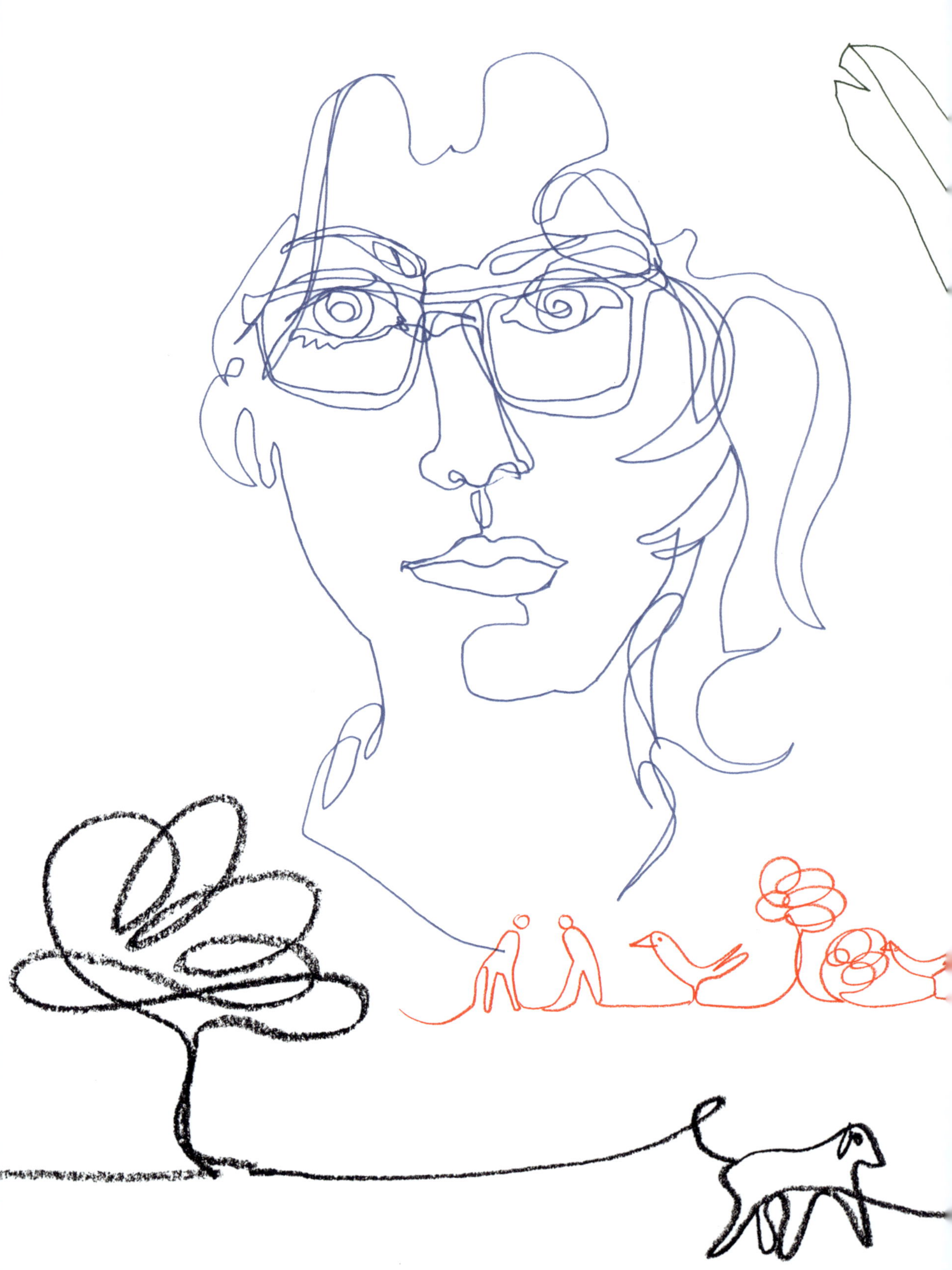

TAKE A LINE FOR A WALK

CONTINUOUS LINE DRAWING

Draw some objects around you or from your imagination using a continuous line in pen or pencil. Don't lift your pen until the drawing is complete. This promotes fluid and intuitive drawing, and demands your full attention, which can make it a meditative experience. It's also lots of fun, plus the unexpected results can help your drawing confidence.

Creative exercise

Using a mirror, draw a continuous line self-portrait. Start with a three-minute drawing, then do a ten-minute drawing. This exercise forces you to observe carefully, promotes hand–eye coordination, and boosts trust in your instincts.

Creative inspiration

The drawings of Paul Klee, Quentin Blake and Shantell Martin.

DRAW BIG, DRAW SMALL

CHANGE SCALE

Select a small item nearby. Enlarge it on the largest paper available, aiming to fill the page. Charcoal or brush and ink work better than a pencil. David Hockney talks about drawing as 'an enhanced way of looking', and this exercise really makes you look. I thought I knew what a pencil sharpener looked like until I started trying to draw it.

Creative exercise

Draw tiny human figures in pen or pencil. Small size focuses effort and using simple media imposes limits. People don't stand straight – they lounge, sway, slouch. Capture movement for realistic characters. I used London street photos for these drawings.

Creative inspiration

The work of William Kentridge and Andrea Bowers.

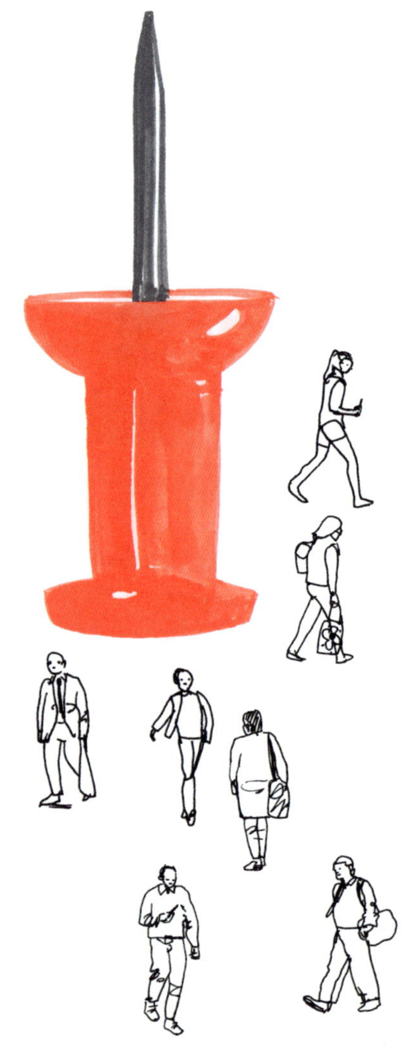

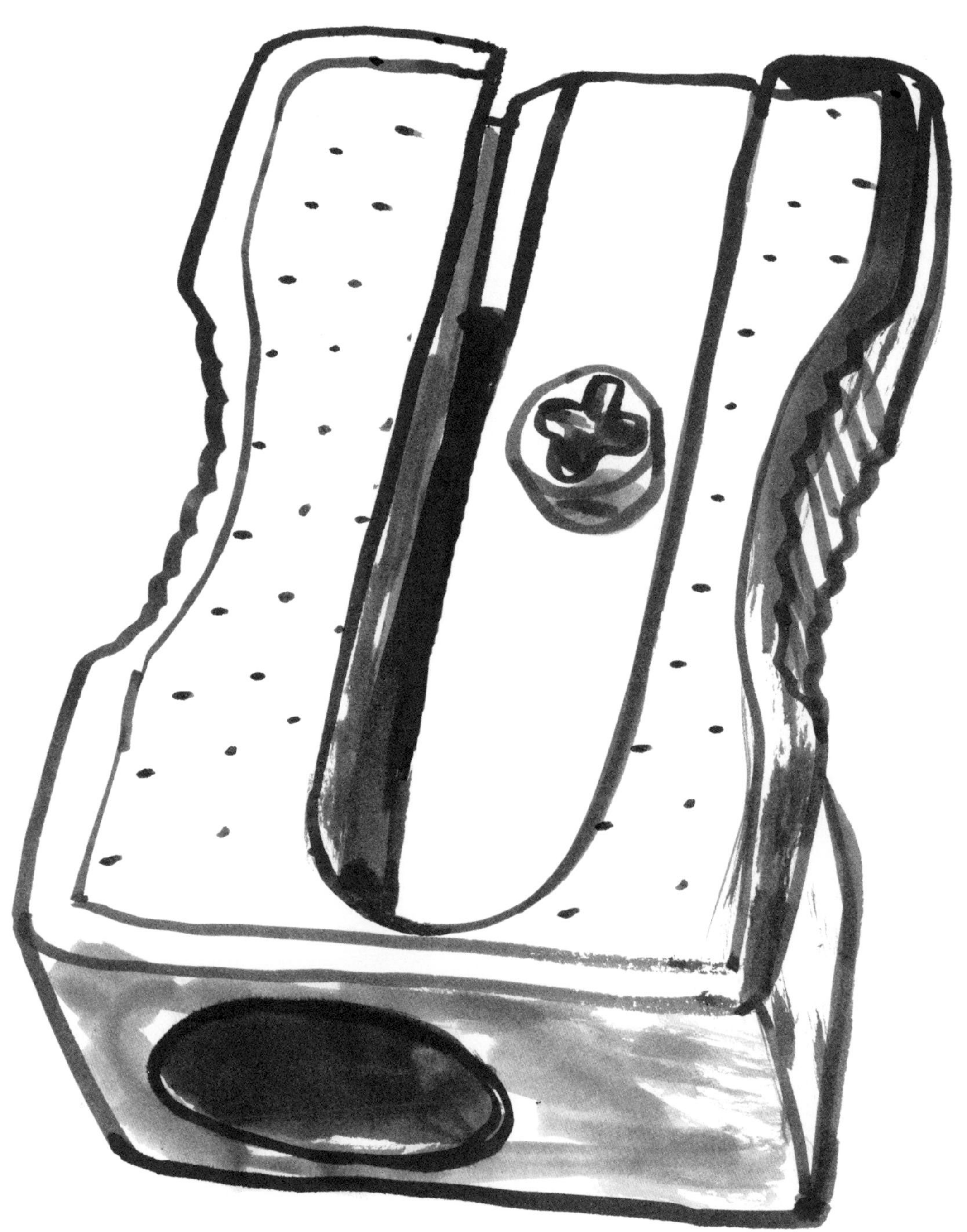

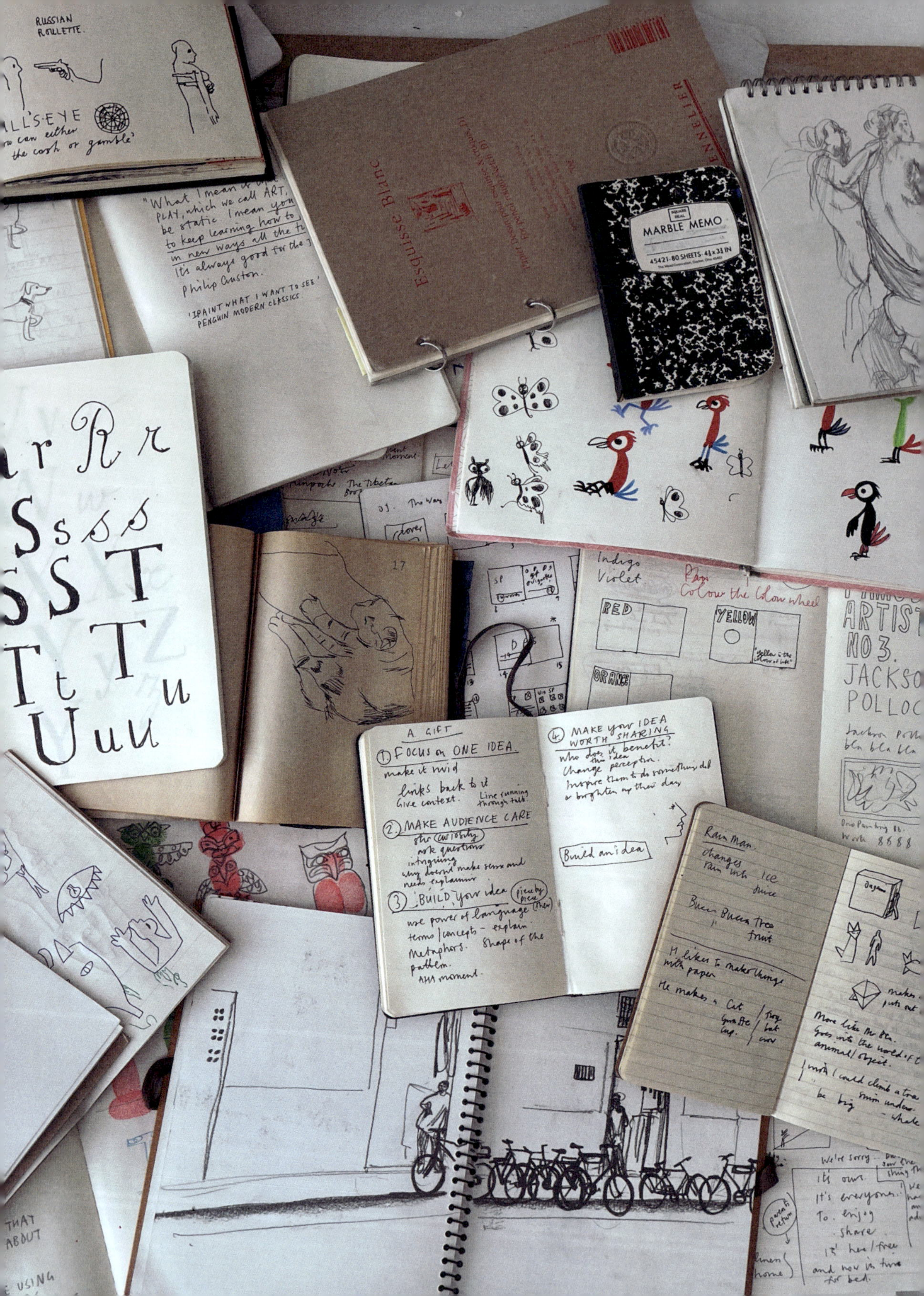

SKETCH BOOK

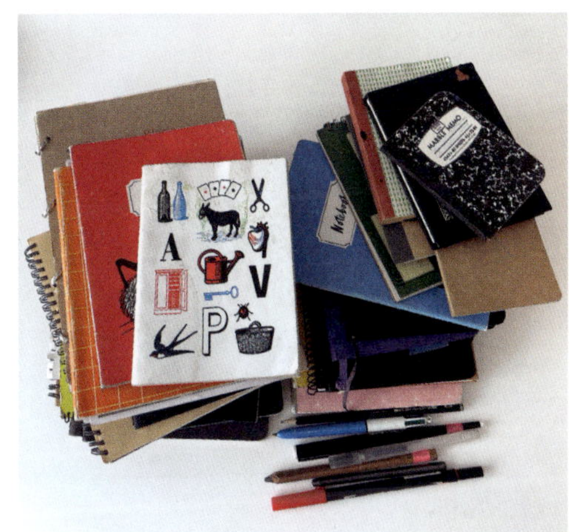

DAILY PRACTICE

I'm rarely without a sketchbook or notebook. It's not a precious thing, and I don't necessarily make beautiful drawings in it, but it is a way of putting down my thoughts, ideas and observations. Sketchbooks can also act as a visual diary. I love that mine often include shopping lists, dentist appointments and general things to do. To make art it's important to fill up your 'well of ideas' and this is a great place to start. Most things I've made or created have grown from a note or sketch in one of these books.

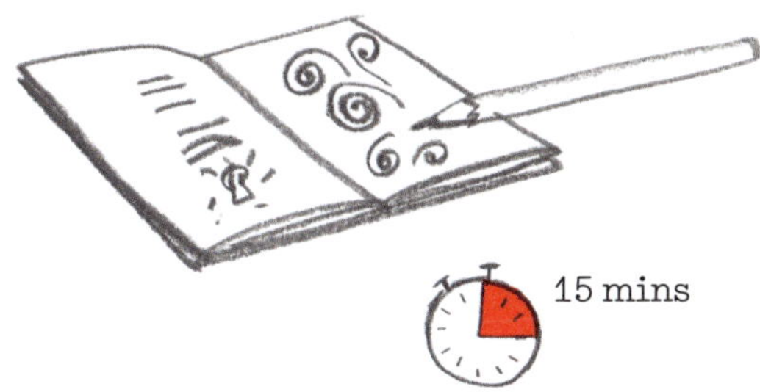

15 mins

Creative exercise

Spend 15 minutes drawing or writing in your sketchbook every day for a week. Don't worry if it's not 'important' – doodles, marks, collages or even descriptions of movies or books are great. The act of documenting is the important part.

Creative inspiration

The sketchbooks of Ed Fella and Frida Kahlo.

Make a PLAY DESK

Make a space in your home for creativity.
It can be a room, a corner, a desk or a box, but it
has to be yours. I have a desk I call my 'play desk'.
It has many different paints, pens, pencils,
coloured pencils, crayons, etc. Working in this way,
with found materials, pigments, sticks and drawing
implements of all descriptions, is something
humans have done for millennia. Brian Eno said that
'children learn through play, but adults play through art …
I don't think we stop playing. I think we just carry on
doing it, but we do it through this thing called art.'

CIRCLE PRINTS

PRINTING WITH LIDS

I really like to print from recycled things. If I can ink it, I'll print from it. Here, I collected lots of different lids from jars and bottles, dipped them into saucers of paint and ink and pressed them down on to a white sheet of paper. The solid circles are printed from the top of the lids, the linear ones from the underside. Give it a try, printing the lighter colours first, slowly building up layers, and adding the darker colours on top.

Creative exercise

Paint a design directly on to a jar lid. Press paper on to the lid to transfer the paint and create a unique monoprint.

Creative inspiration

The work of Sonia Delaunay, Sophie Taeuber-Arp, and Howardena Pindell.

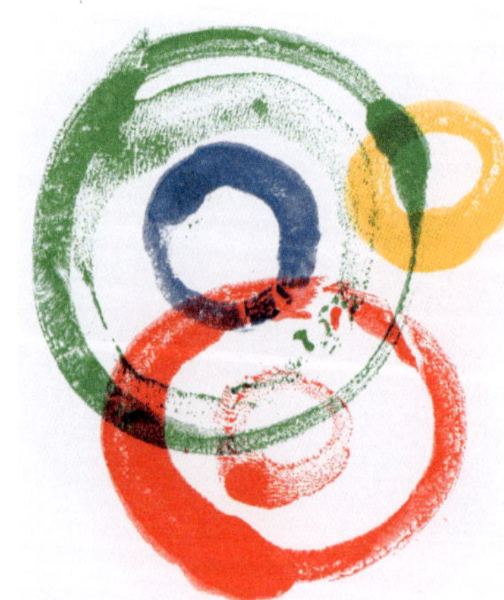

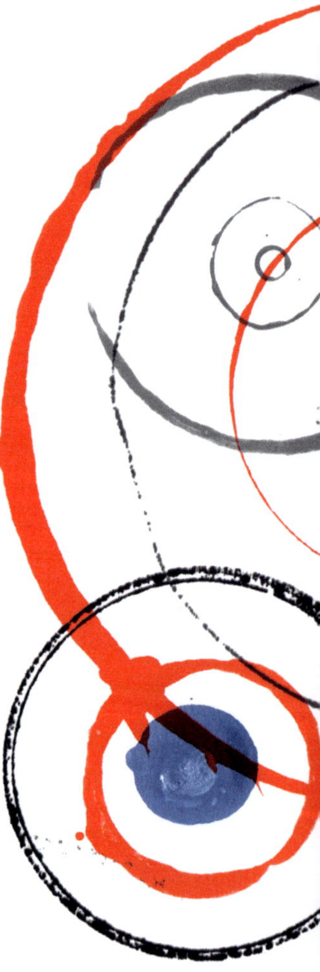

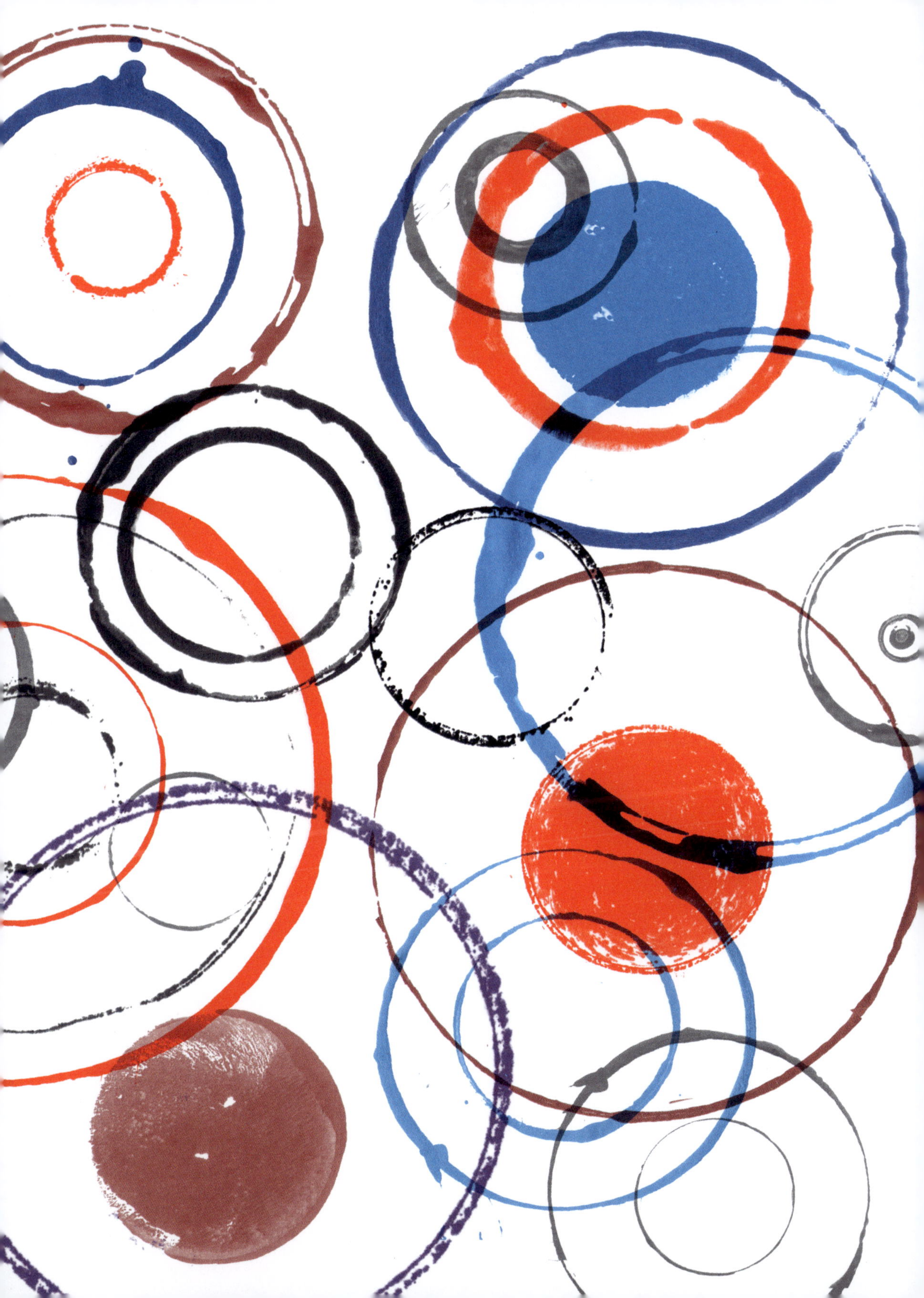

BRUSH LOVE

MAKE YOUR OWN BRUSH

I had as much fun making these brushes as I did using them. Collect flowers, grasses, and things around the house, and attach them to sticks, using tape, string or elastic bands. I've used a bamboo stick from the garden, cut into roughly 15cm (6in) lengths with secateurs.

From left to right: paper clips, plant, grass, newspaper, dried bamboo leaf, wool, stalks, cardboard, cotton buds, rosemary, daisies, denim, leaf.

Creative exercise

Dip your handmade brushes into ink or paint and try to draw with them. On the following pages you can see how I've used mine to make some marks and hand lettering. The unpredictability is what makes these brushes interesting!

Creative quickie

Take an old household brush and cut the bristles to make it wonky. Dip in ink and make some marks.

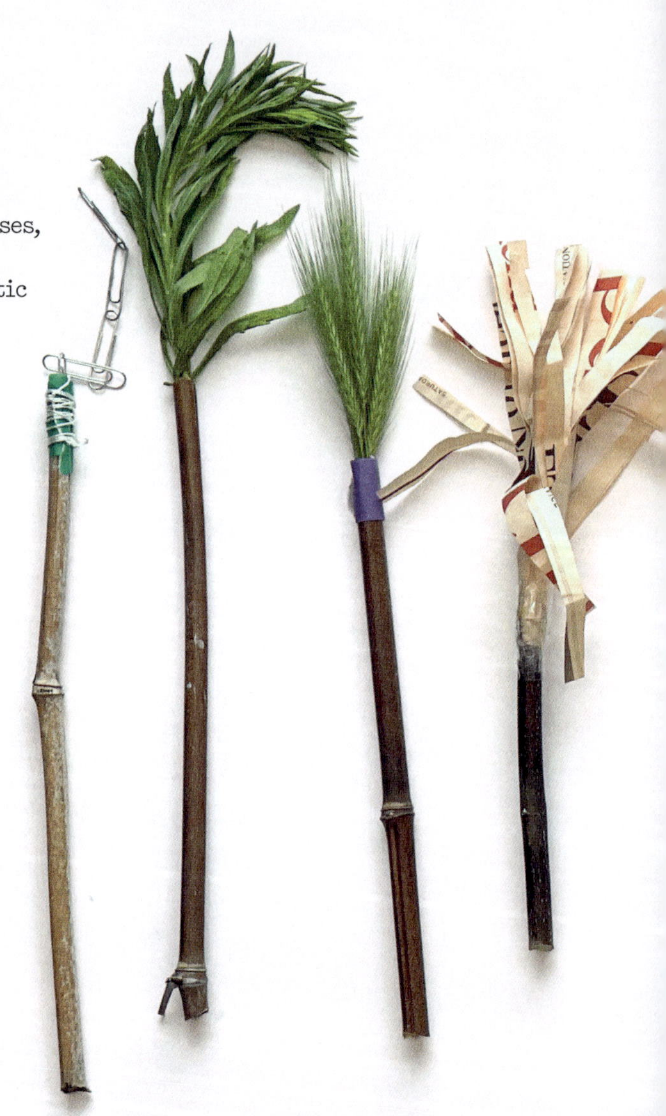

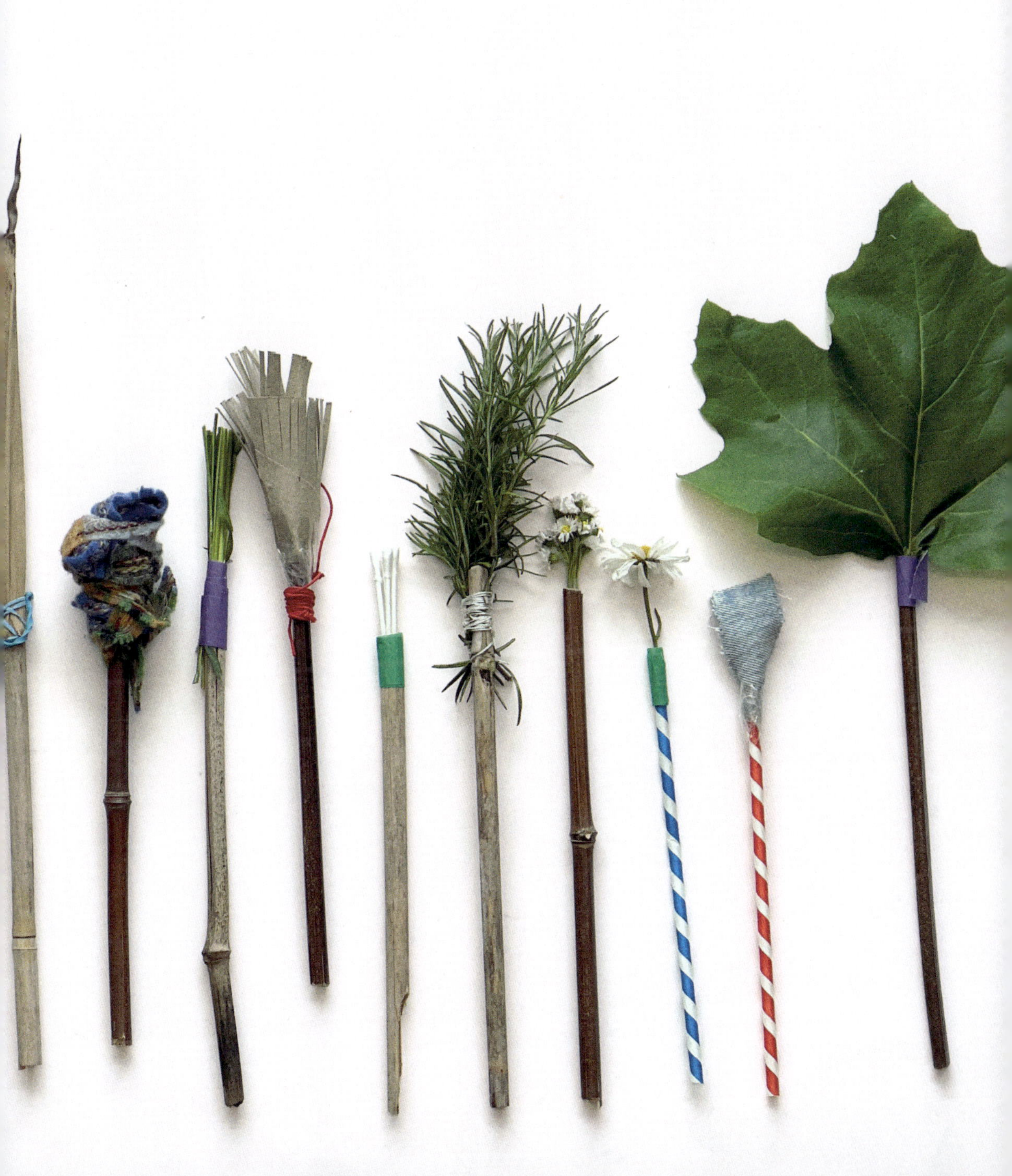

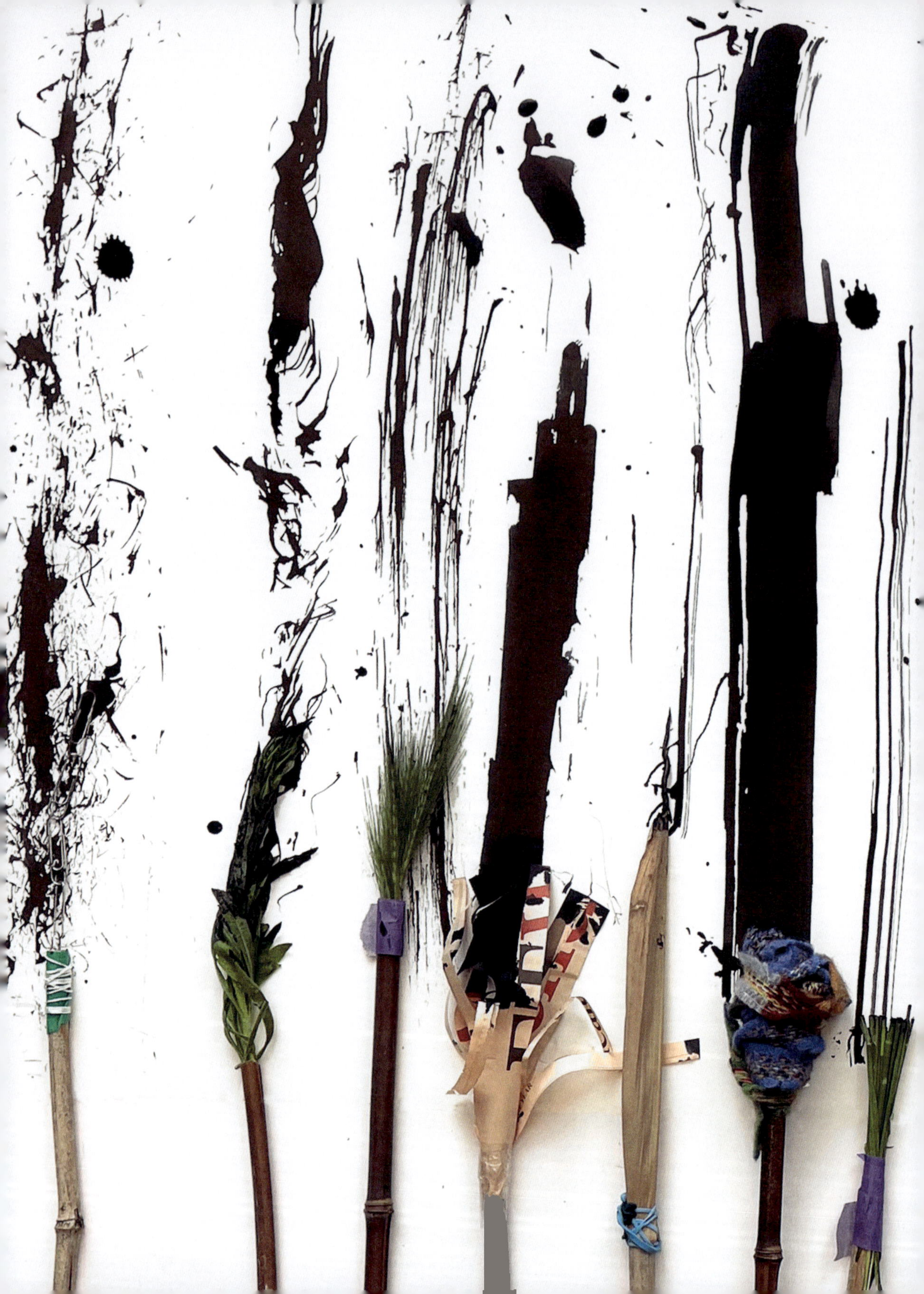

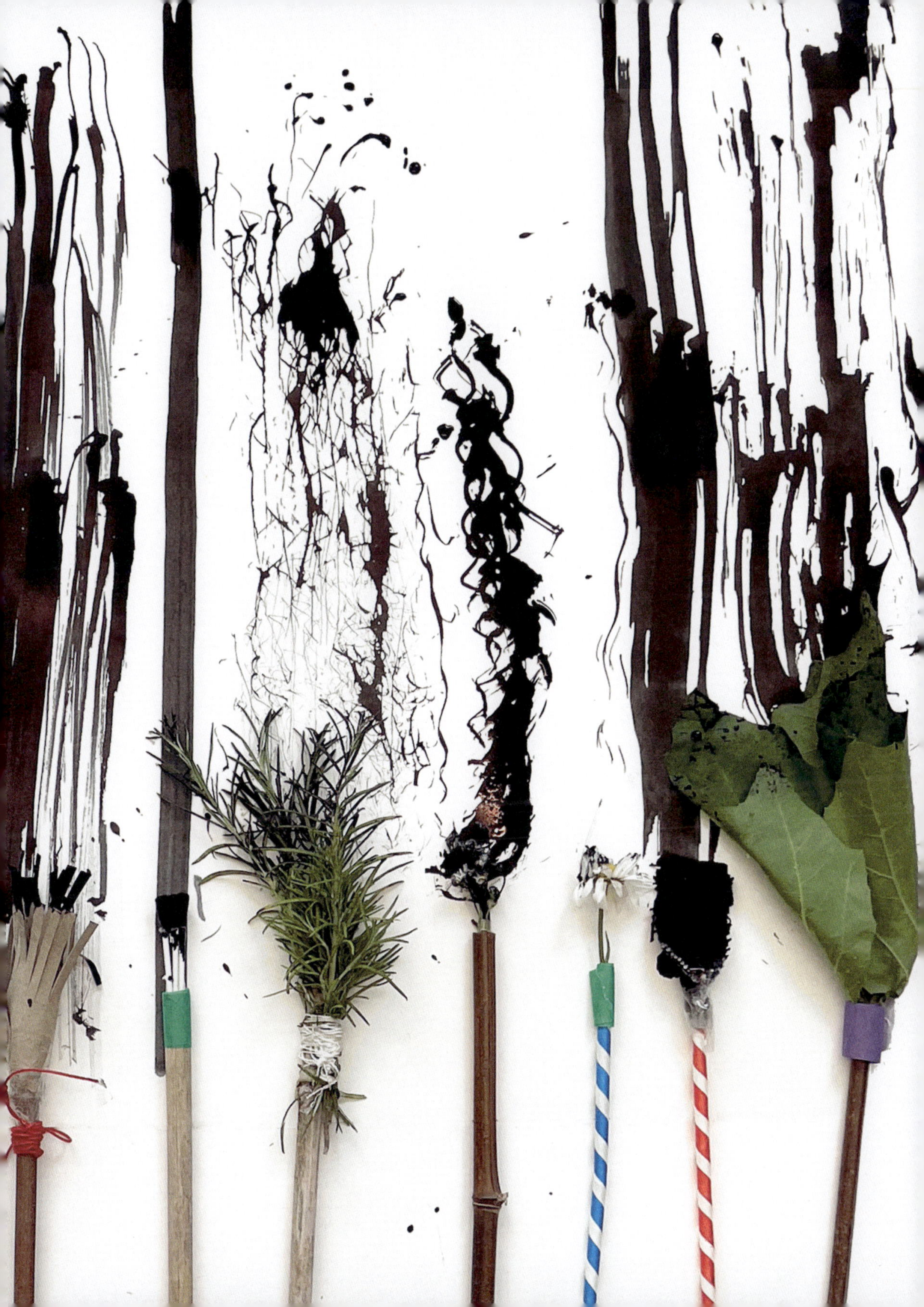

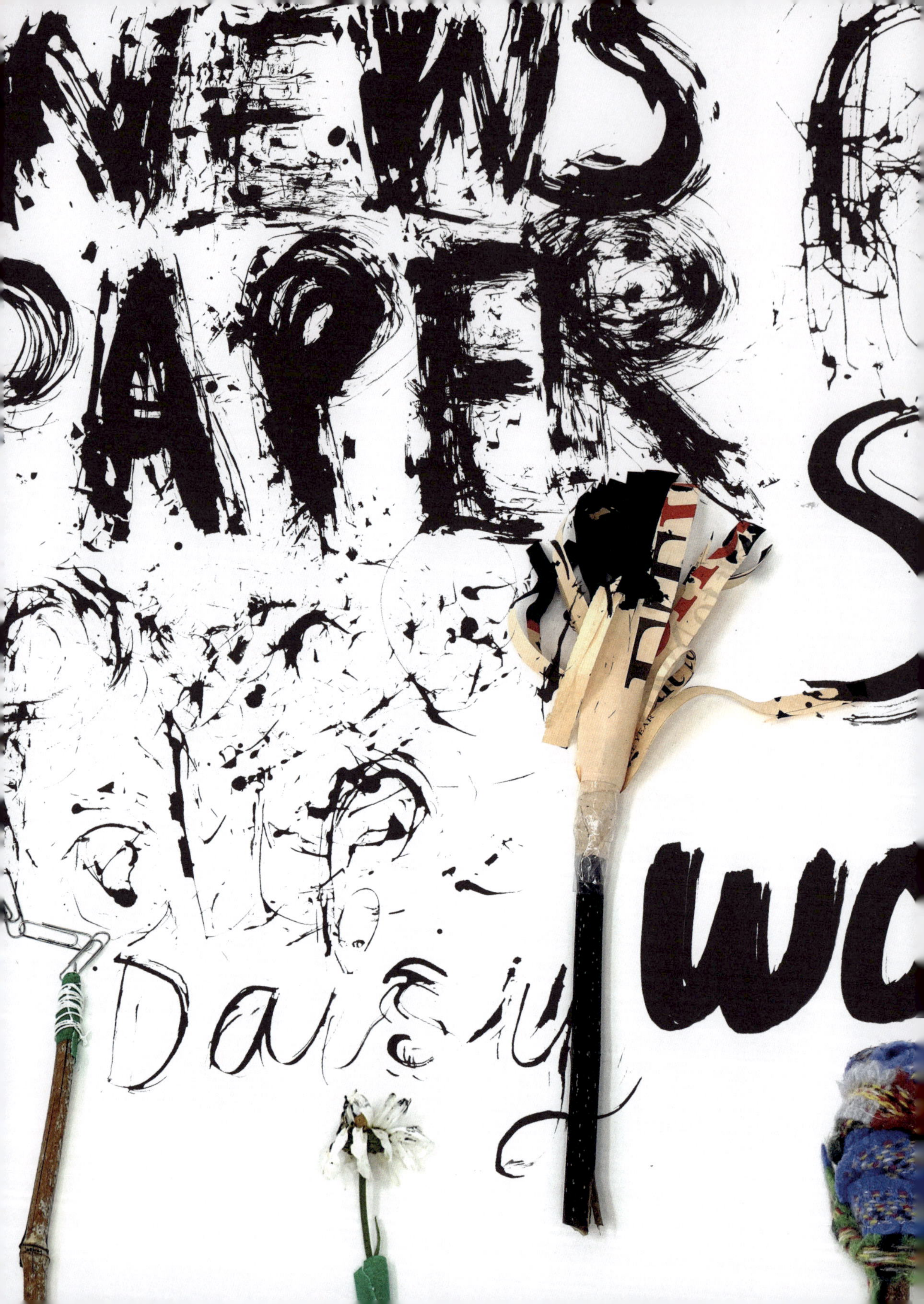

NEWS
PAPERS
Daisy

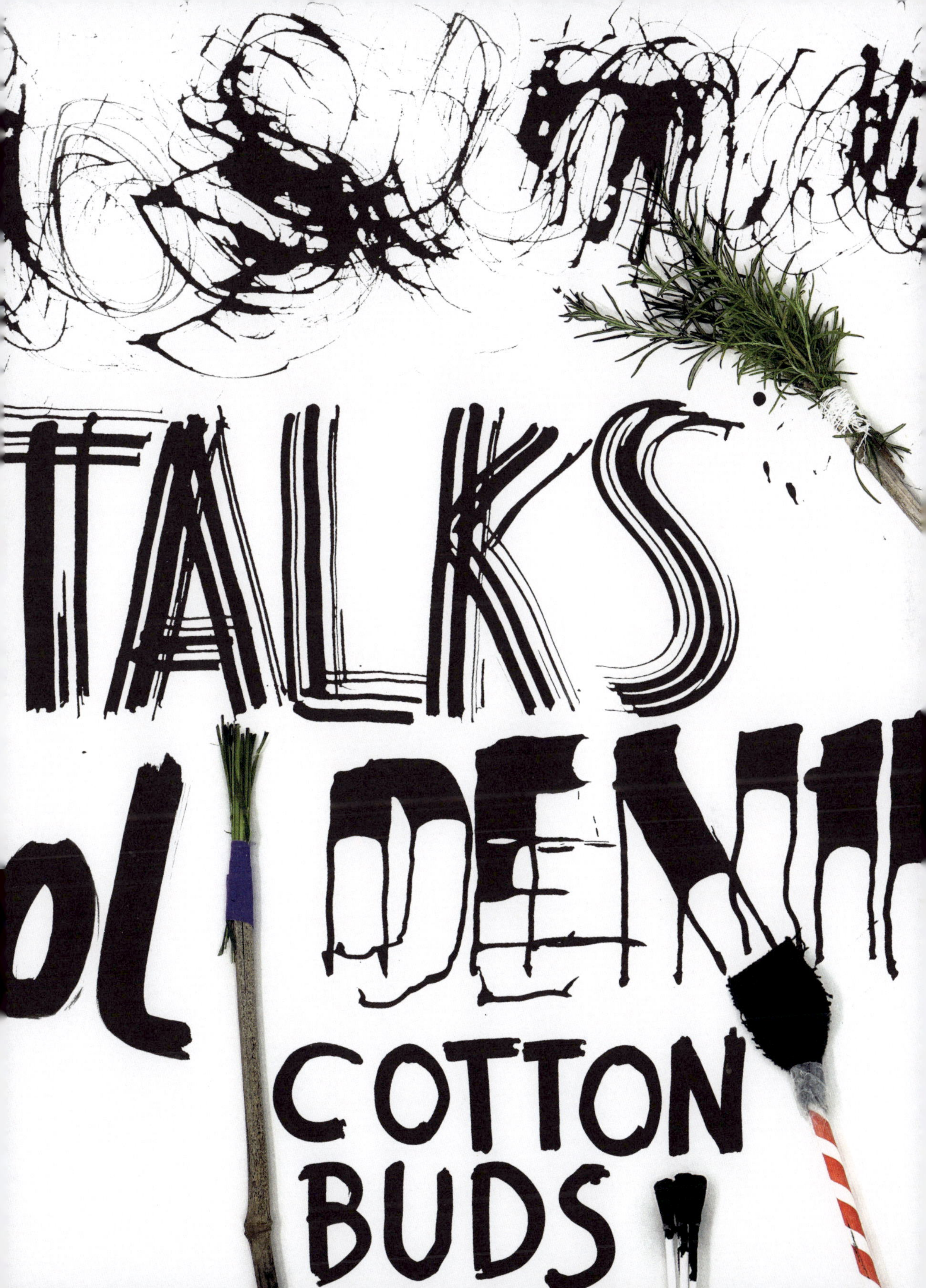
TALKS
COTTON
BUDS

PAPER CUT

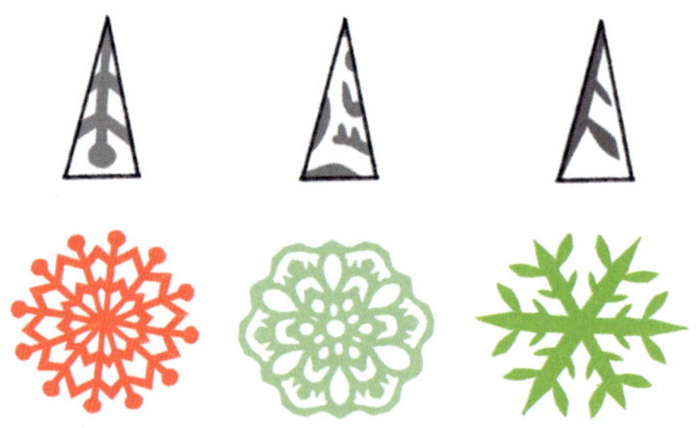

NOT JUST A SNOWFLAKE

As a child, I loved making paper snowflakes, and there's no reason to stop as an adult. This activity is universally engaging and great for concentration and dexterity. Beginners can start with basic patterns, while those that are more adept can experiment with intricate designs. The beauty is their uniqueness – no two designs are ever the same.

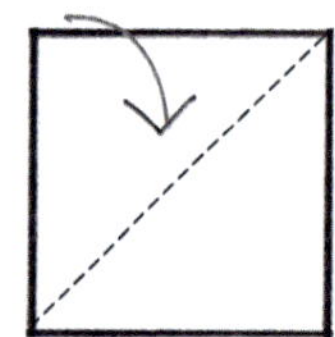

1. Fold over a square of thin paper to make a triangle.

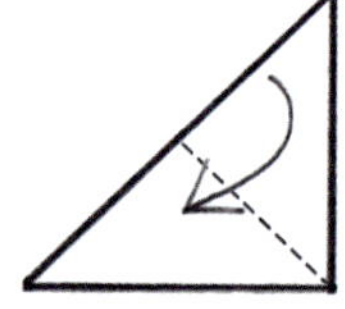

2. Fold in half again to make a smaller triangle.

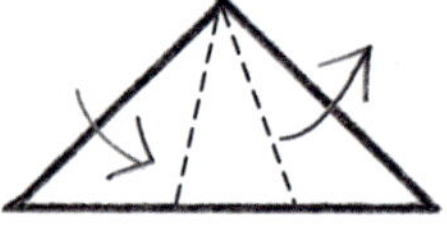

3. Fold it lightly into thirds then firmly fold the left triangle forward and the right triangle back, as shown.

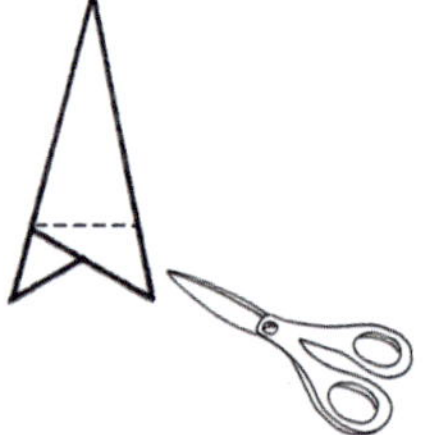

4. Trim the overlapping points at the bottom.

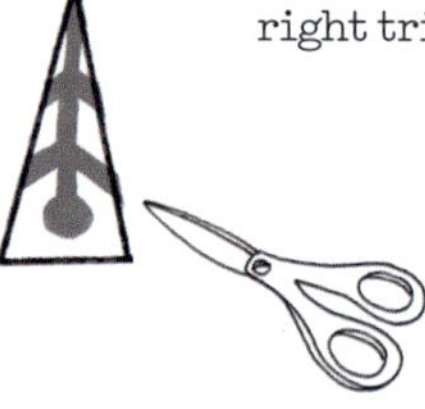

5. Draw shapes on the edges and cut out (in the ones above, the white parts were cut out). Unfold to reveal the snowflake.

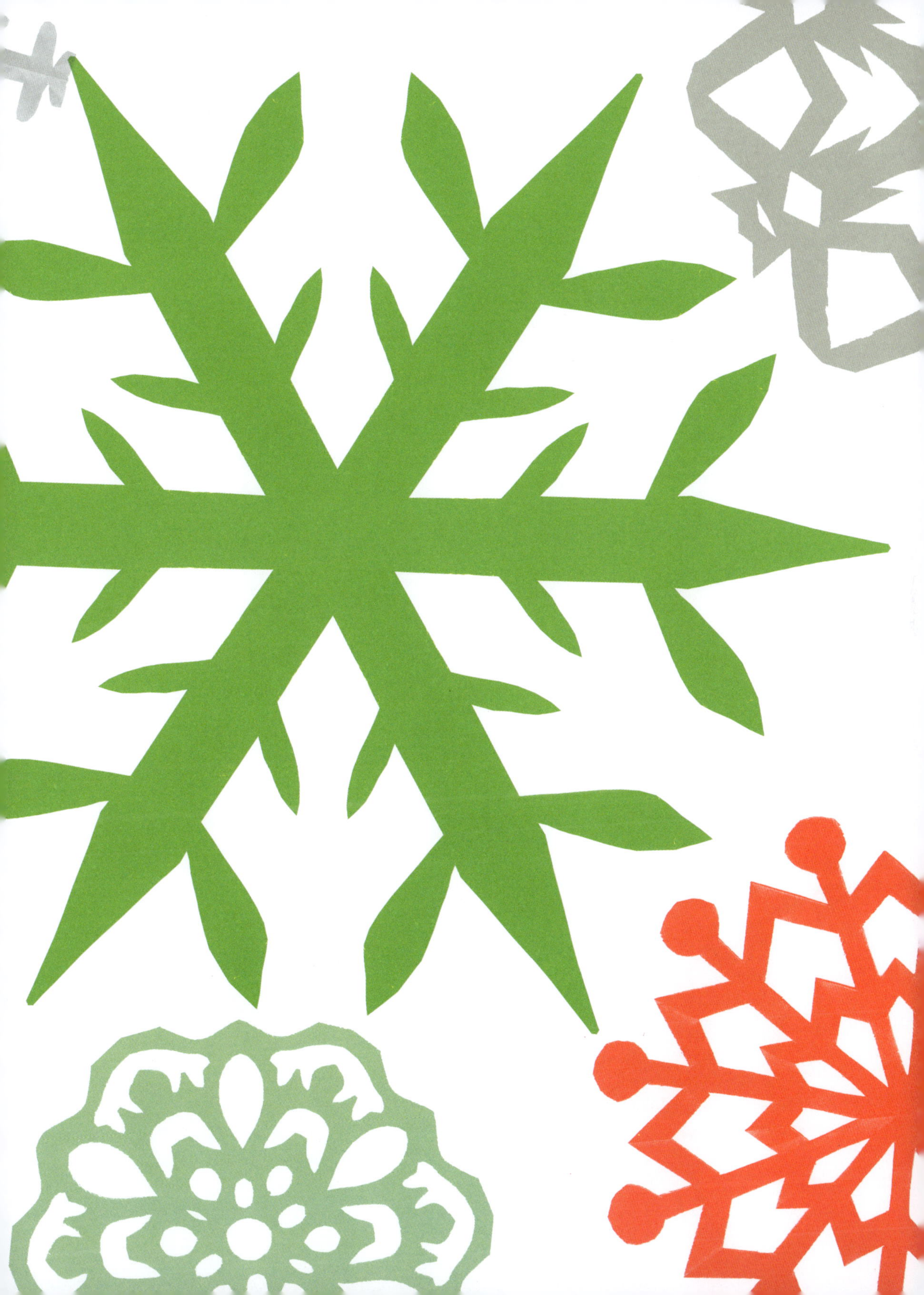

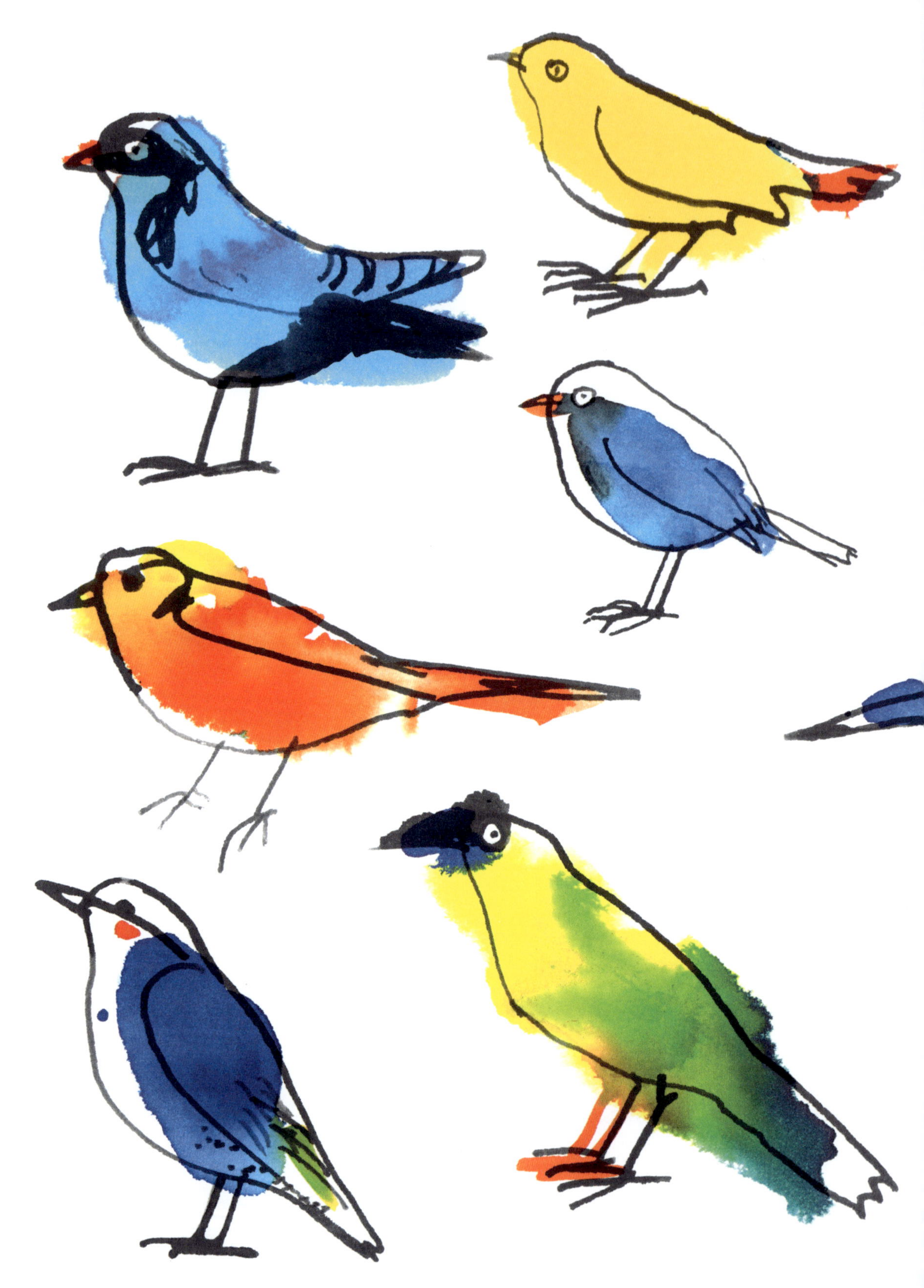

BIRD BLOTCHING

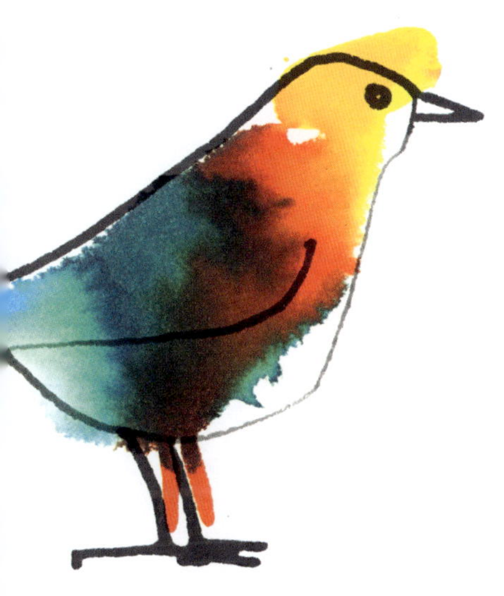

PLAYFUL WATERCOLOUR AND INK

I enjoy drawing birds because the variety of shapes and colours to choose from is endless, and minor mistakes are easily forgiven! I usually start on mixed-media paper, add water splotches and drip coloured inks on top. Once dry, I draw the bird in black waterproof ink. Alternatively, I start with the ink drawing and reverse the process. The unpredictability of how they will turn out is part of the joy.

Creative exercise

Trace bird shapes on thick paper or stencil paper. Cut out the bird (don't make the legs too thin!). Using a small, stiff brush and thick paint, stencil bird shapes on to a sheet of paper. You can also try stippling and making patterns within the stencil shape.

Creative inspiration

Bird paintings and drawings by Edward Lear, Georges Braque and Pablo Picasso.

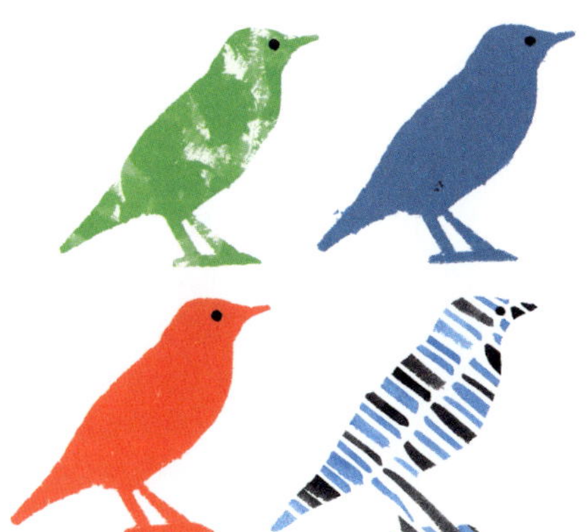

CURIOUS CREATURES

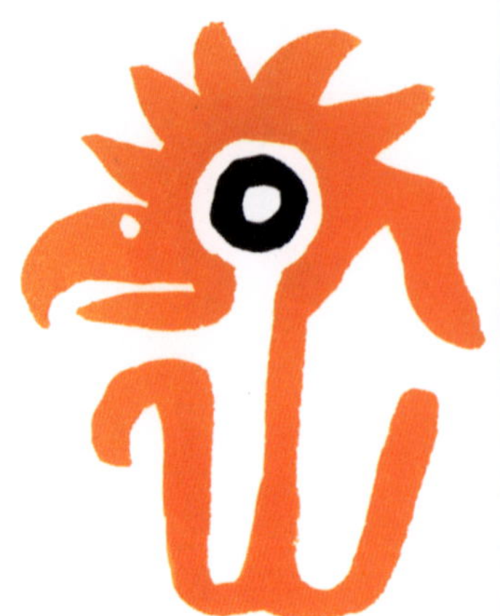

INSPIRATION FROM AFAR

Look beyond your own culture for unique references. I looked at ancient Mexican carvings, searching for distinctive creatures, then drew and coloured my own versions. I like to draw birds and so was intrigued by the bird interpretations – the carvings had unfamiliar characteristics and ways of drawing that I would never have imagined by myself. Try exploring other sources, like medieval manuscripts, indigenous Australian art or Peruvian sculptures.

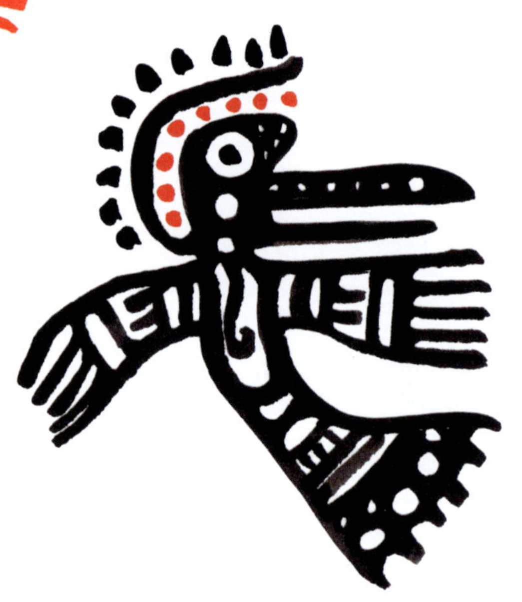

Creative exercise

Paint or draw a curious creature in a fitting spot at home: maybe above a switch in a utility room, or hidden under a table. Use paint pens or water-based paint. Give it a name and write a short story for it.

Creative inspiration

Aztec wall carvings and alebrijes: Mexican folk-art fantasy animal sculptures.

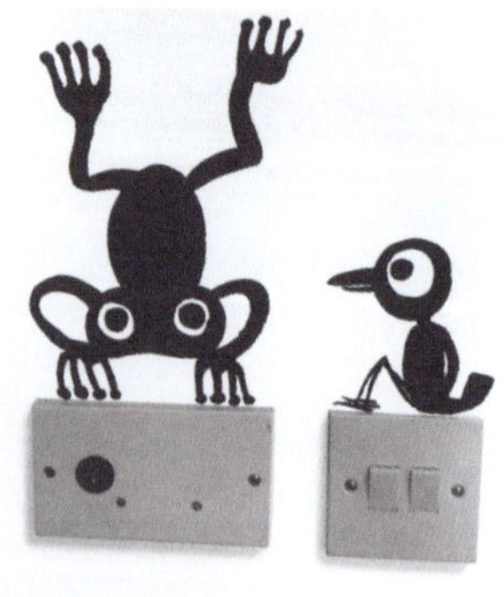

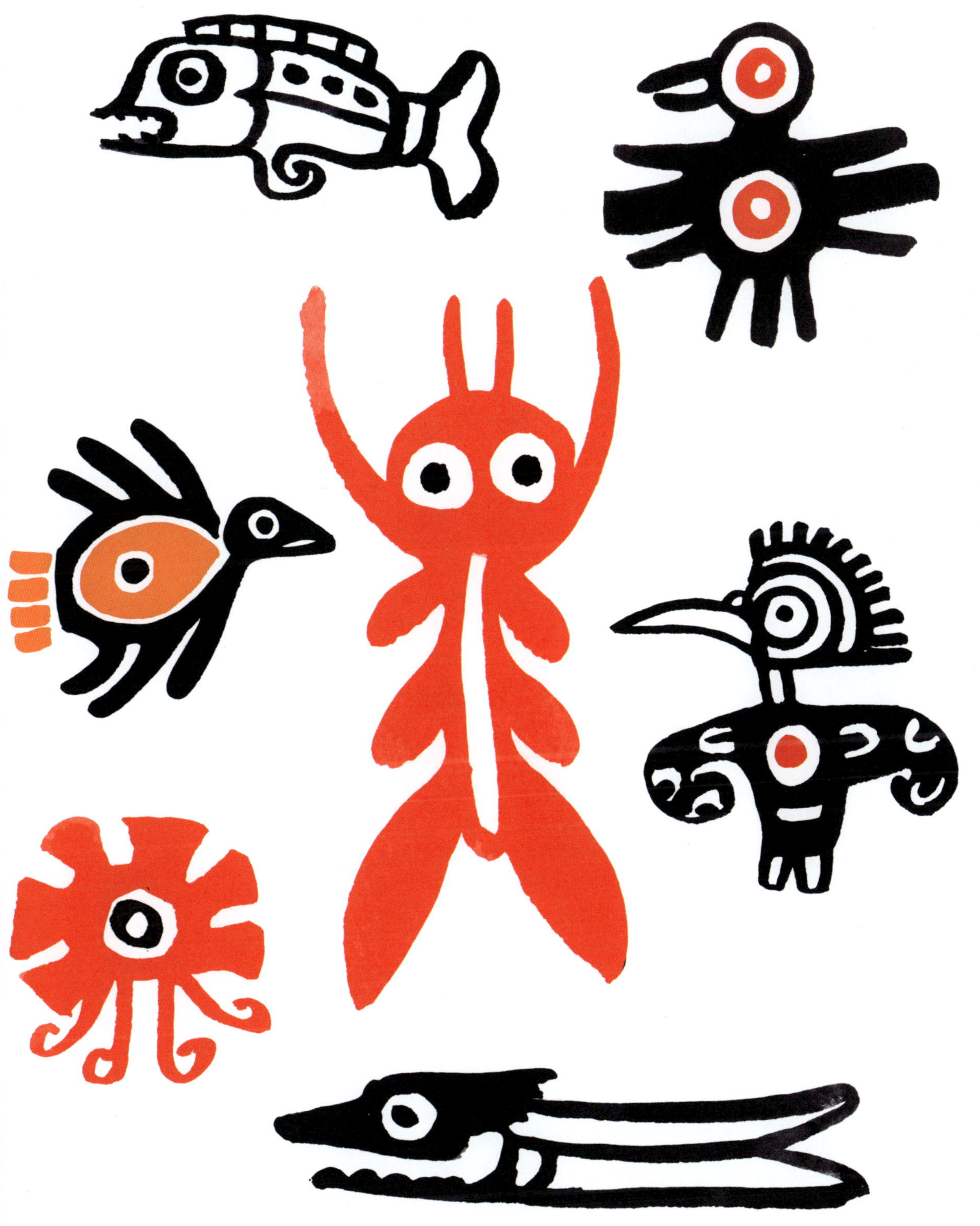

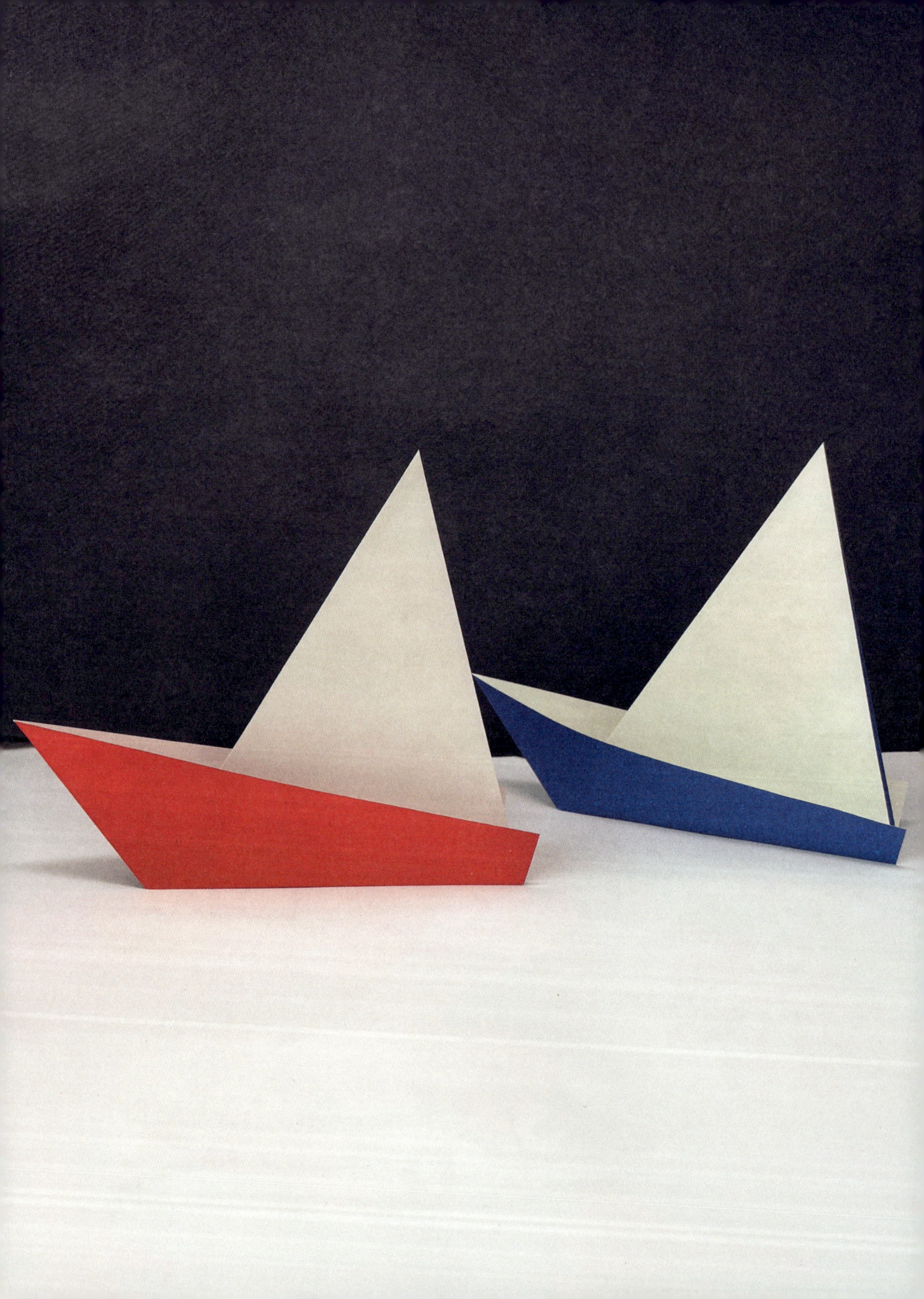

PAPER YACHT

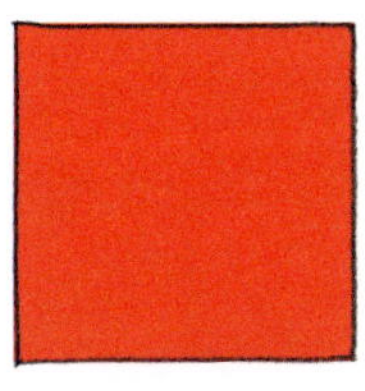

1. Start with a square piece of paper, ideally with colour on one side only.

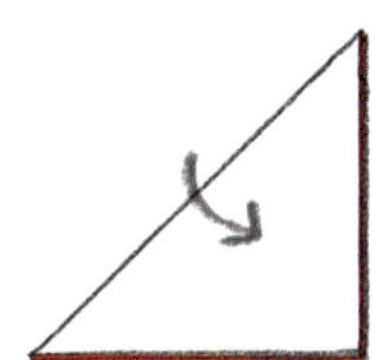

2. Fold along the diagonal.

EASY ORIGAMI PAPER YACHT

These little boats are extremely simple to make, but very elegant. I have a whole fleet of them in many different colours in my studio. They bring joy!

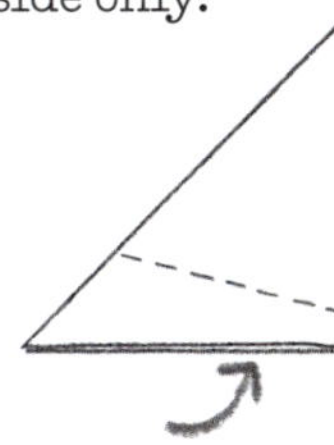

3. Fold up the bottom edge on an angle, to create the hull.

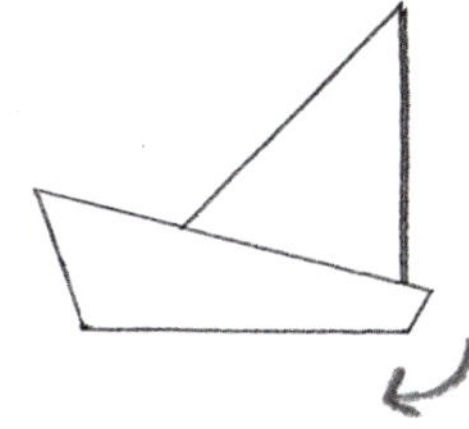

4. Undo the last fold.

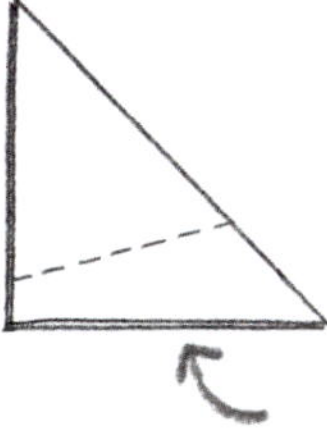

5. Turn the paper over to the other side and repeat step 3.

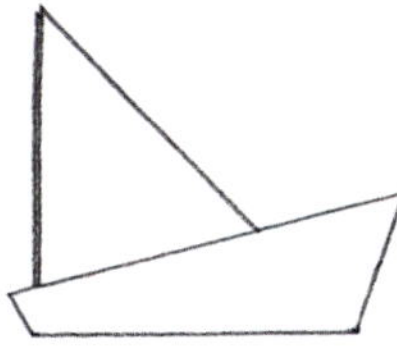

6. Unfold the whole sheet and place flat with the white side up and the creases orientated as shown in the next step.

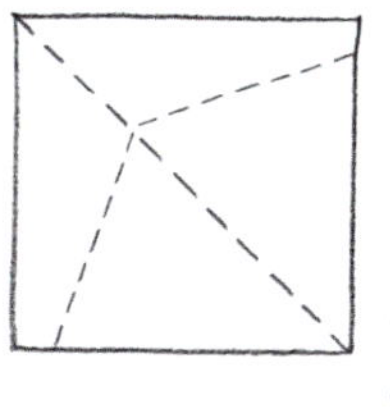

7. Pinch the top left corner to form the front and, at the same time, push up the bottom right corner, allowing the central crease to come forward.

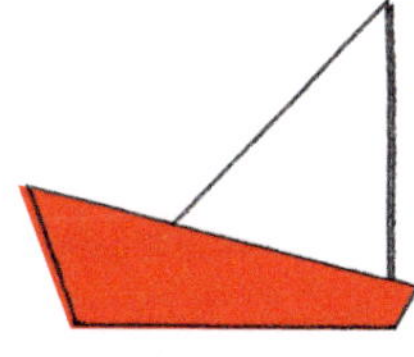

8. Fold flat. The front is closed and the back is open. Now enjoy your finished paper yacht!

CUT AND STICK

COLLAGE WITH PAPER AND EPHEMERA

Collect old postcards, stamps, coloured paper, photos and ephemera, from junk shops or around your house. Play around with the elements on a sheet of paper. On the next page I've used an old piece of cardboard as my background. It's good to have a 'focal point' about a third into the image: strong colours, letters or figurative elements work well for this.

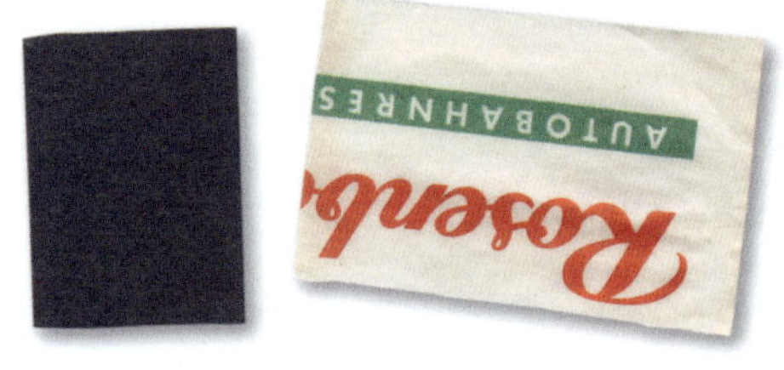

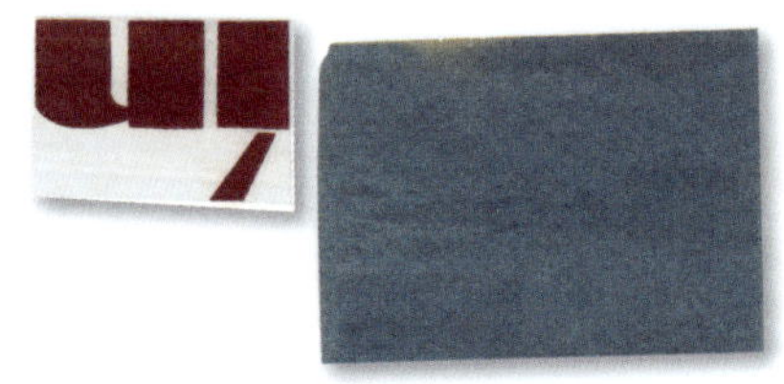

Creative exercise

Collect printed ephemera. Use low-tack tape to temporarily stick down your collage pieces and, when you're happy with the final composition, use a glue stick. Now create a mixed-media work by adding drawn or painted elements to complete your design.

Creative inspiration

The work of Kurt Schwitters, Robert Rauschenberg and Joseph Cornell.

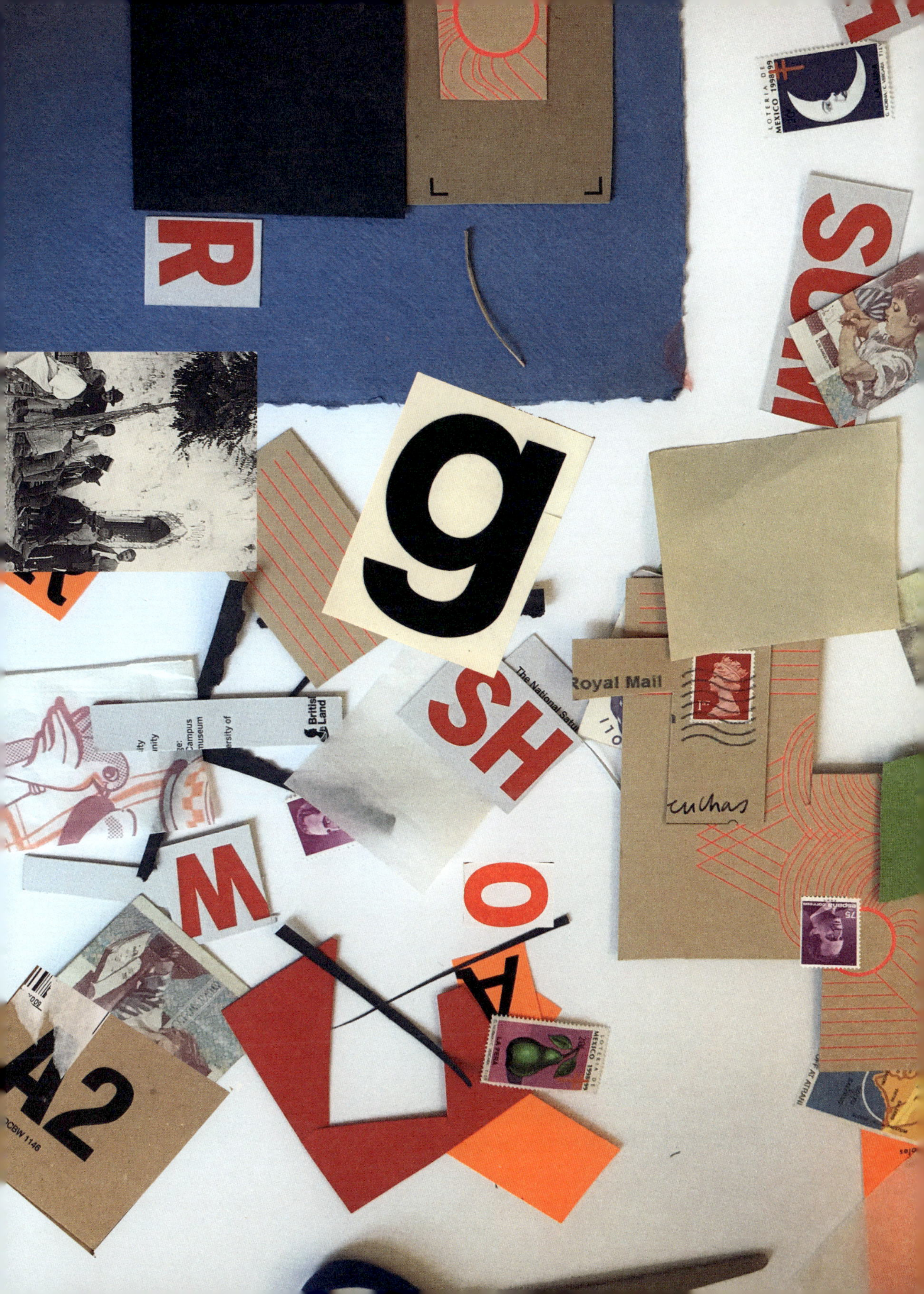

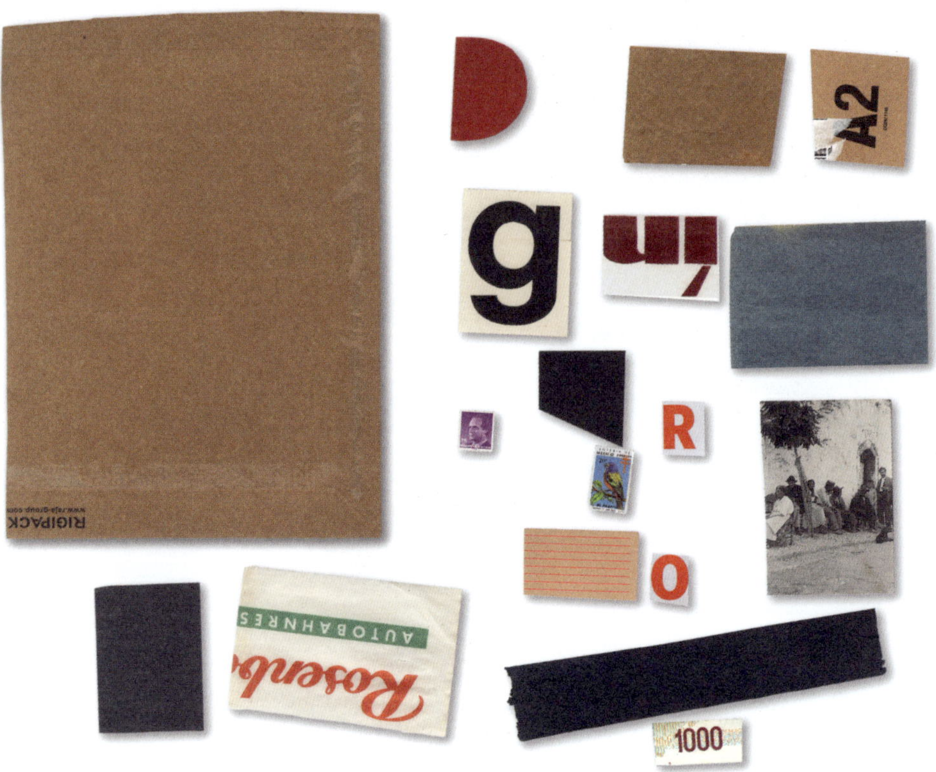

The elements

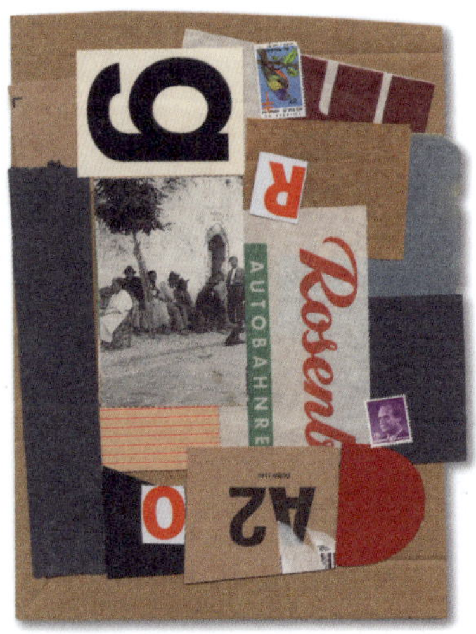

Variation 1

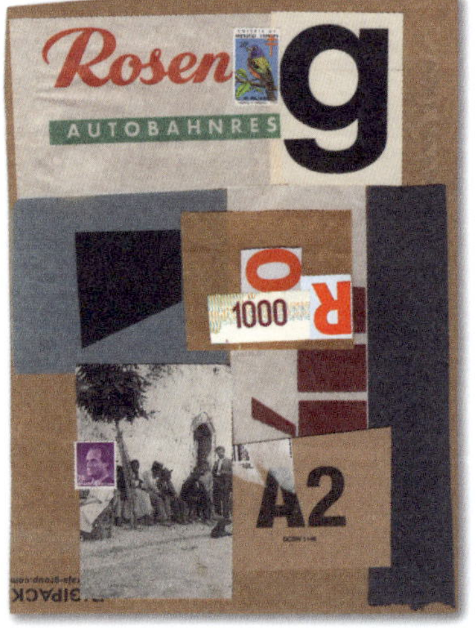

Variation 2

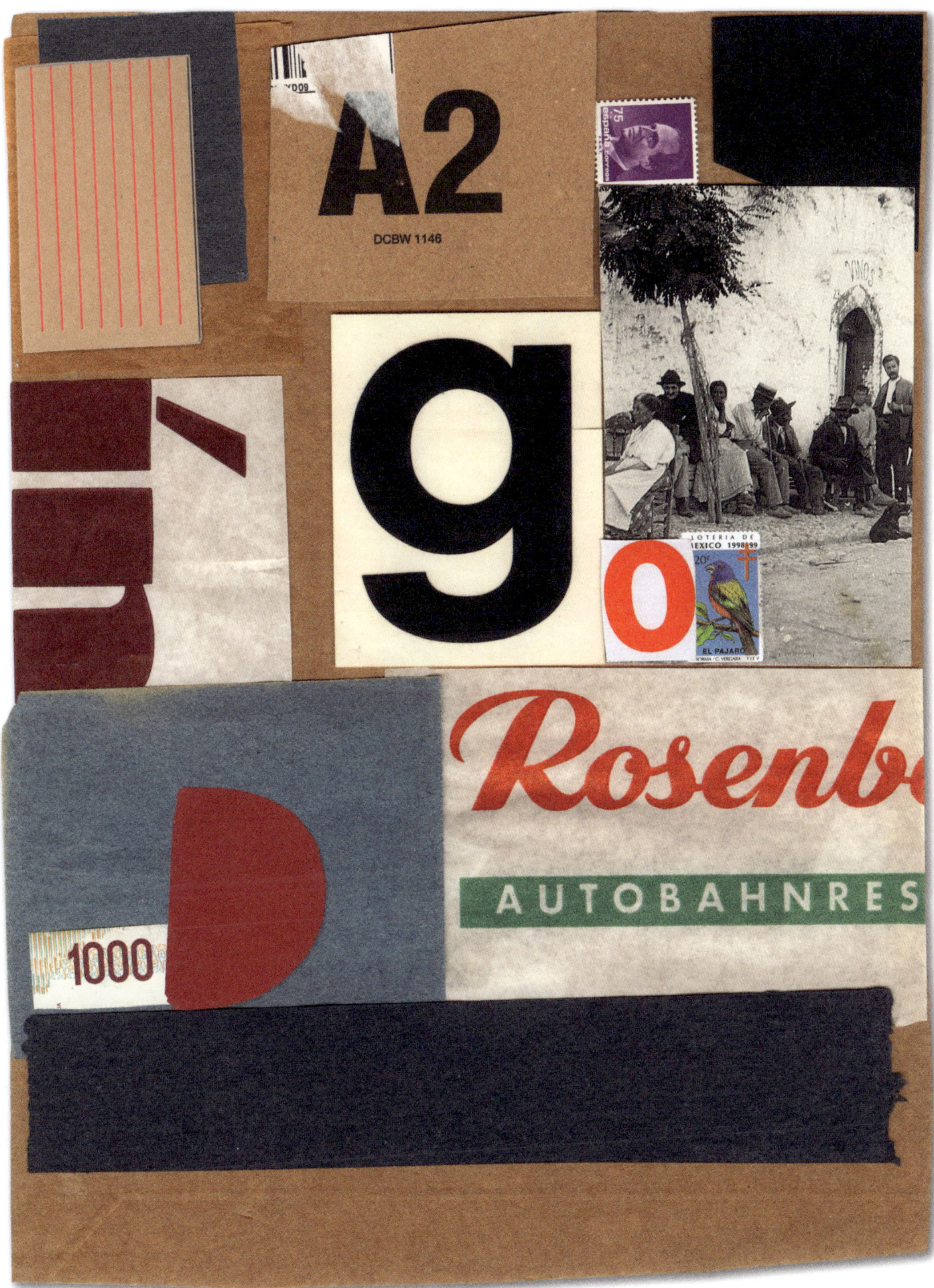

Variation 3

SHELLS

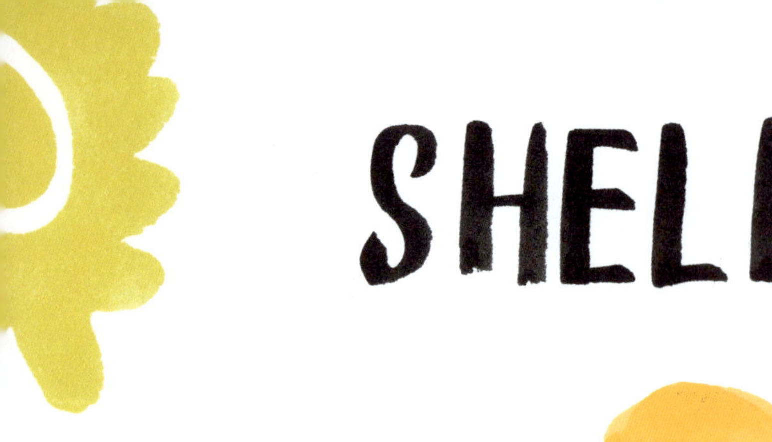

SHELL TEXTURE STUDIES

Nearly everyone has picked up a shell and put it in their pocket, each one a little treasure. They are a rich source of inspiration for all kinds of artists. Their diverse shapes, textures and colours offer endless possibilities for exploration. Each shell is unique, making you really look closely as you draw. Observe the intricate patterns, ridges and contours of shells, and try to replicate those textures using various art media: pencil, charcoal, ink or even digital art tools.

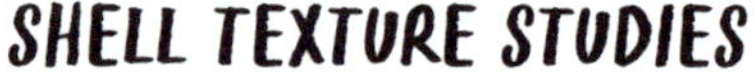

Creative exercise

Observe a single shell for five minutes, focusing on its texture, shape and patterns. How do you imagine it feels, smells, tastes? What thoughts does it inspire? Now draw it.

Creative inspiration

The work of Georgia O'Keeffe and Ernst Haeckel, and the sculptures of Henry Moore and Barbara Hepworth.

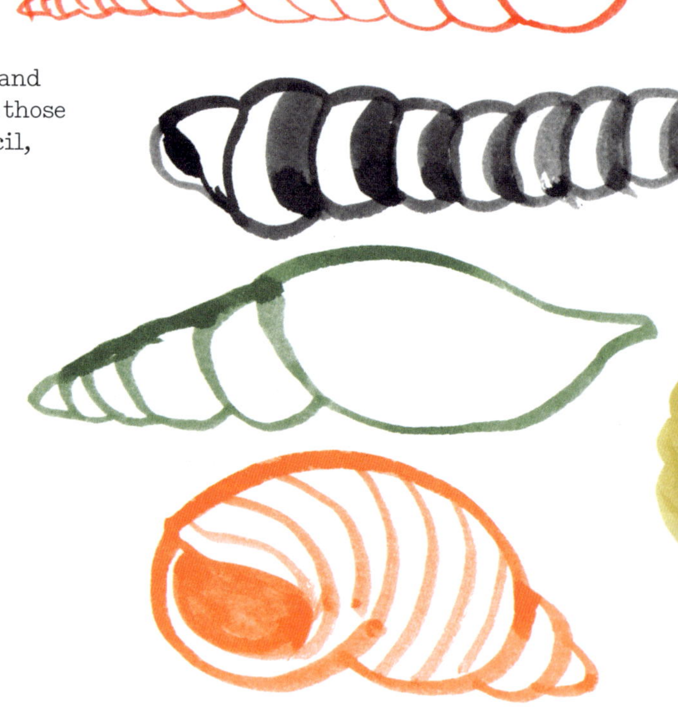

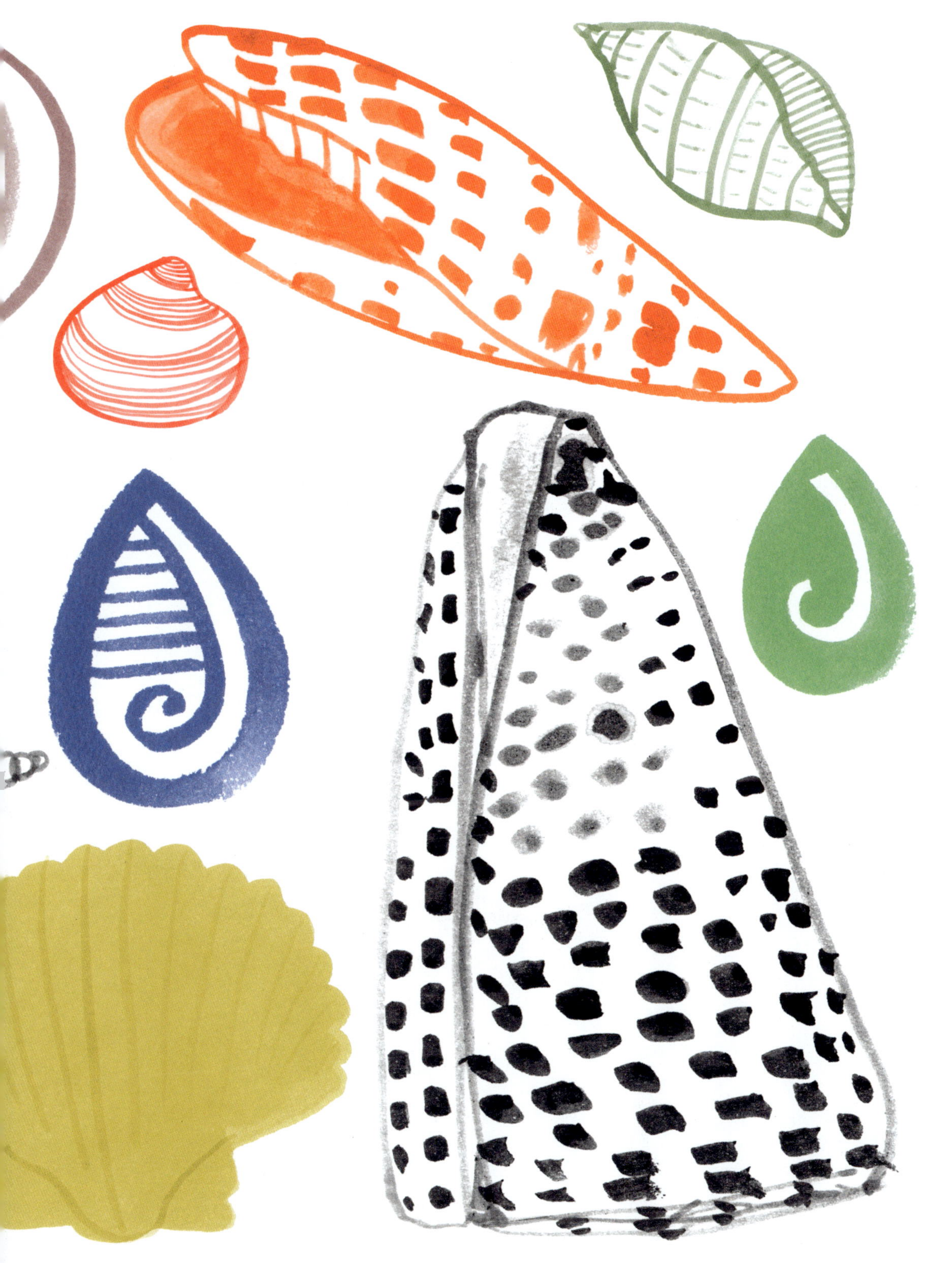

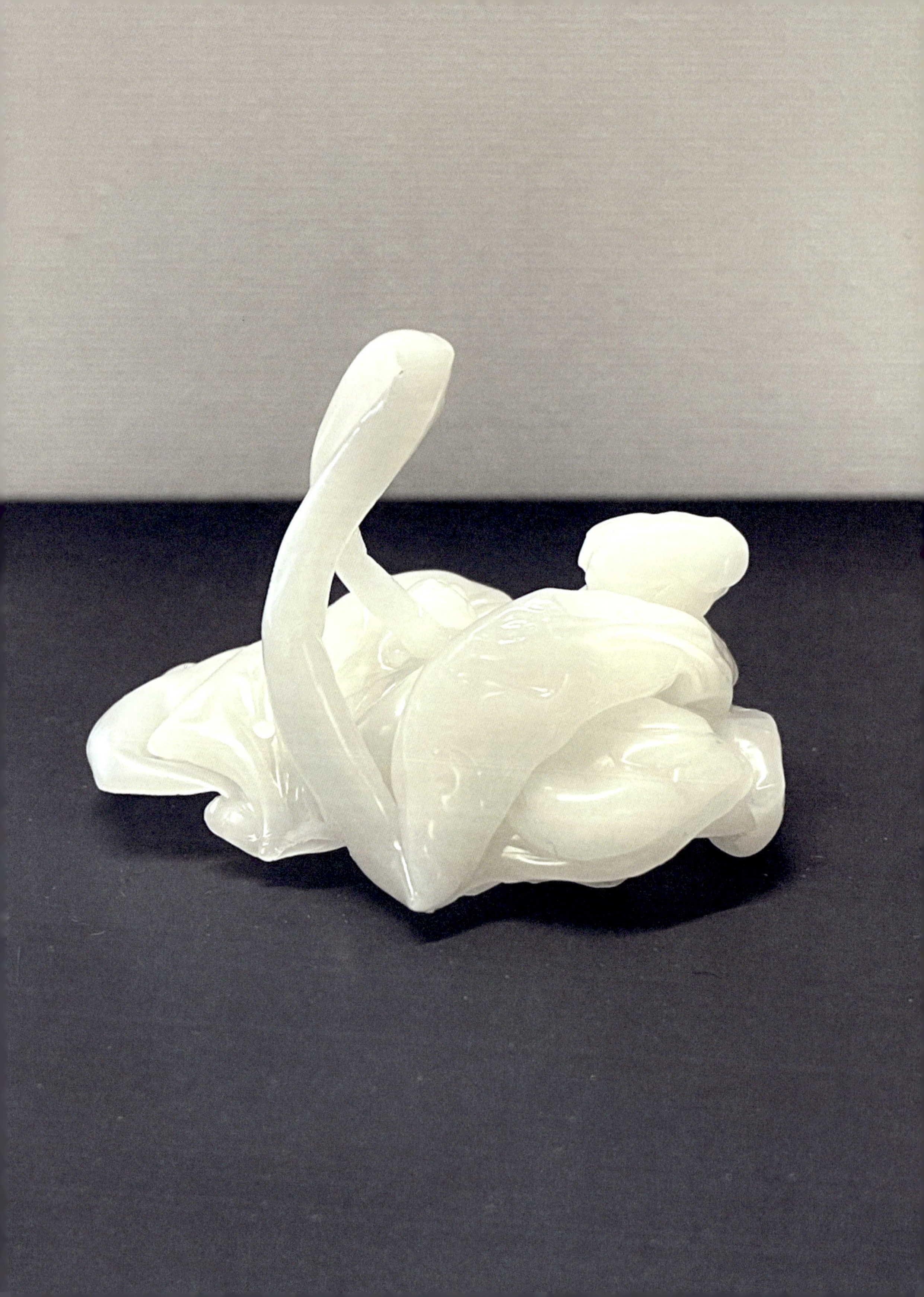

COULAGE

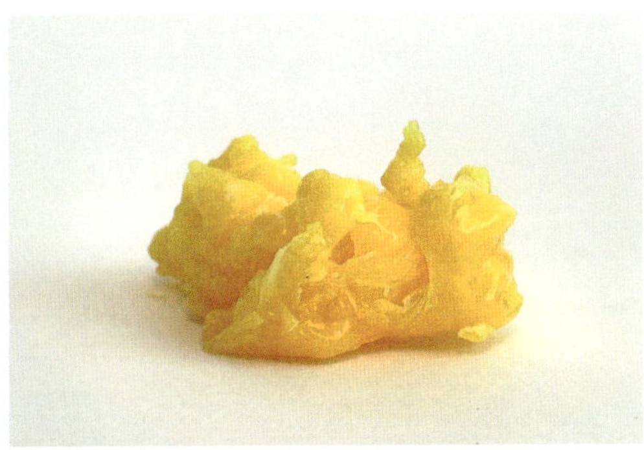

WAX MELT SCULPTURE

Melt wax flakes or an old wax candle (after removing the wick) in a bain-marie. Pour the molten wax into cold water. As the wax meets the water, it solidifies into unpredictable, dreamlike forms. The Surrealists used to do this, and it's fascinating to watch. Once cool, display your sculpture. This exercise is good to do with chocolate too!

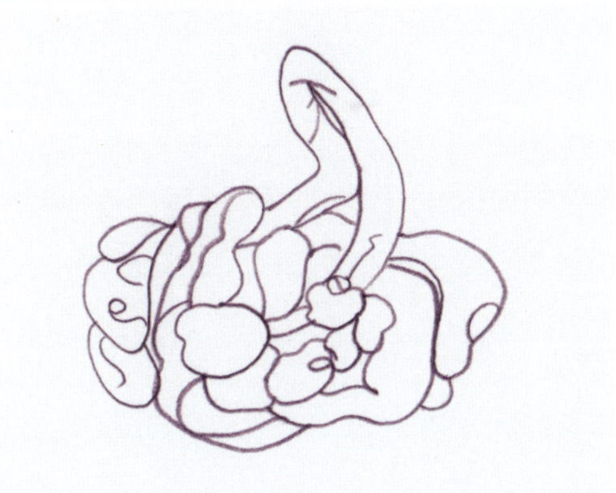

Creative exercise

These sculptures can be very interesting to draw. Their unique forms will ensure you've never drawn anything like it before! It will test your observation skills.

Creative inspiration

The work of Surrealists Dora Carrington and Max Ernst.

CALM the CRITIC

There's a persistent voice inside all our heads, often telling us what we can and cannot do – especially when we start making art. Sometimes I feel like I'm arguing with a strict teacher. It's our logical mind attempting to set boundaries. To truly embrace creativity, you must quiet that critic and trust your instincts. That's when the good stuff happens.

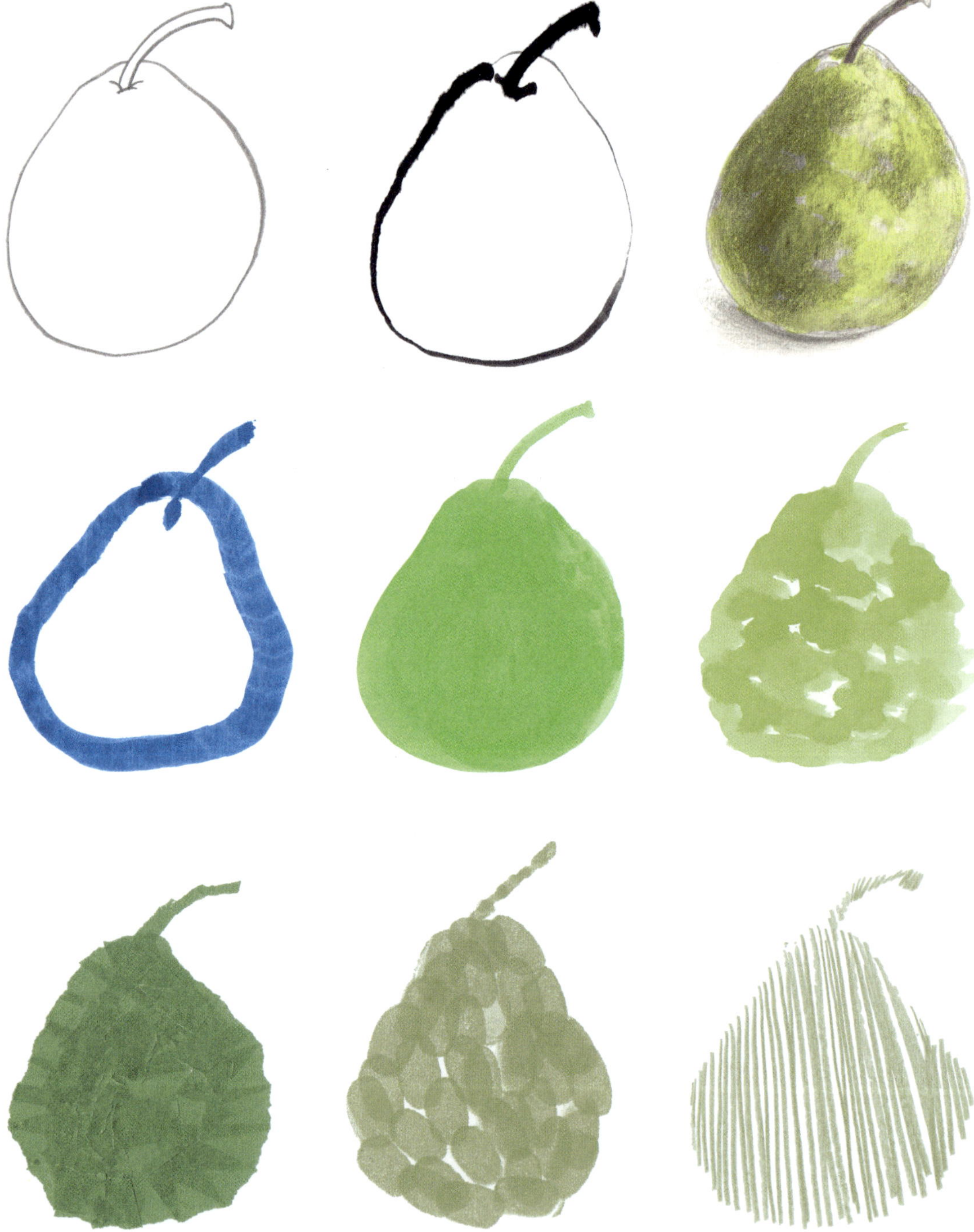

PEAR SHAPED

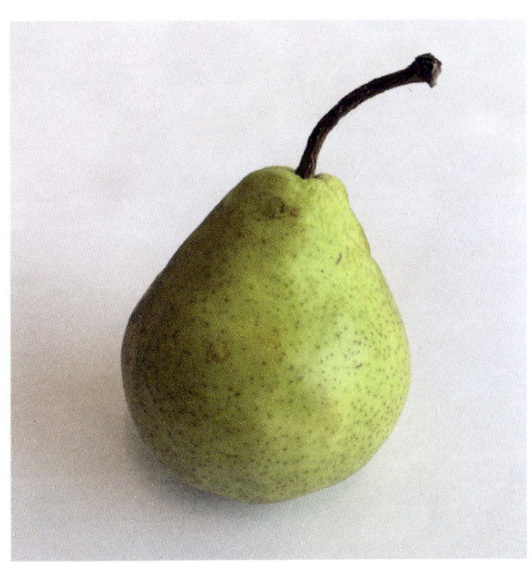

PEARS DRAWN NINE WAYS

Trying different media is a very positive way of gaining confidence in using materials. Choose a subject, for example a piece of fruit, and try to draw it with at least nine different drawing tools. In the pear drawings opposite I've used, from top left: pencil, stick and ink, pencil and watercolour, acrylic paint, gouache paint, watercolour, tape, fingerprints and coloured pencil.

Creative exercise

Once you've drawn with nine different kinds of materials, combine three of them into one drawing. Now you have a mixed-media artwork.

Creative inspiration

The still lives of Ben and Winifred Nicholson.

LAZY CATS

PEN AND INK CATS

Think about the shapes rather than focus on the idea of drawing a cat. You can use a real cat or photographs for reference. Use brush and ink or try some sticks or a scratchy pen. The more unpredictable the medium, the better.

Creative exercise

Try drawing cats with ink and brush without looking at the paper. Draw very quickly and fill the page with lots of cats.

Creative inspiration

Andy Warhol's drawings of his cats. Saul Steinberg and Ronald Searle also drew some charming and funny cats.

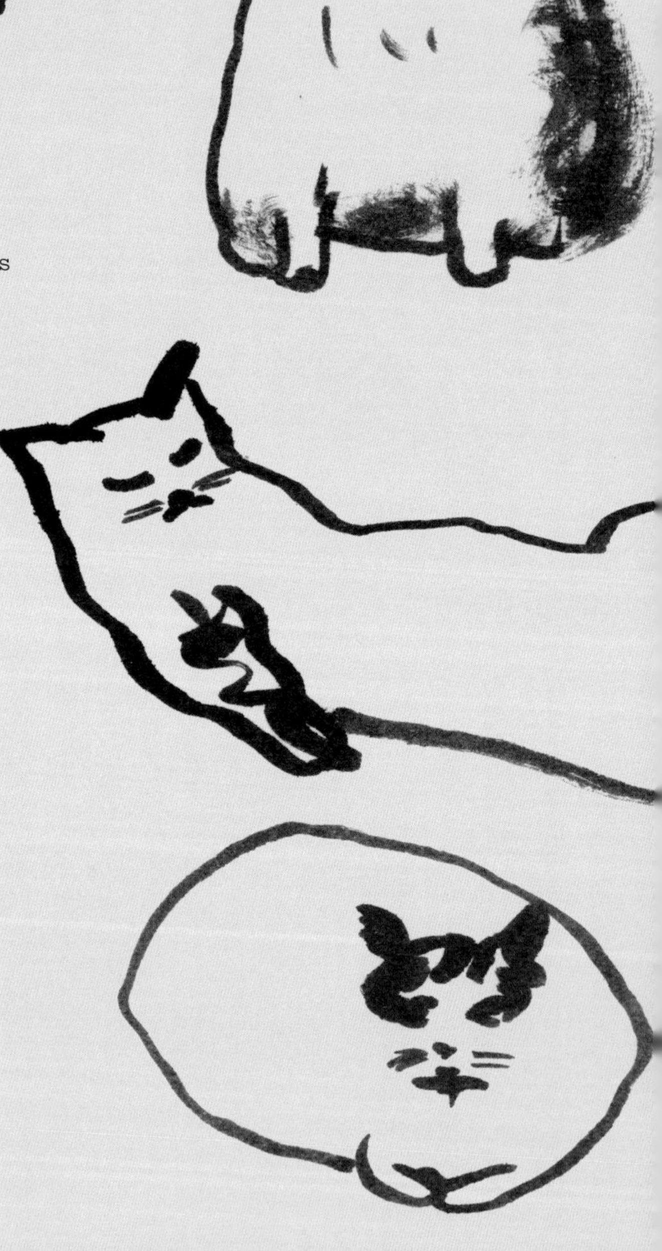

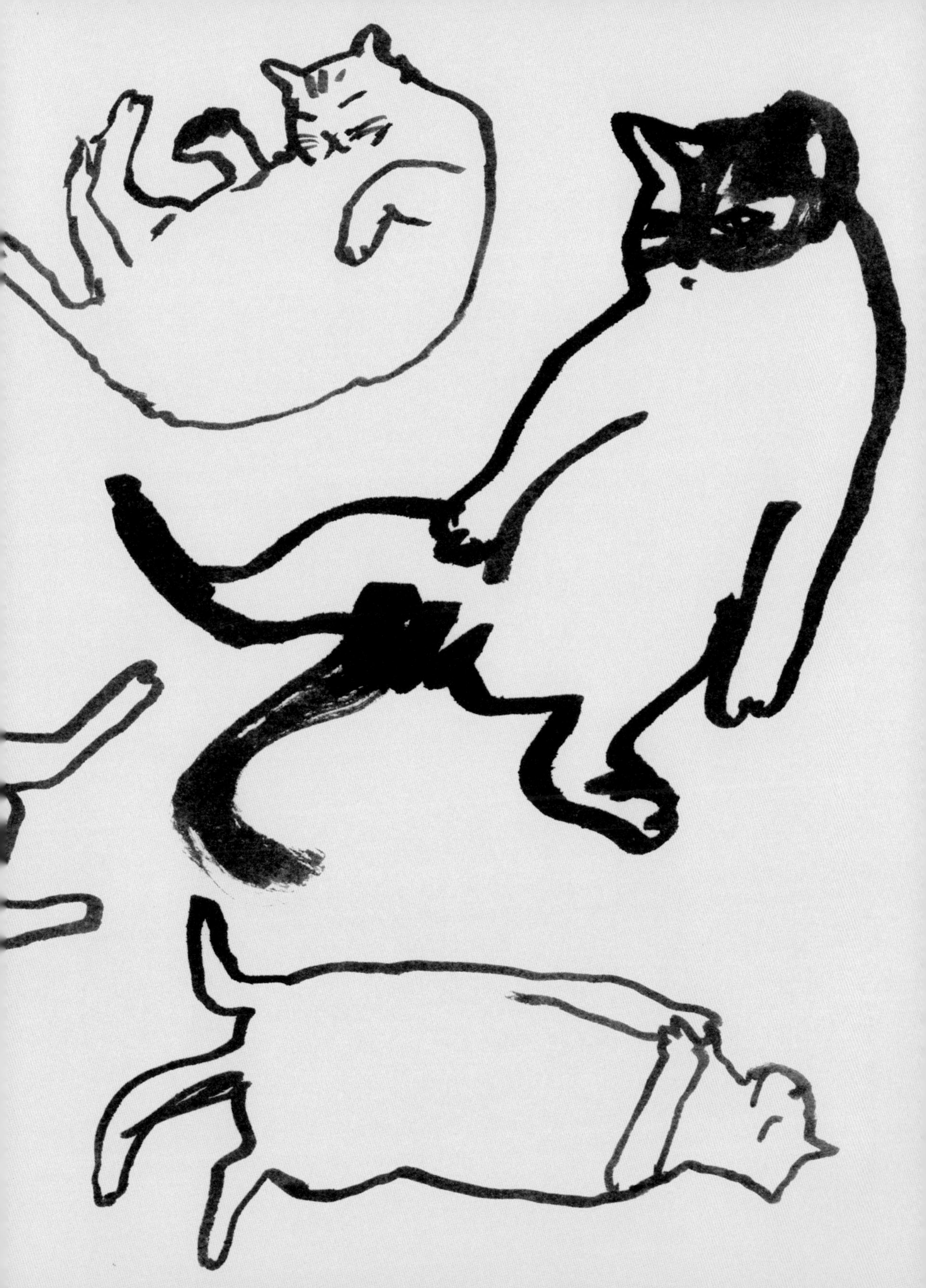

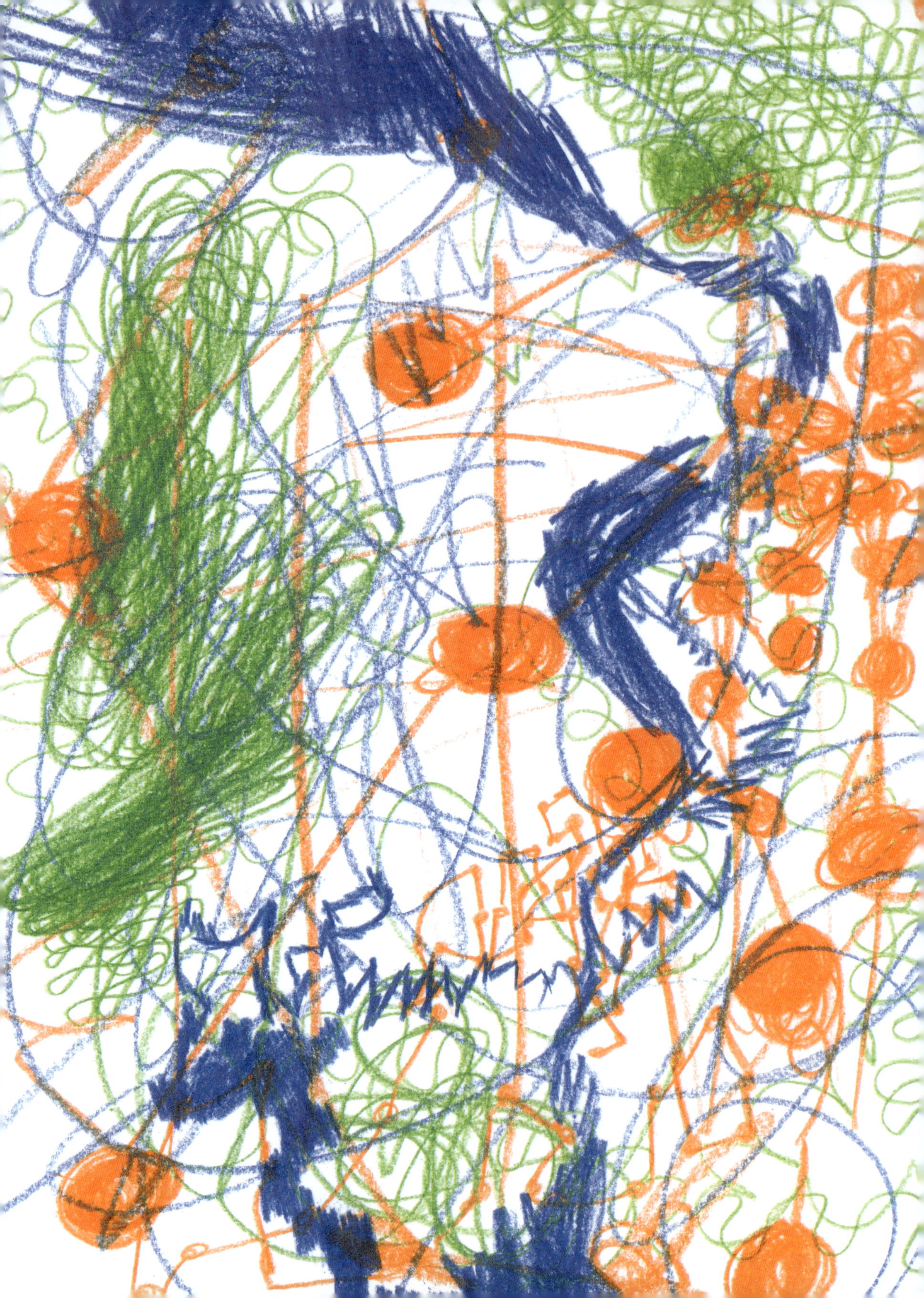

EYES SHUT

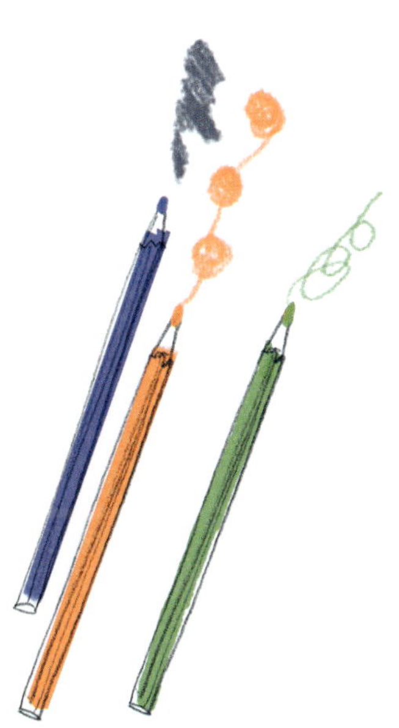

UNCONSCIOUS DRAWING

If you ever watch a child pick up a pencil and paper, it is amazing to watch their lack of fear in making that first mark. Be inspired by that and use coloured pens or pencils to make random marks and scribbles. Focus on the sensory experience: the sound, the feel of pen on paper and the movement of your arm. Bypass your logical brain to enjoy unconscious mark making.

Creative exercise

Sketch your own face or any object you can find using your non-dominant hand.

Creative quickie

Hold a two-pencil dance. Hold a coloured pencil in each hand, close your eyes and imagine they are dancing with each other.

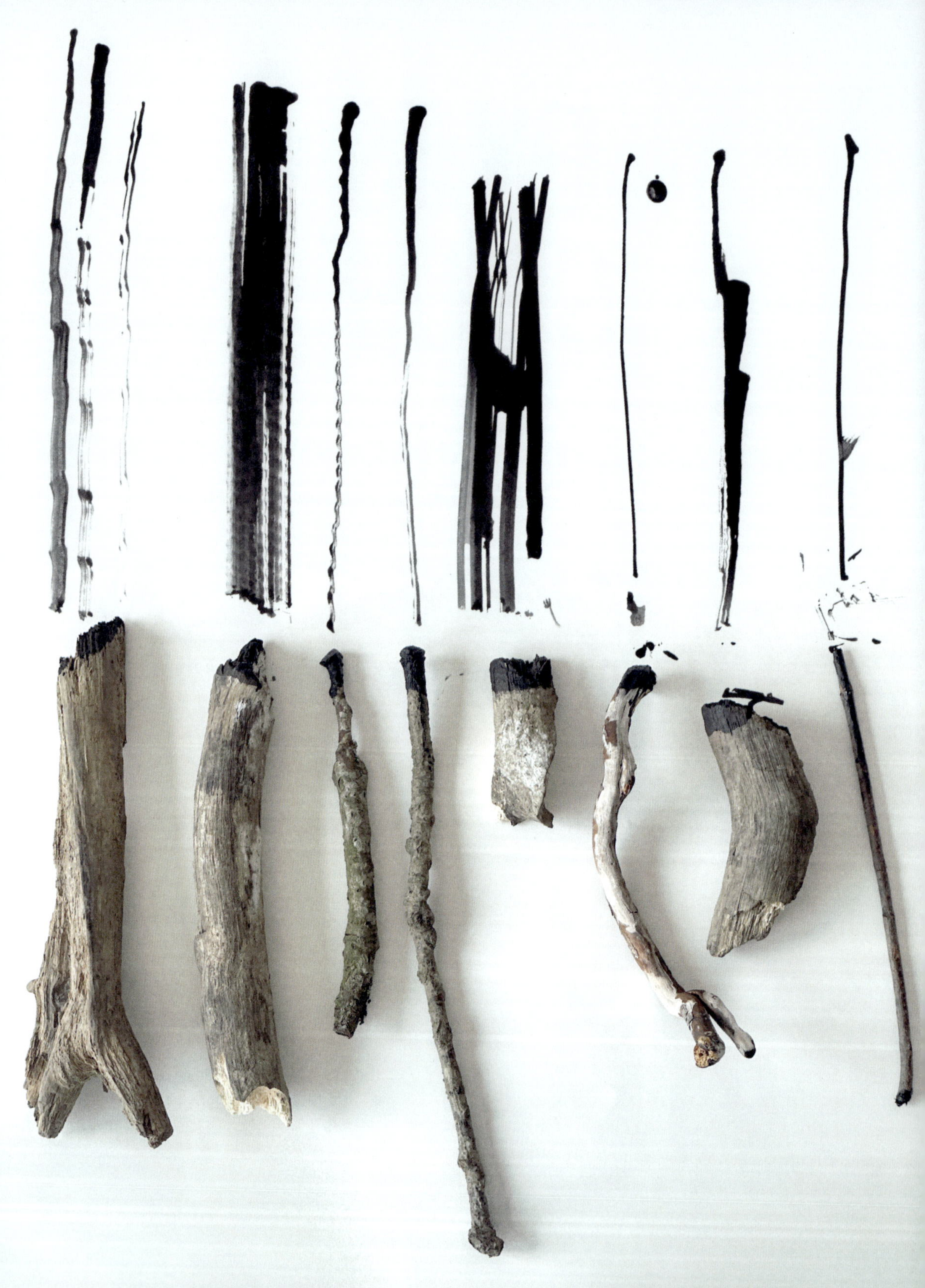

DRAW WITH STICKS

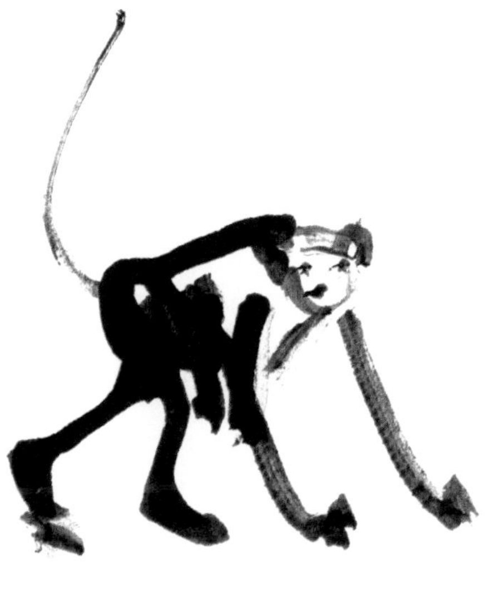

MARK MAKING

Drawing with sticks and ink is a great alternative to conventional art tools. The limitations and unpredictability of the stick can actually enhance your drawing! The lines created are unlike anything you'd normally achieve. Humans have always used sticks to draw, and many cultures still do. Drawing with a stick connects you to nature and ancient practices.

Creative exercise

Collect sticks in different shapes and sizes and experiment with ink marks. Once you're comfortable, try drawing something specific. I started with monkey sketches from reference pictures.

Creative inspiration

The expressive drawing lines of Cy Twombly and outsider artist Bill Traylor.

MOP ART

DRAWING WITH WATER

If you have a dry outside space you can paint with water! All you need is some water, some kind of container to hold it in and a mop or brush. It gives you the opportunity to paint on a big scale without the mess or needing to have the right equipment. Also, if you make a mistake, you can just wait for it to dry and start again! Take a photograph of your finished artwork and watch it slowly disappear as it dries.

Creative exercise

Find a public space where you can paint some images or messages with water. Choose a warm, dry day and a surface that has a good contrast when water is applied.

Creative quickie

Buy some Chinese water-writing fabric, commonly used to practise Chinese calligraphy – it's also great for drawing on as a portable painting surface.

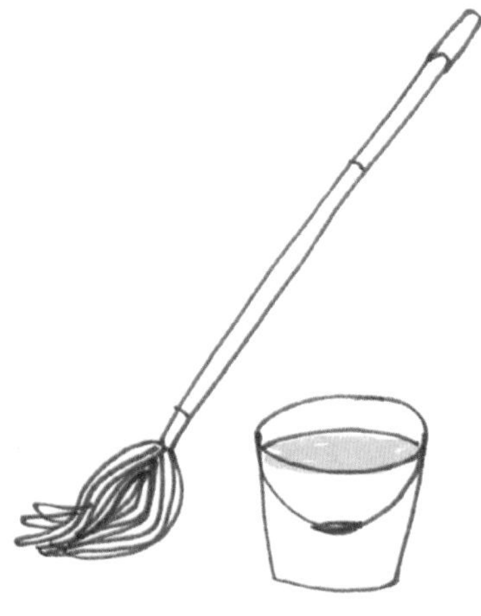

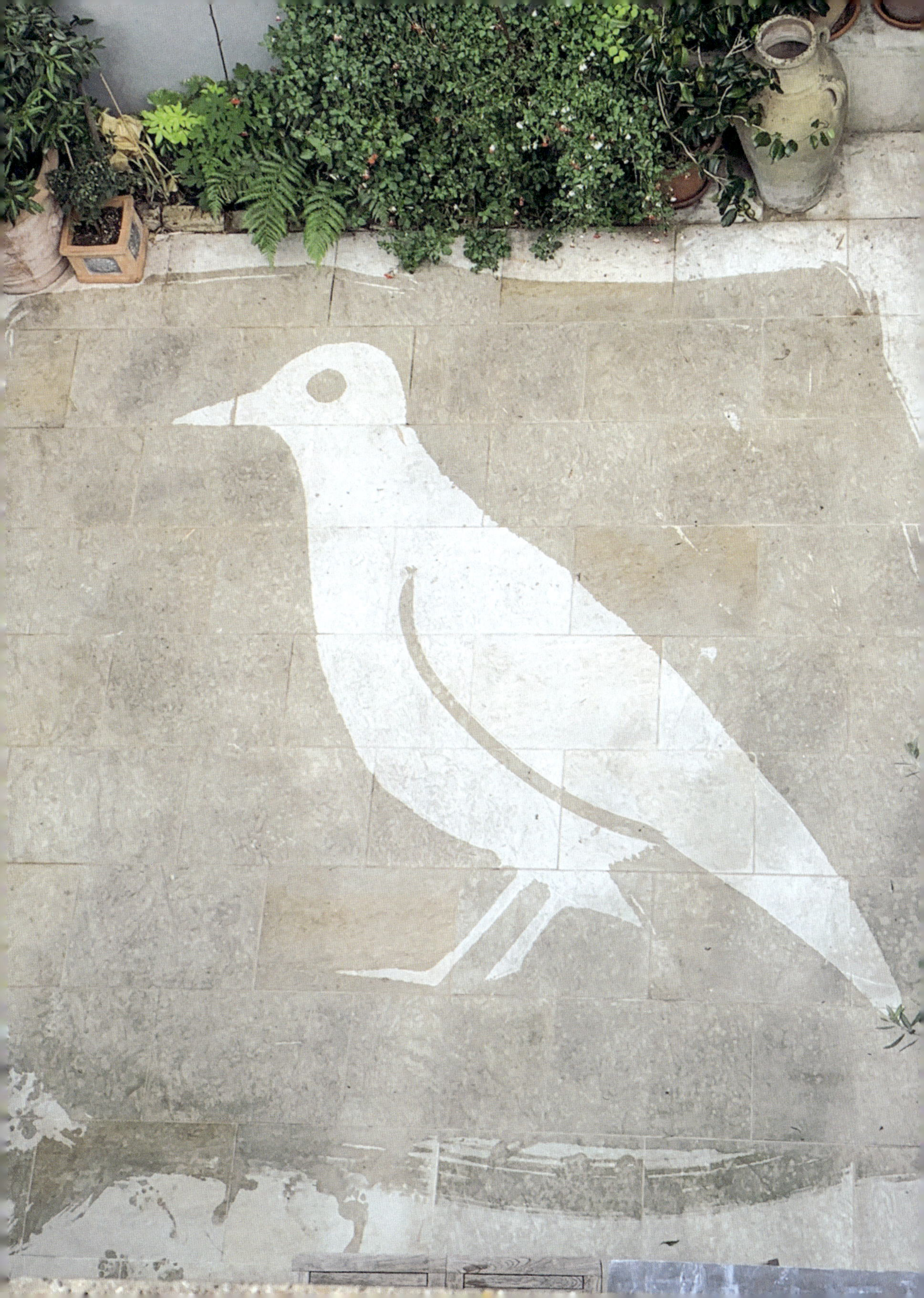

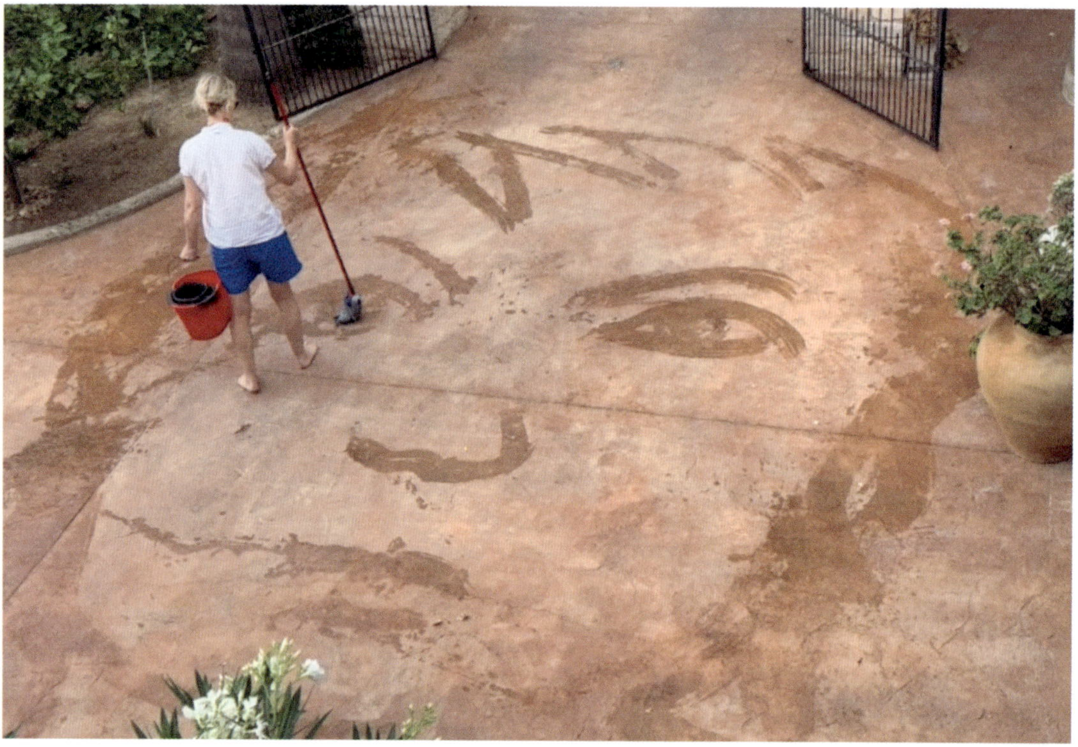

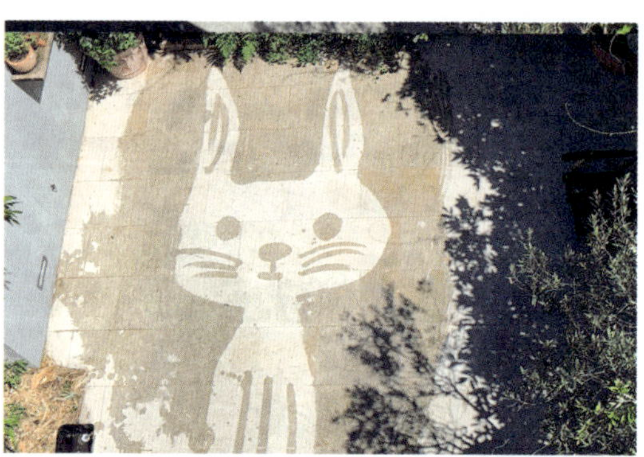

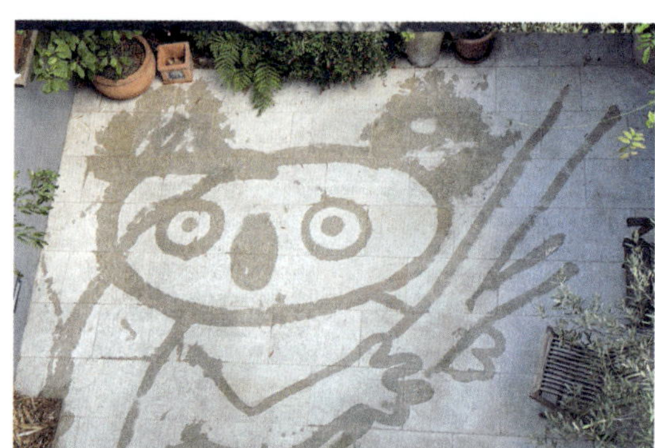

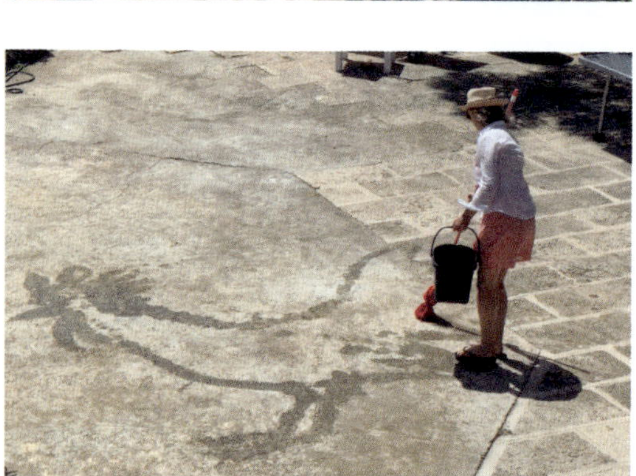

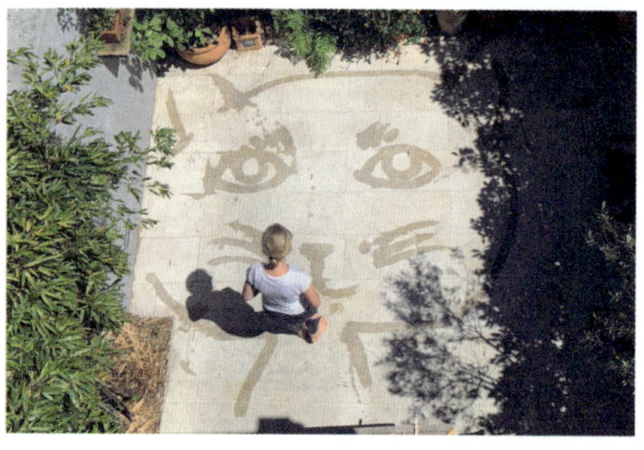

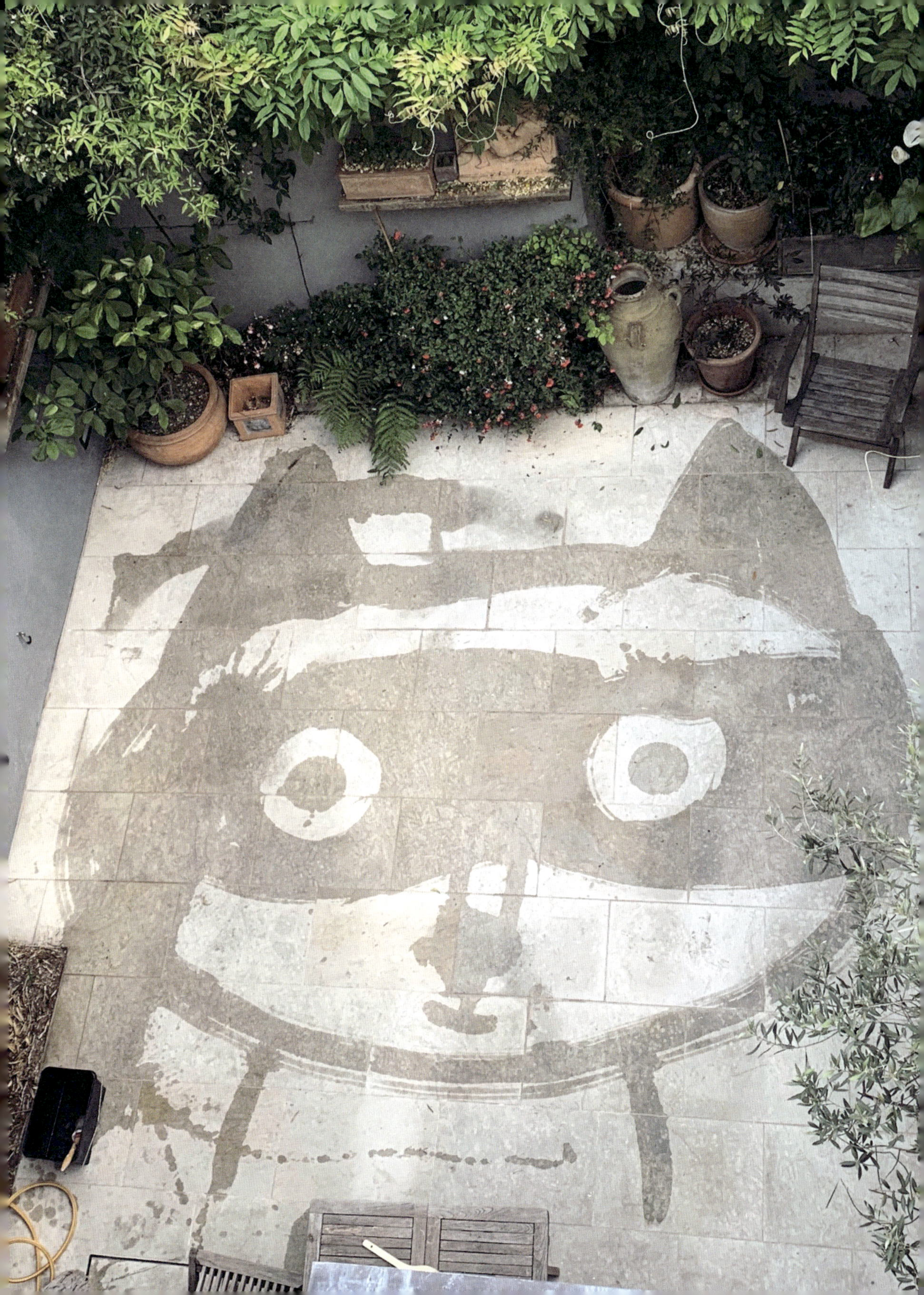

EXQUISITE CORPSE

A DRAWING GAME

This Surrealist game, for two to four players, is great for imagination and collaboration. Fold a piece of paper into equal parts, one for each person. The first person starts drawing in the top section and extends it slightly into the next. The paper is then folded to hide the drawing, and the next player continues the line. Repeat the process until everyone has contributed. Unfold to see some unpredictable artwork.

Creative exercise

Instead of drawing on each section, use mixed media, colour or collage. Remember to use the same overlap principle.

Creative inspiration

The exquisite corpse drawings of the Chapman brothers and Kerry James Marshall.

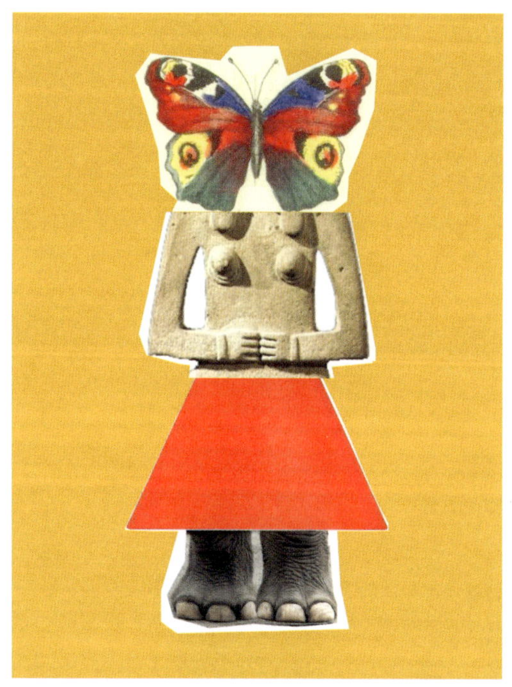

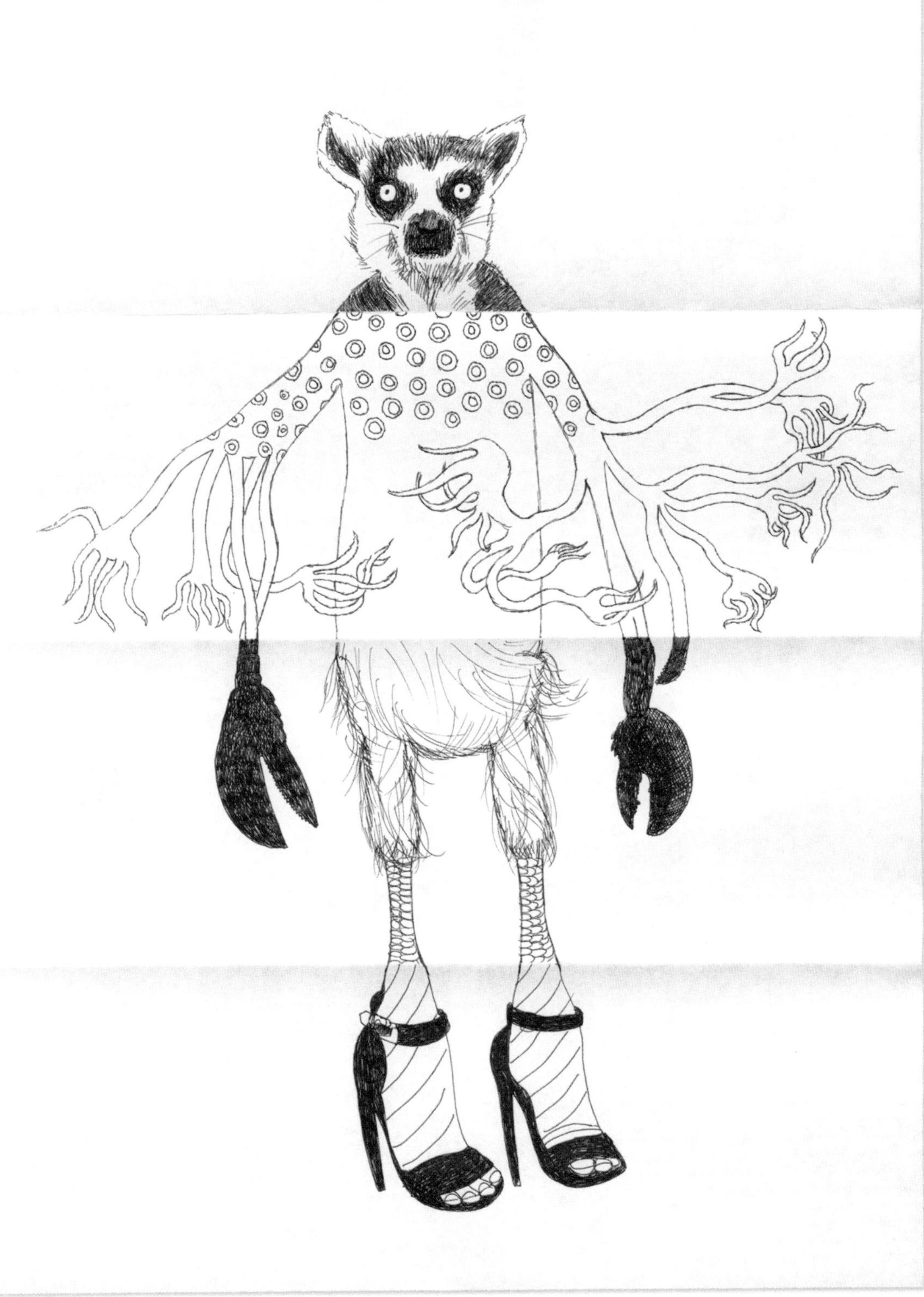

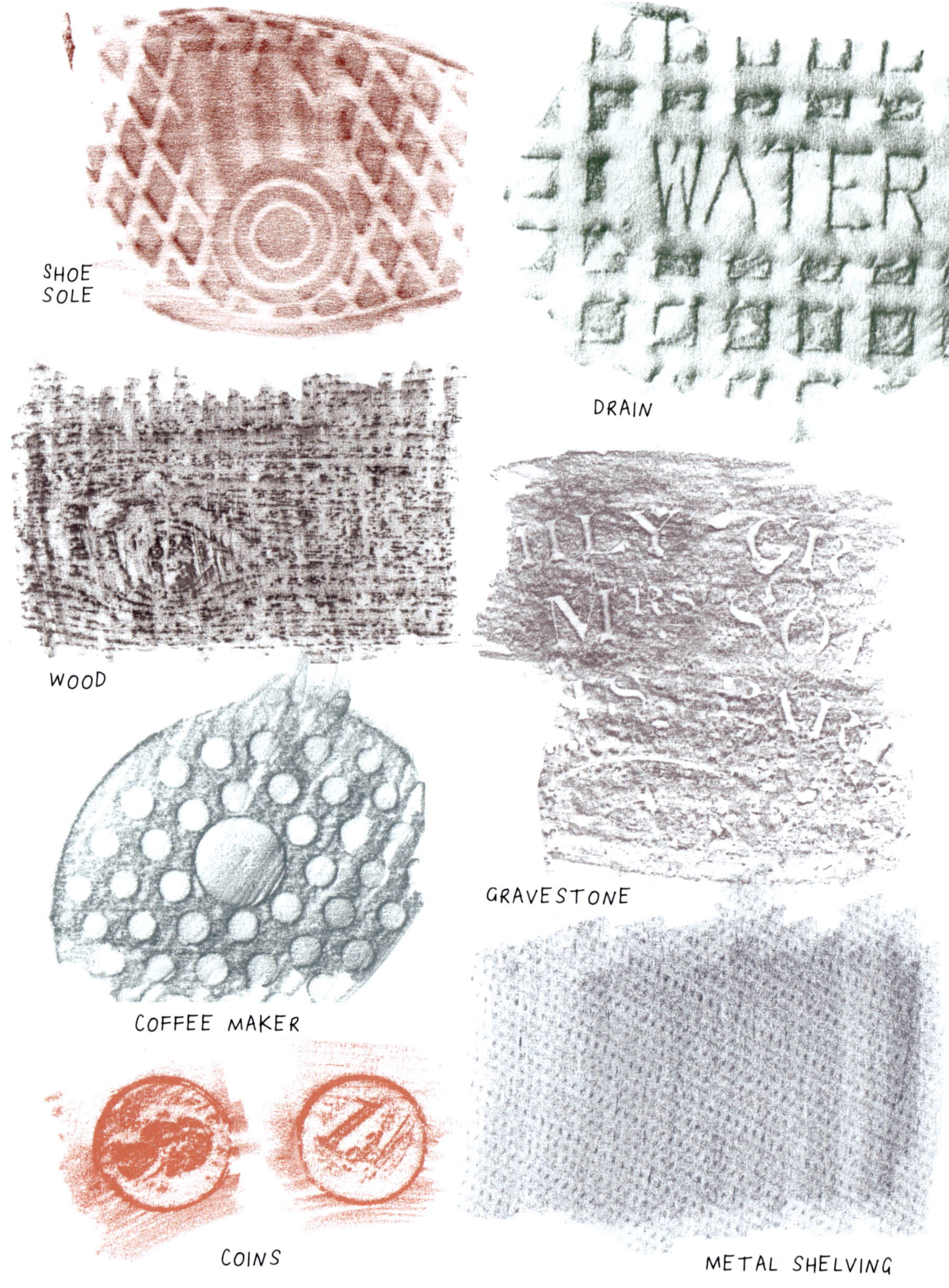

SHOE
SOLE
DRAIN
WATER
WOOD
GRAVESTONE
MRS
COFFEE MAKER
COINS
METAL SHELVING

FROTTAGE

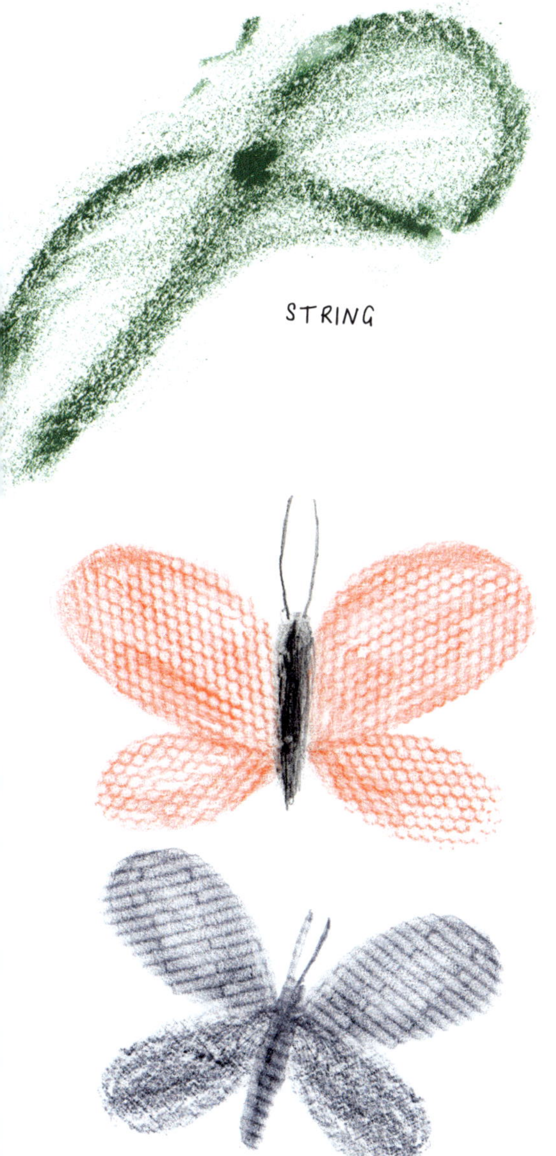

PENCIL RUBBINGS

I remember making rubbings of trees and gravestones when I was a child – this direct contact with materials is sensory and magical. You can use any kind of textured object for frottage art: try leaves, bark, rocks or coins. Experiment with different objects and materials to see what kind of images you can create. You can also incorporate some of these marks into artworks, like the butterflies here.

Creative exercise

Place a piece the paper on a raised, textured surface or object. Rub a pencil or crayon firmly over the paper and lift it to reveal the image. Find as many different objects and surfaces as you can.

Creative inspiration

The frottages of Max Ernst, Mona Hatoum and Eileen Agar.

AFTER IMAGE

OPTICAL ILLUSIONS

On the opposite page, look at the green and blue circles briefly, then shift your gaze to the blank space below. Watch the colours transform: green to red and blue to yellow. Now look at the white star on this page, then down to the white rectangle below it to see a red star. These are after-images and it's useful to be aware of them when making art. They're also fun!

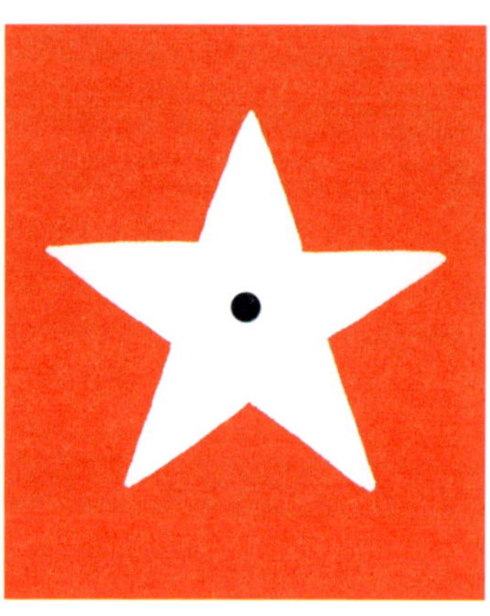

Creative exercise

Try making an artwork using complementary colours: orange and blue, red and green or yellow and purple. Complementary colours are so called because the colours work harmoniously together.

Creative inspiration

The work of Josef Albers, Anni Albers and Yayoi Kusama.

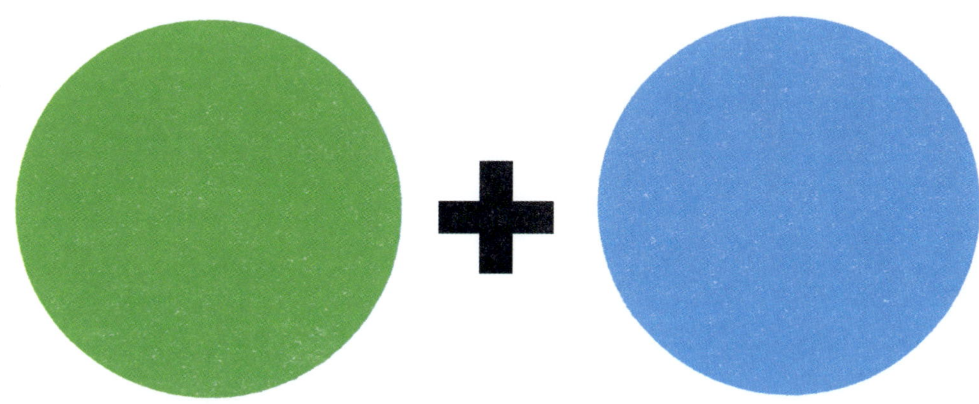

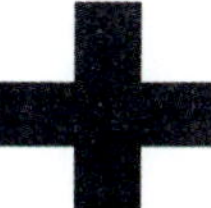

I SEE FACES EVERYWHERE

PAREIDOLIA

Face pareidolia, the tendency to see faces in everyday objects, is hardwired into the human brain. This was one of the first projects I did at art school, and it really helped change my perspective on the world around me. Imagining something that isn't there – in this case, seeing shapes or faces where they aren't – is what creativity is all about.

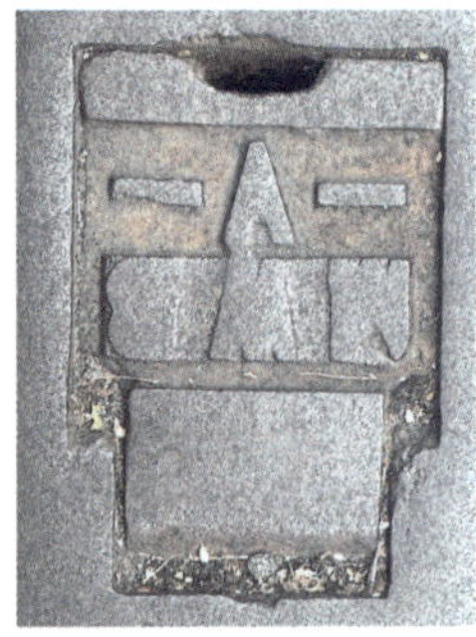
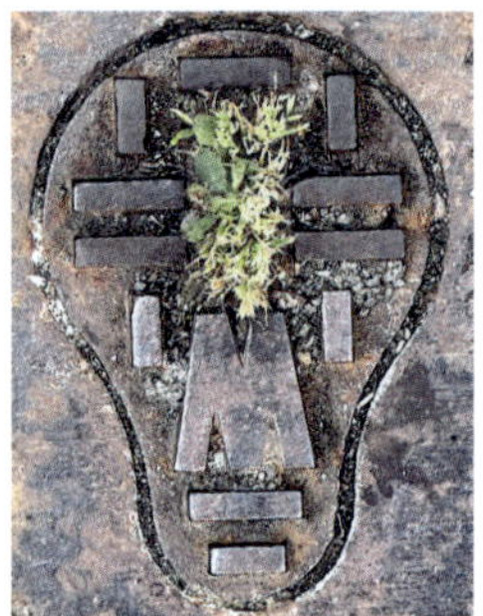
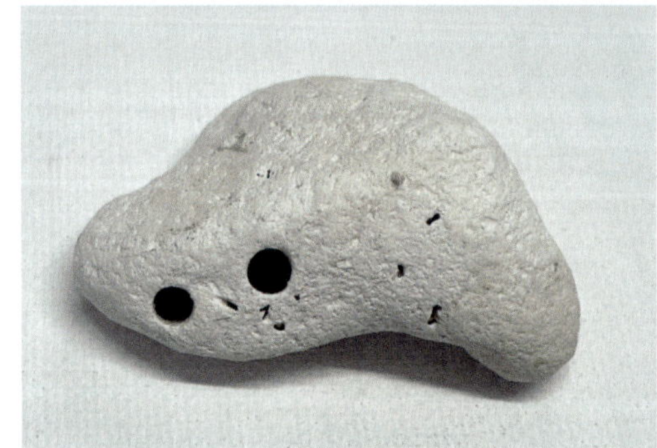

Creative exercise

For a week, use a camera to take pictures of 'faces' you see around you. If you can, print the photos and arrange them side by side to create a gallery of characters.

Creative inspiration

The work of Christoph Niemann and Saul Steinberg.

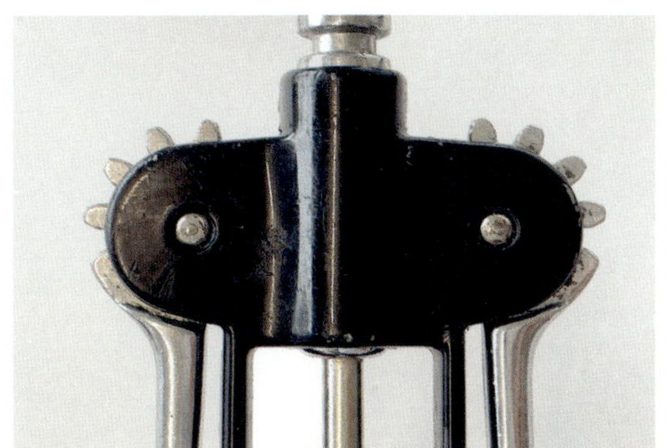
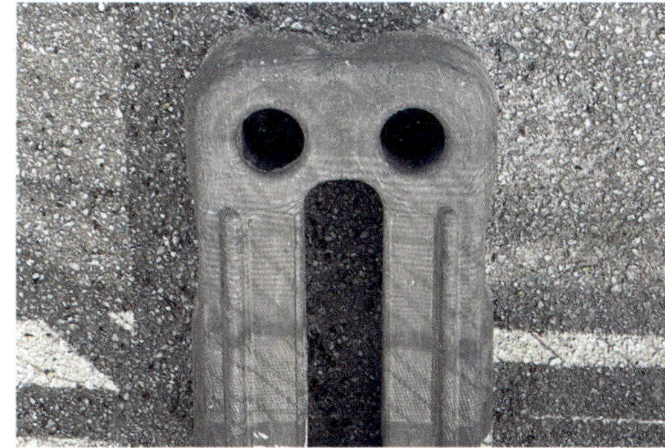
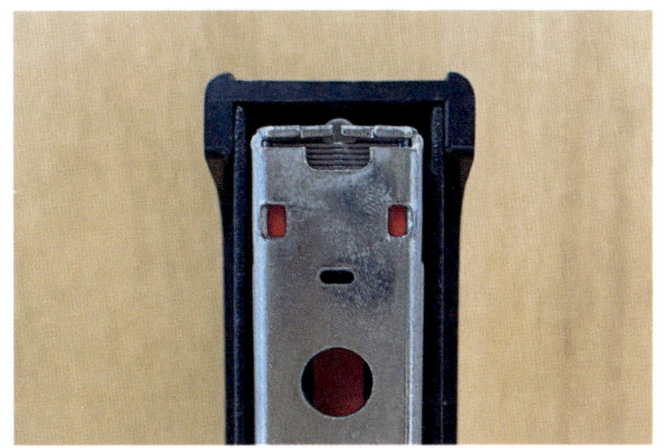
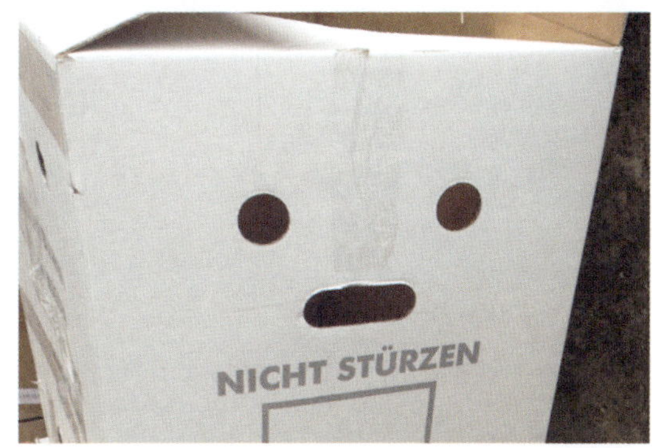
NICHT STÜRZEN
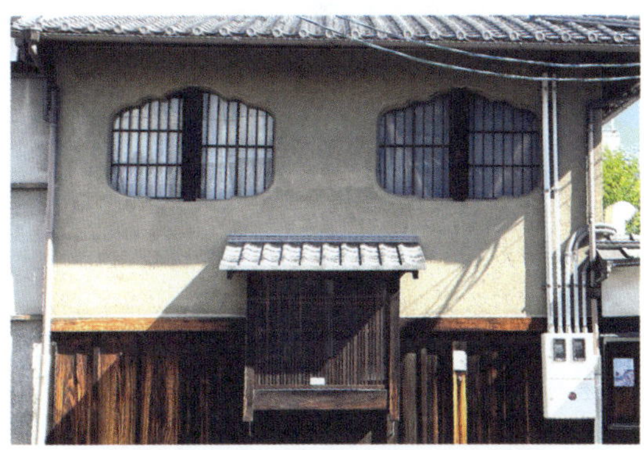
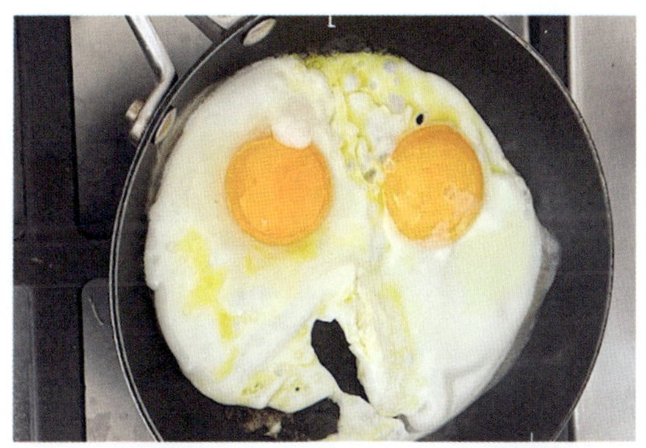
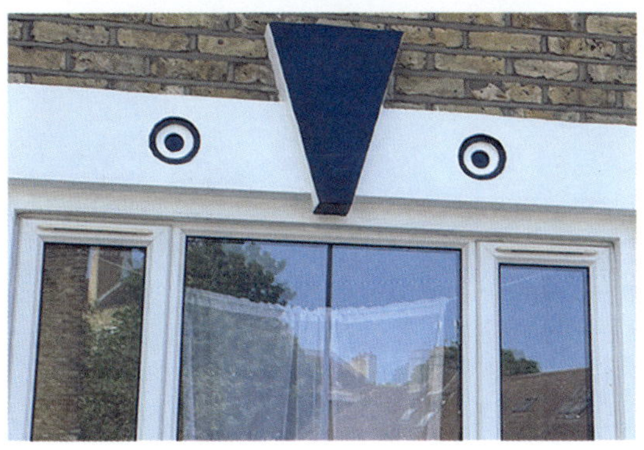
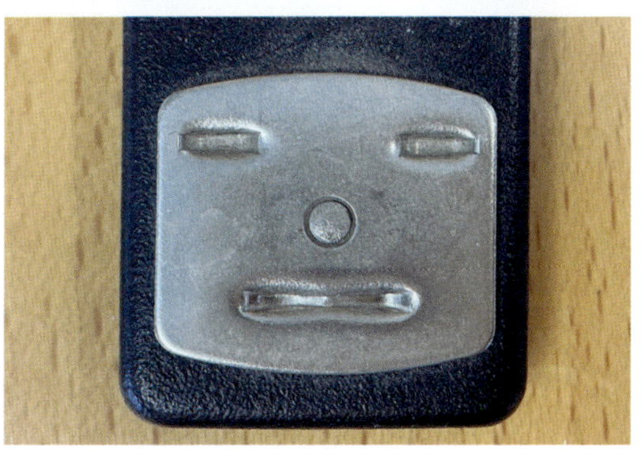

MISTAKES are GOOD

In the words of Bob Ross, 'there are no mistakes, only happy accidents'. Some remarkable discoveries – like penicillin and the colour mauve – actually began as mistakes. I find that my best work often emerges in the moments when I permit mistakes to happen. This is a specific mindset. When I'm on the computer, my inclination is to correct my errors immediately. However, when I'm working with traditional drawing materials, a spilled bottle of ink or an unexpected mix of colours becomes an opportunity for experimentation and play. The key is to embrace this approach and to tune into this way of working.

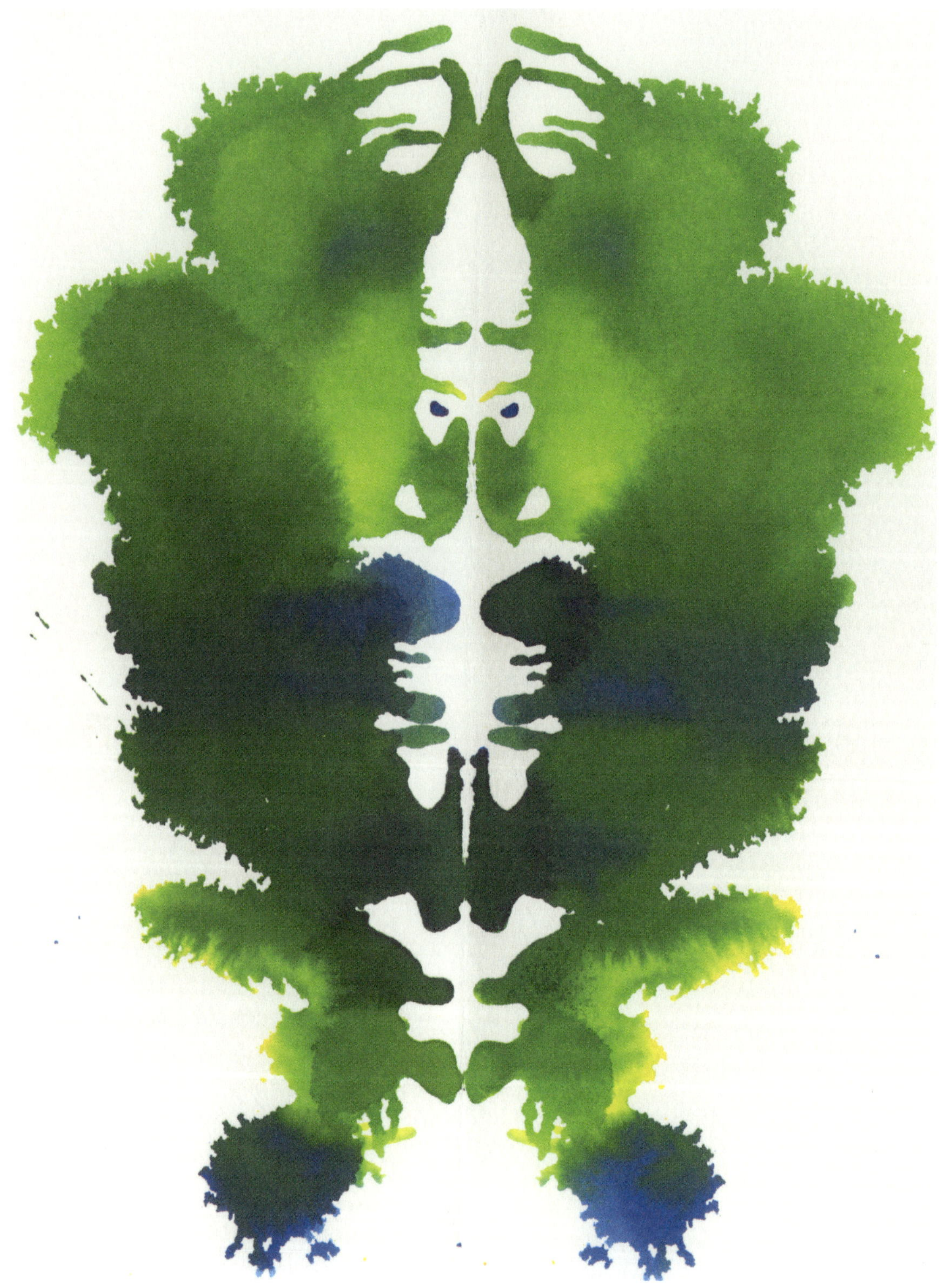

SPILL SOME INK

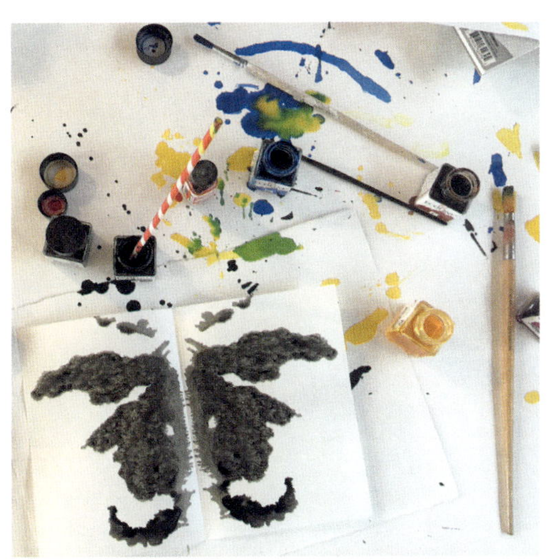

INK BLOT ART

An ink blot or Rorschach test is a psychological evaluation in which your interpretation of an ink blot is used to reveal something about you, but ink blot patterns and artworks can also be appreciated for their beauty alone. So much about making and enjoying art is the element of surprise, and the ink blot technique is great for creating it. You can use black ink or coloured inks or paint.

Creative exercise

Fold a sheet of watercolour paper in half, open it out and use a brush or straw to place some ink blobs on one side only. Fold over and press lightly. This creates unique shapes and creature-like marks.

Creative inspiration

The ink blots of Cornelia Parker and Mary Wagner.

FLOWER POWER

DRAWING AND PAINTING FLOWERS

'When you take a flower in your hand and really look at it, it's your world for the moment.' I love this quote from Georgia O'Keeffe, who painted many beautiful flowers in her lifetime. These simple poppies were made with watercolour, dropping colour on colour to build up texture. We can always find flowers to look at or draw, even weeds growing on the pavement often have beautiful flowers. As O'Keeffe also said, 'to see takes time,' so take a little time to be inspired by a flower.

Creative exercise

Try and draw or paint some flowers or weeds from life. Take the time to really study the leaves, stalks and colours, and make some studies in your sketchbook. Find out their names and write them down next to the drawings.

Creative inspiration

The flowers of Alan Fletcher and Georgia O'Keeffe, and the beautiful botanical drawings of Michael Landy.

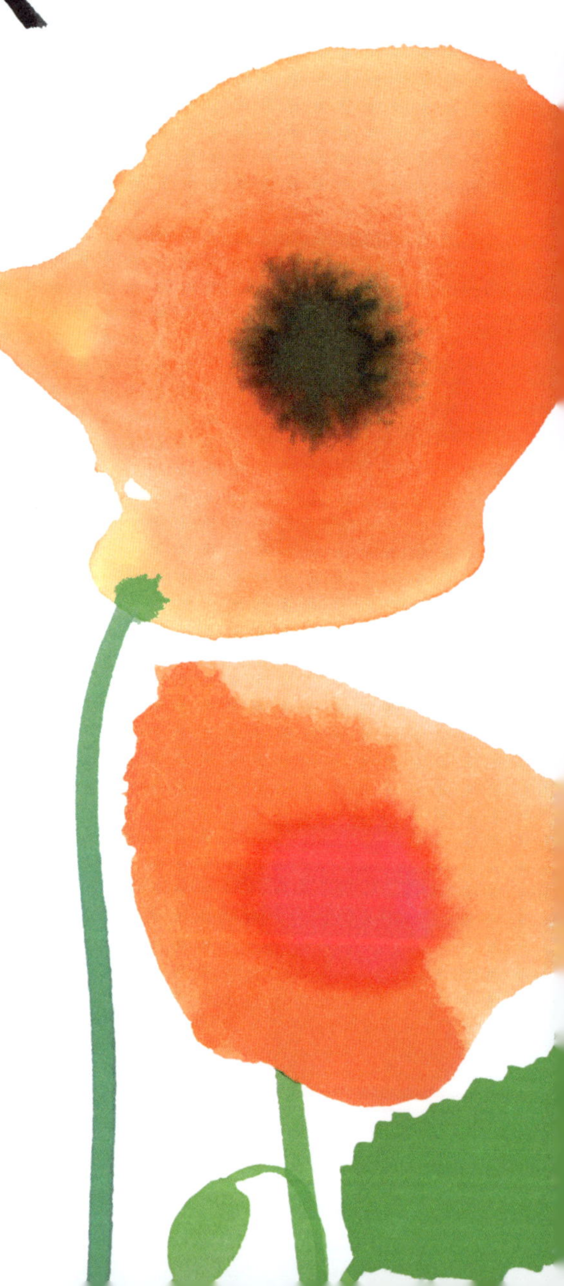

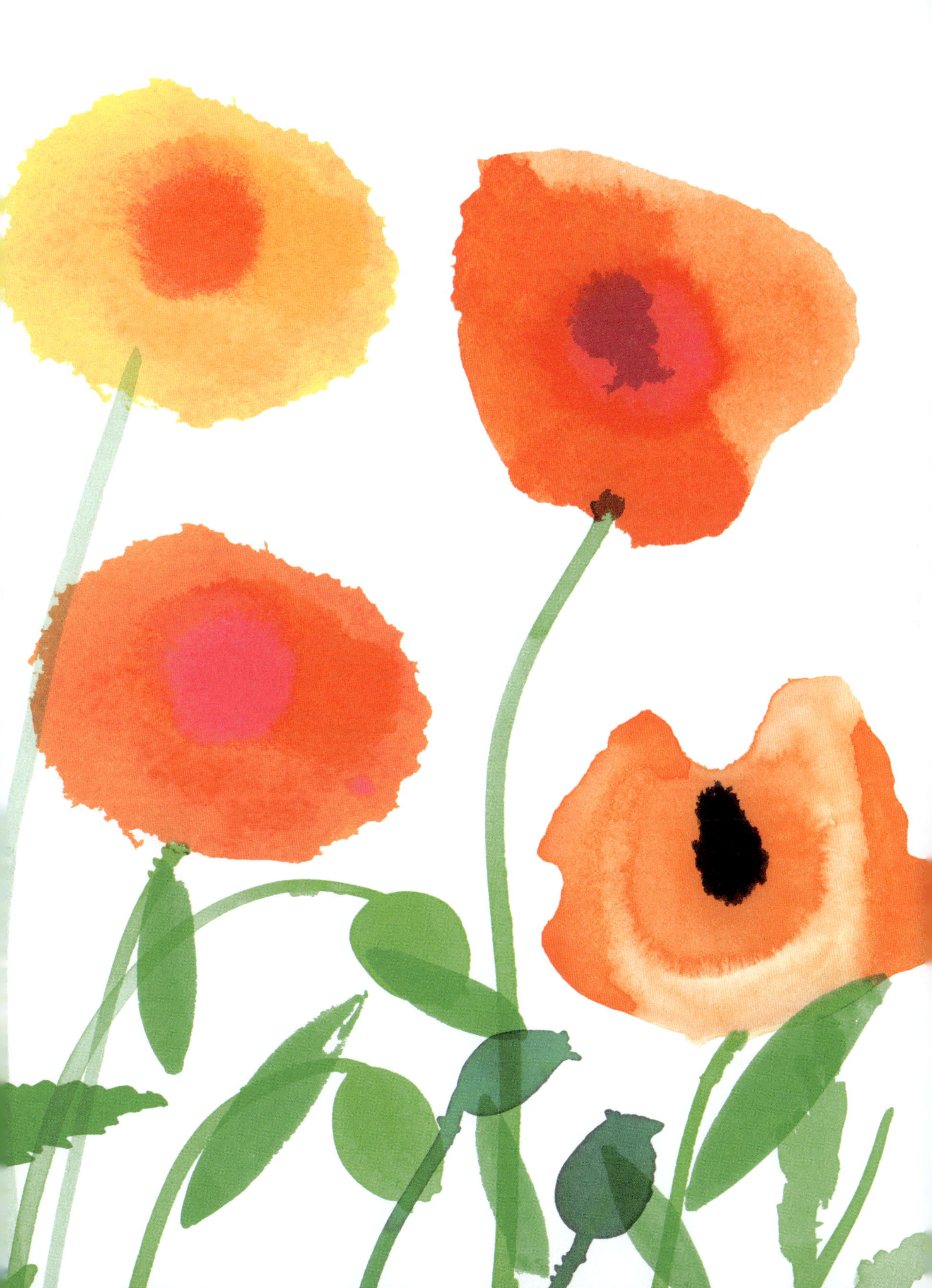

GLITCHY INK LINE

INK BLOT TECHNIQUE

Interesting line work is half of what makes
a successful drawing. The glitchy lines on
this dog drawing take inspiration from
Andy Warhol's ink blotting or monoprint
technique. To achieve this, draw with a
dip pen and ink on a shiny paper or glass
surface. Press a clean sheet of paper on top,
rub gently then lift carefully. The resulting
reversed image, with its irregular splodges
and broken lines, is made of unpredictable
marks, but this is its charm.

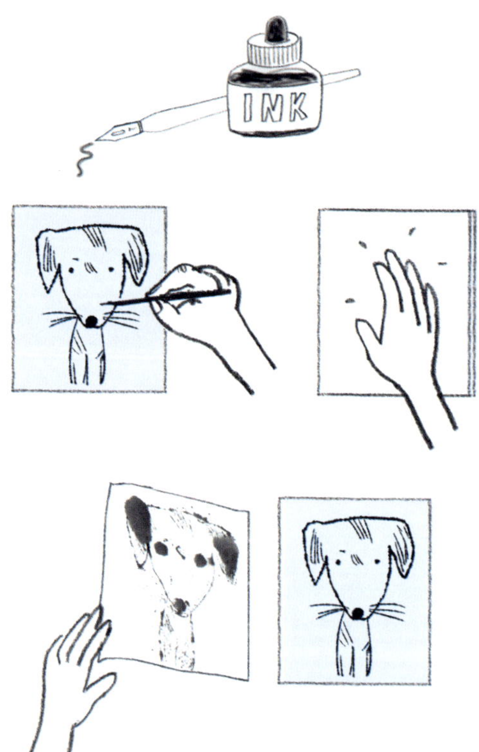

Creative exercise

Experiment with pen and ink drawings
using the ink blot technique. If you
tape the blotting paper to the glass
along one end to make a hinge, you can
draw it in parts more slowly to build
up the image.

Creative quickie

Use copy carbon paper for drawing.
It gives a beautiful blue or black
smudgy line.

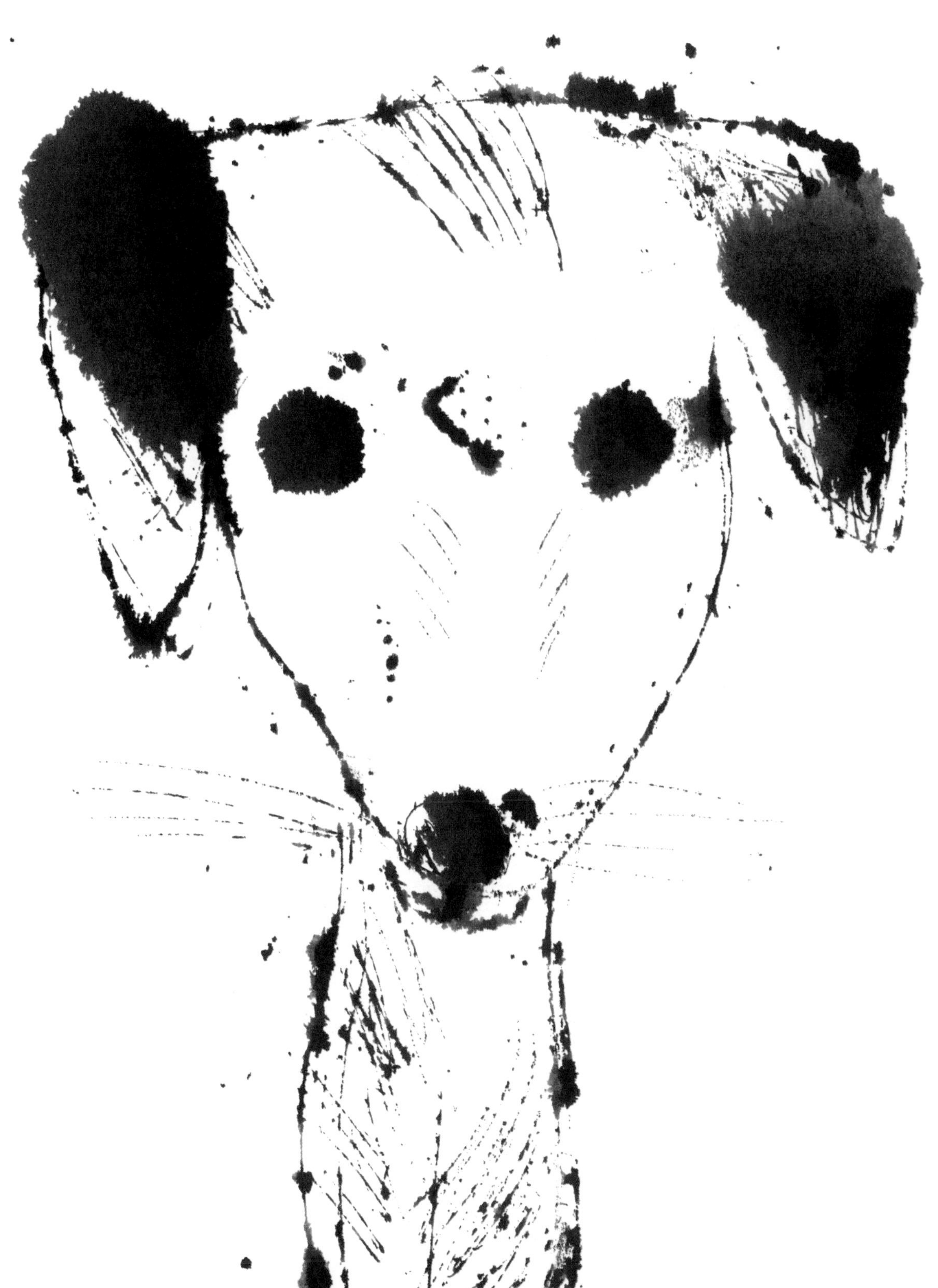

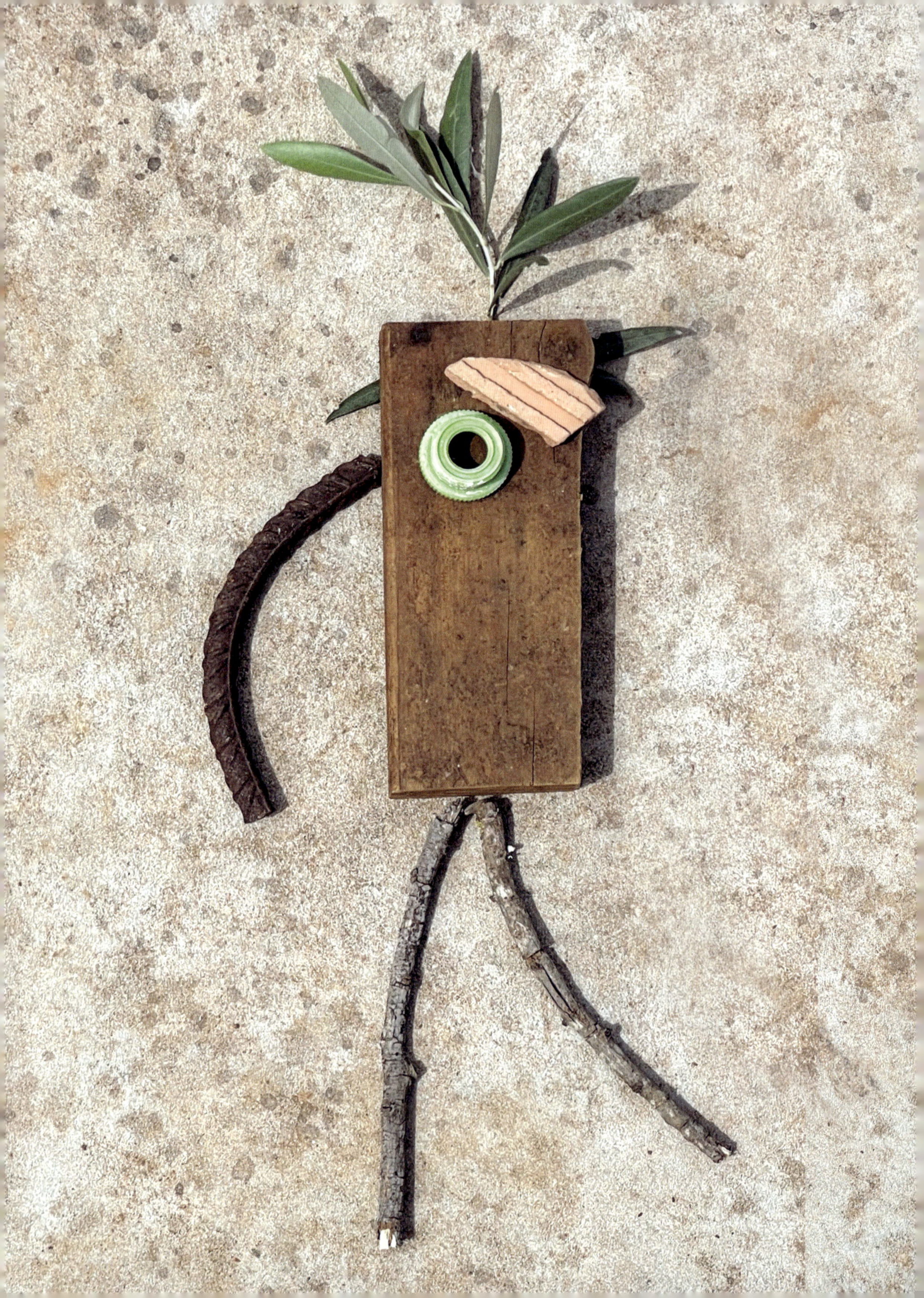

FOUND OBJECTS

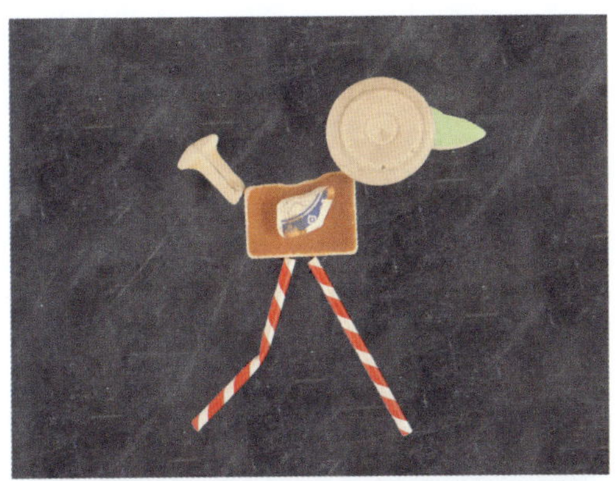

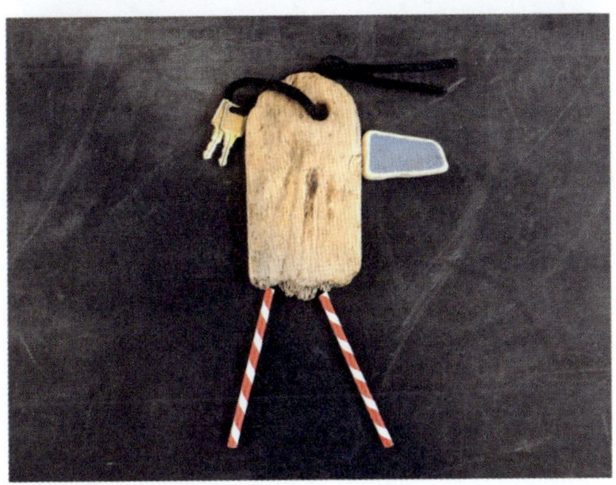

ASSEMBLAGE

I love making art from found objects. The characters I've created here are made from items found around the house, street, beach and junk shops: wood fragments, antique keys, straws and rubbish. This hands-on project encourages you to create wherever you are, and helps you to rediscover the world around you. You'll find that anything can be transformed into art.

Creative exercise

Gather your own objects and arrange them on different coloured backgrounds or surfaces. You can also experiment with lighting. Take photos of your work.

Creative inspiration

The work of Joseph Cornell and Rosalie Gascoigne.

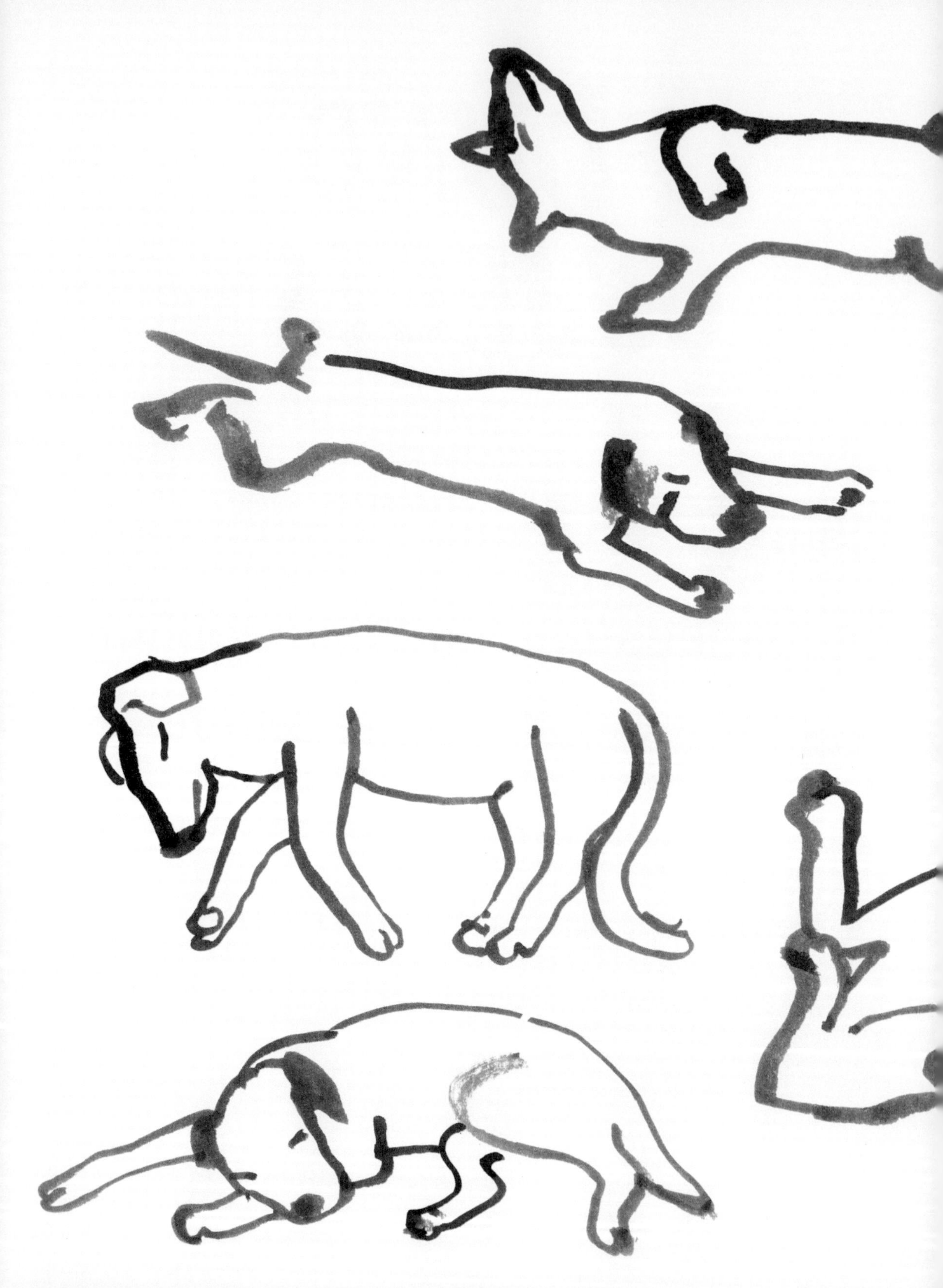

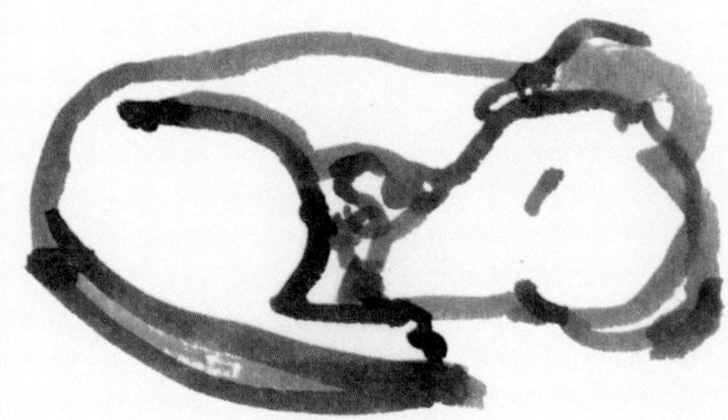

SLEEPY DOGS

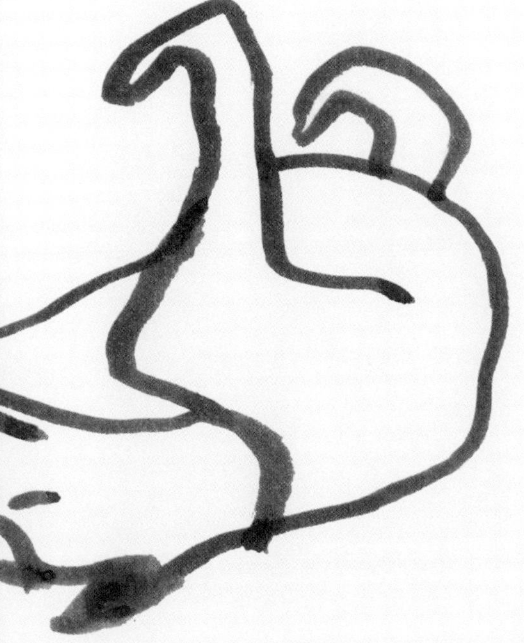

INKY DOG DRAWINGS

Dogs can be very hard to draw, so try it when they are asleep. Concentrate your attention on how they are feeling and try to capture that, rather than making an accurate anatomical drawing. It's the sentiment that you're trying to capture. I drew these dogs with a round brush and black ink, watered down to give a bit more texture. I used a mixture of photographs and my own dog, who often lies next to me when I'm working.

Creative exercise

Choose at least three very different mediums – for example, paint, collage and coloured pencil – and try to draw sleeping dogs in as many different ways as possible, but all on the same sheet of paper.

Creative inspiration

The dog drawings and paintings of David Hockney and Sally Muir.

LEAF CIRCLE

DRAWING WITH NATURE

I love it when the leaves change colour in autumn. Make use of this fleeting time to create art with them. I've arranged these maple leaves in a circle, blending the colours. Collecting the different gradated colours is part of the pleasure. Use two sticks to help form the circle: push one into the ground as the centre and move the other around like a clock dial to help position the leaves accurately.

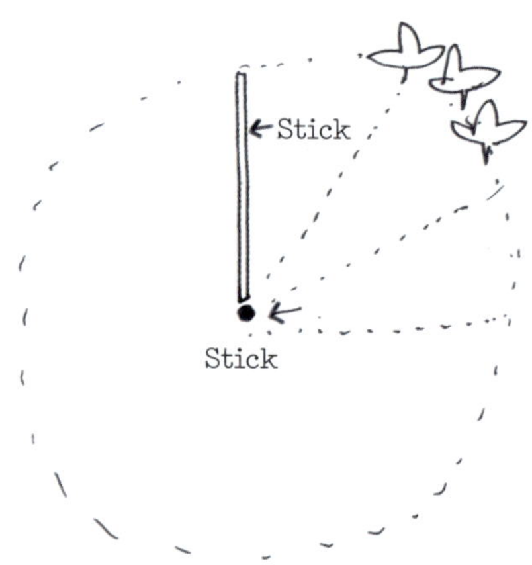

Creative exercise

Collect and sort leaves by colour to create various artworks large and small, like this rainbow path, for example. Part of the fun is when you make something in nature for others to discover.

Creative inspiration

The work of Andy Goldsworthy, Ai Weiwei and Jenny Kendler.

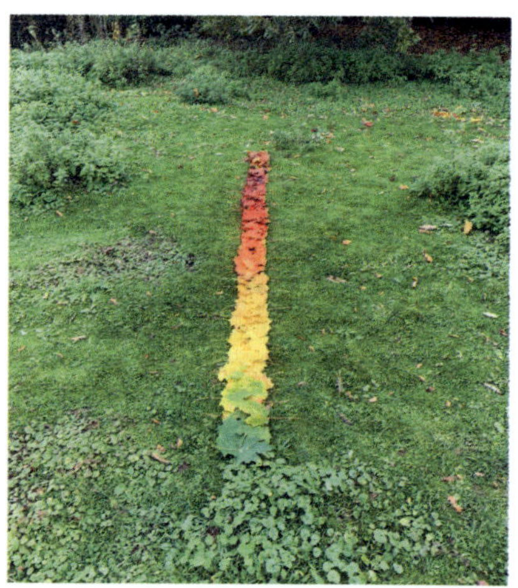

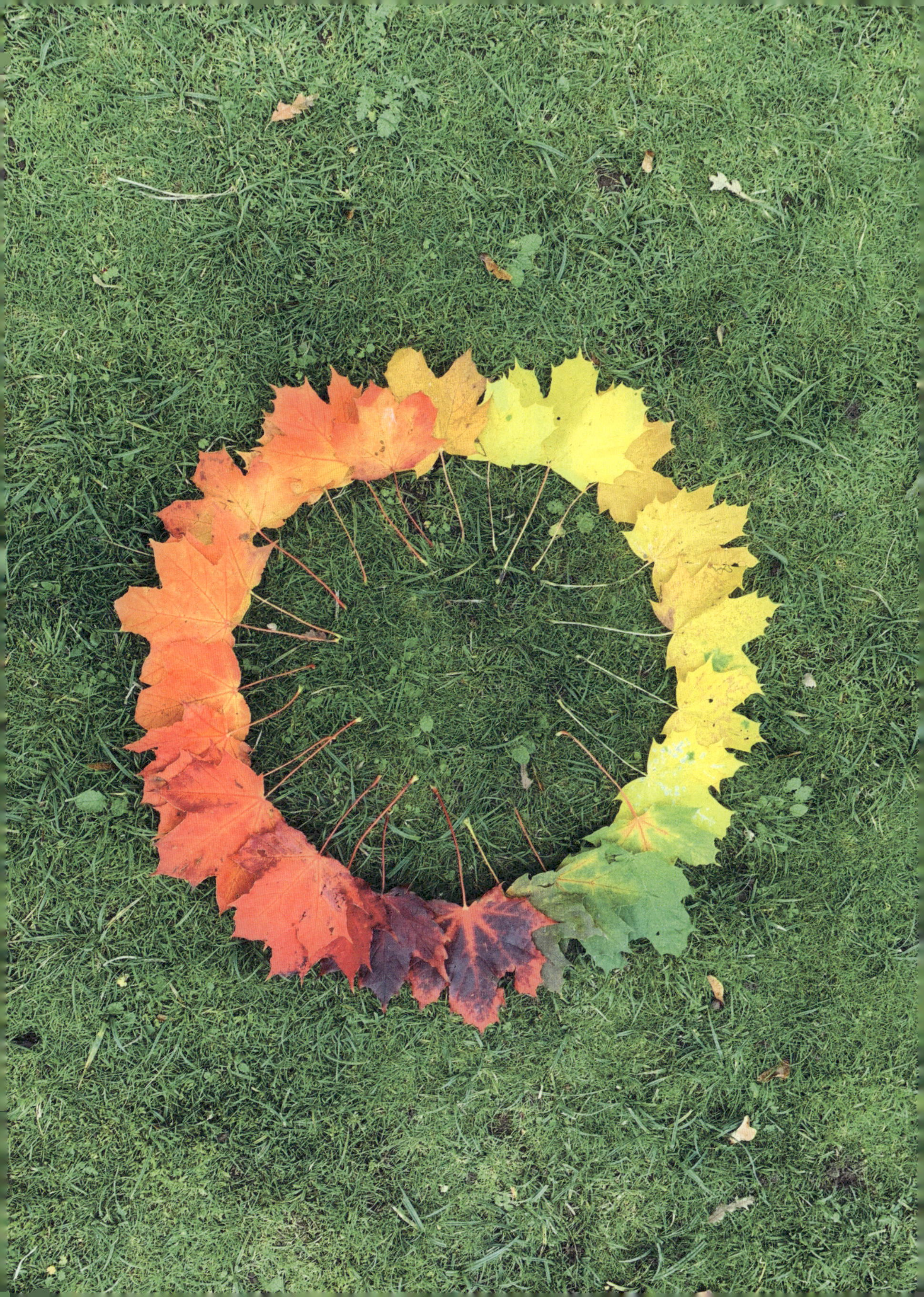

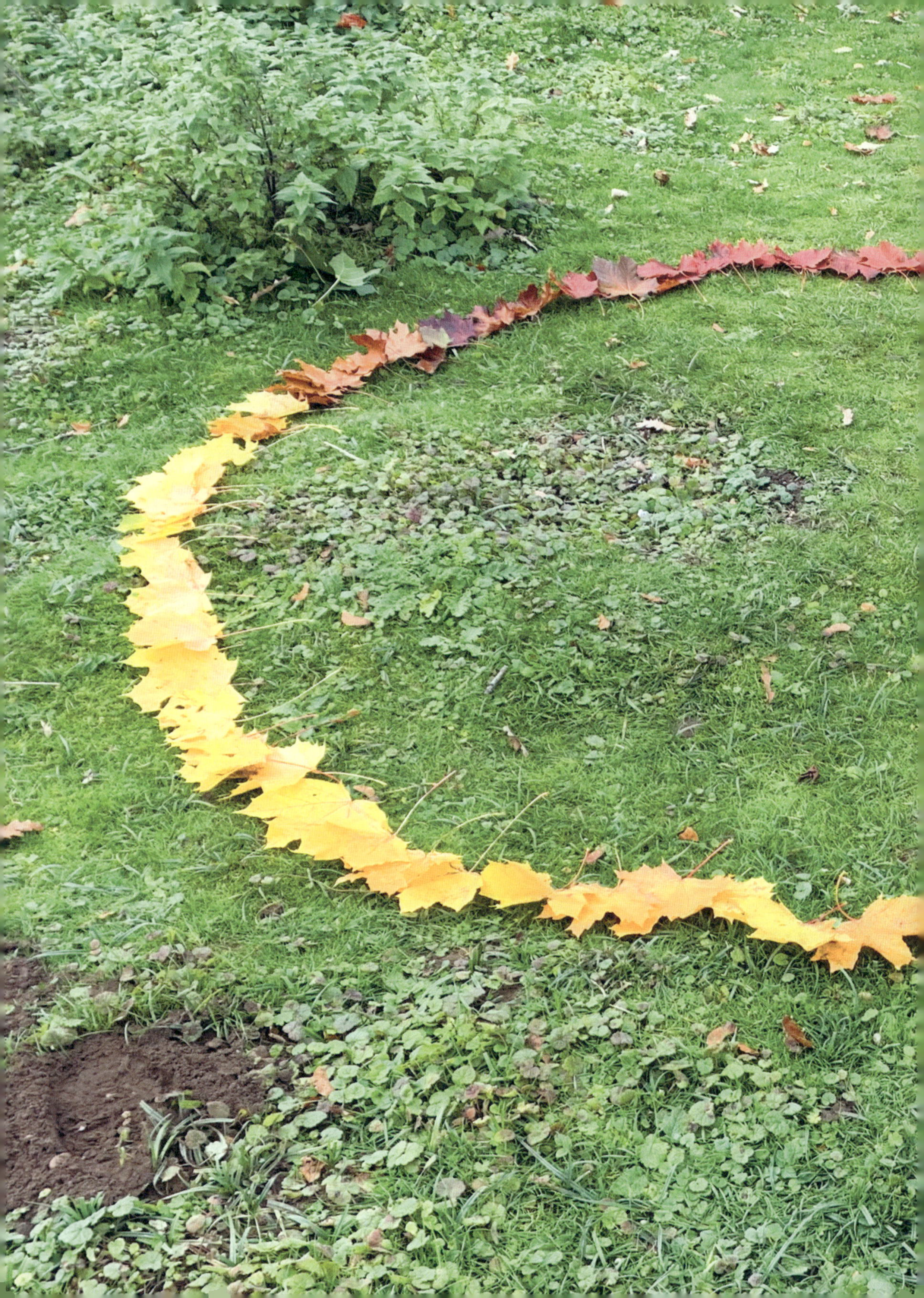

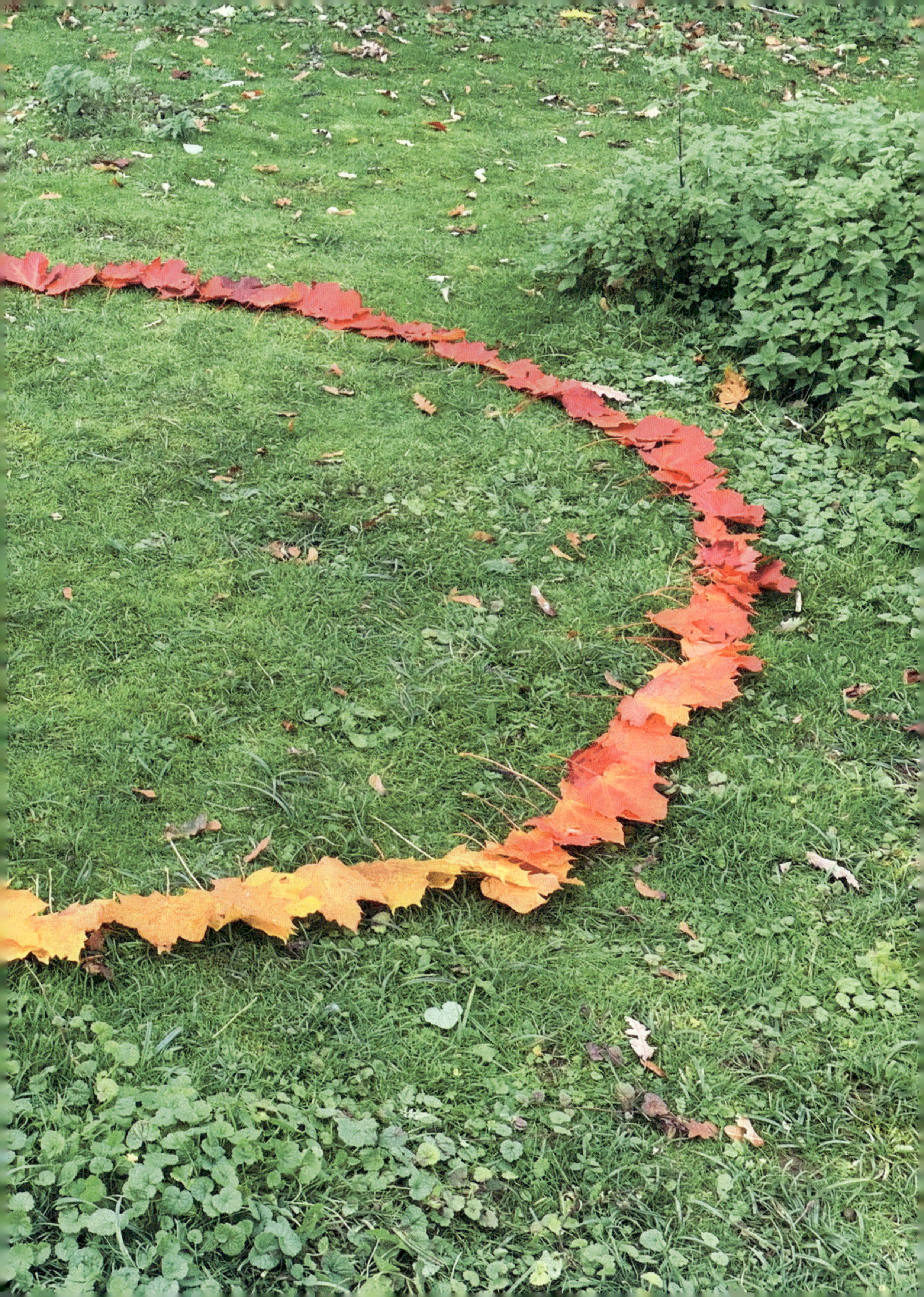

TYPE EVERYWHERE

LOOK FOR LETTERS

Look around you: letters are everywhere! From street signs to shop fronts, each has its own style and history. Use a camera or smartphone to capture these unique fonts. You'll start seeing the world in a new way, noticing the small details that make each letter special. It's a fun and simple way to explore – or defamiliarize – your surroundings.

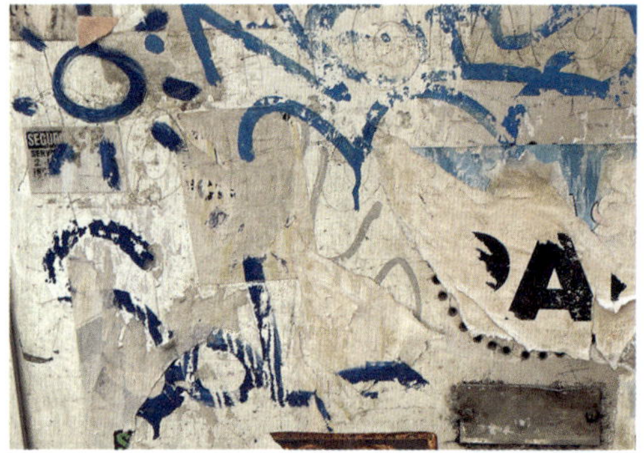

Creative exercise

Make your own compilation of photographs of examples of lettering all around you. Lay out the images in a way that enhances the contrast between styles. This could be done digitally or physically.

Creative quickie

Take photos of distressed walls. Here you will find all kinds of artworks! Many artists have been influenced by the patina and colours of walls in our cities and streets, including Robert Rauschenberg.

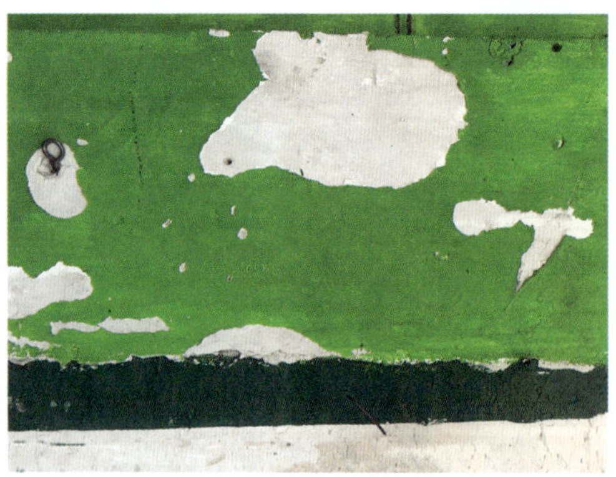

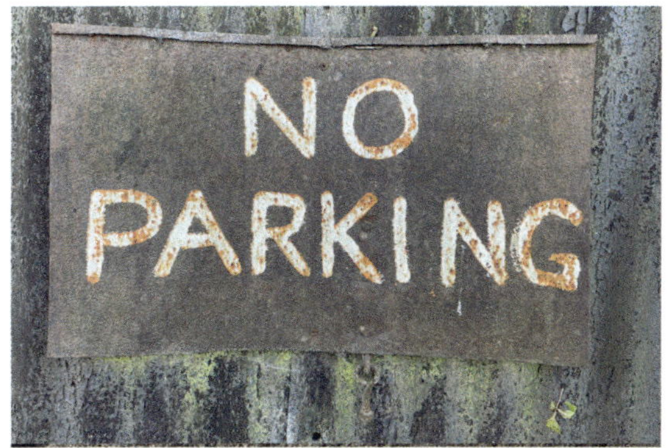
NO
PARKING

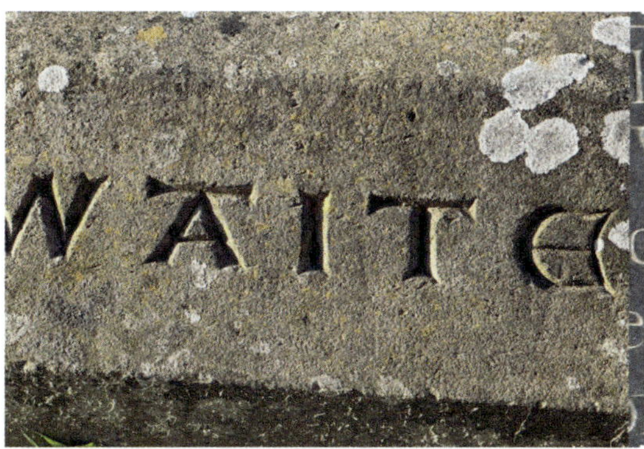
WAITC

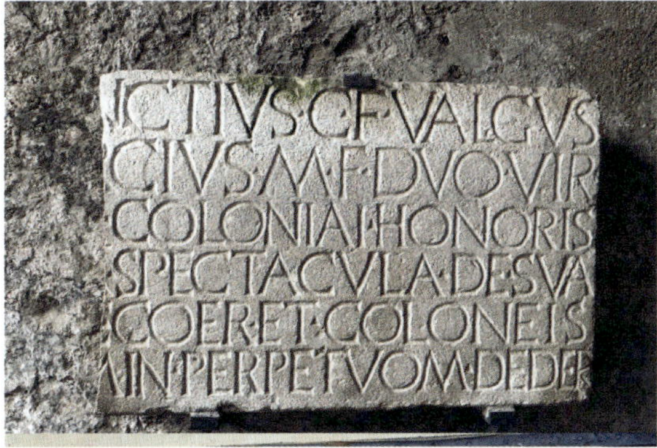
ICTIVS·CF·VALGVS
CIVS·MF·DVO·VIR
COLONIAI·HONORIS
SPECTACVLA·DESVA
COERET·COLONEIS
AINPERPETVOM·DEDER

BO

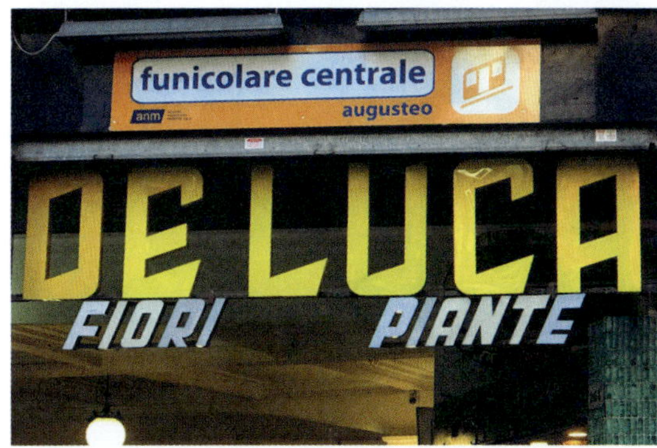
funicolare centrale
anm   augusteo
DE LUCA
FIORI   PIANTE

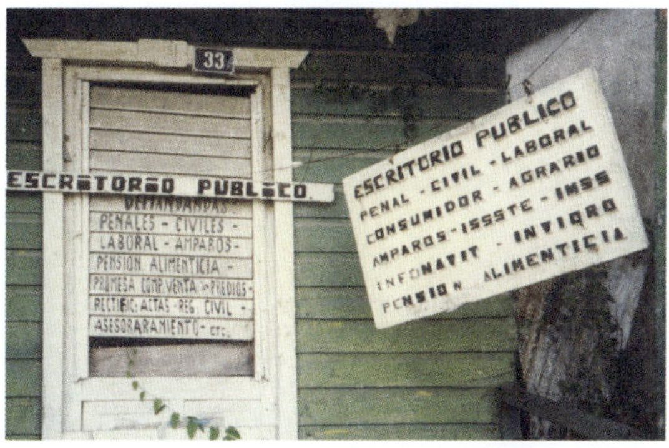
33
ESCRITORIO PUBLICO
DEMANDANDAS
PENALES · CIVILES
LABORAL · AMPAROS
PENSION ALIMENTICIA
PROMESA COMP VENTA PREDIOS
RECTIFIC. ALTAS REG. CIVIL
ASESORARAMIENTO · CTS.
ESCRITORIO PUBLICO
PENAL · CIVIL · LABORAL
CONSUMIDOR · AGRARIO
AMPAROS · ISSSTE · IMSS
INFONAVIT · INIIQRO
PENSION ALIMENTICIA

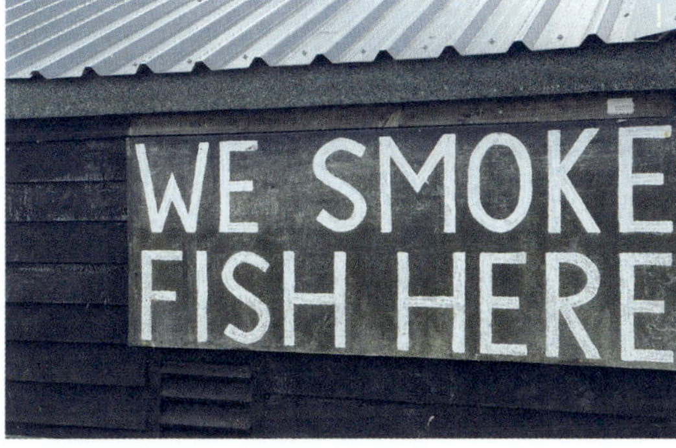
WE SMOKE
FISH HERE

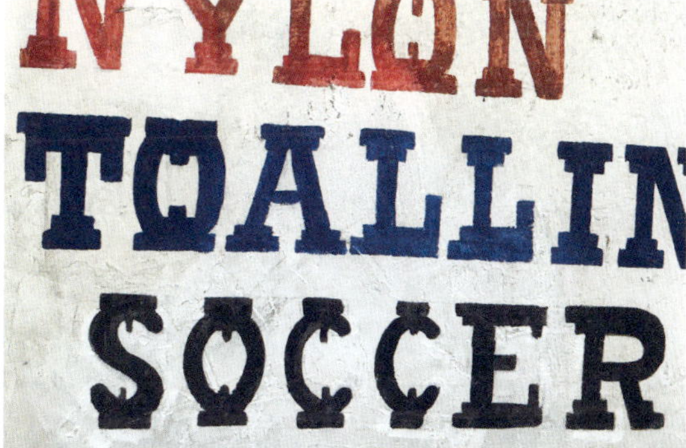
NYLON
TOALLIN
SOCCER

HAND LETTERING

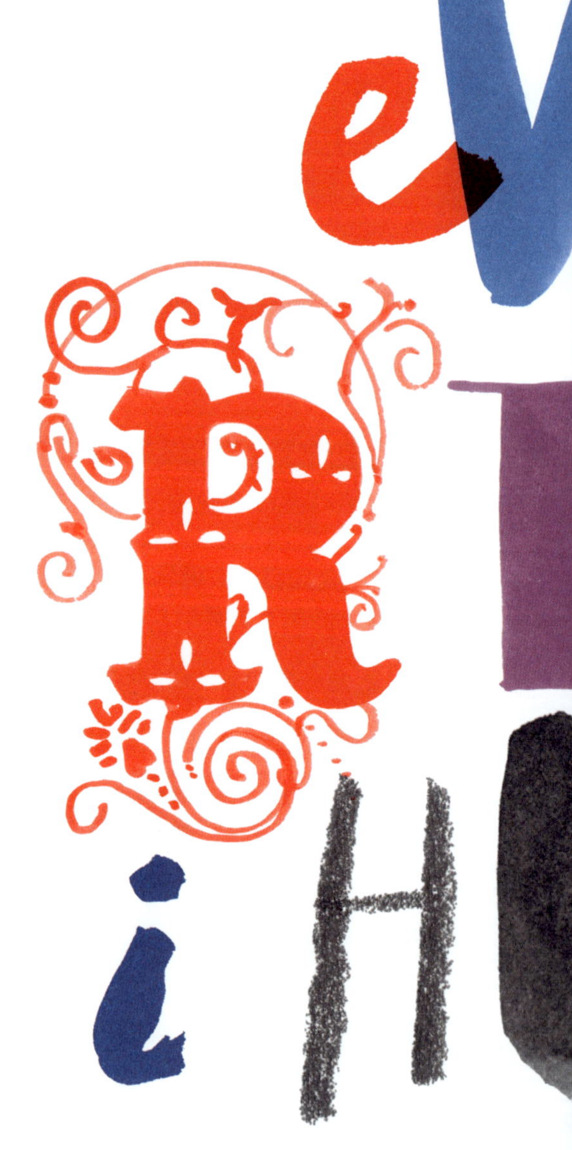

DRAW YOUR OWN LETTERS

I use a lot of hand lettering in my work because it feels personal and alive. Unlike standard fonts, there are no hard rules, so it's a fun way to push boundaries and create a unique voice. For me, hand lettering stands out in a sea of fonts. It cuts through the visual clutter with a human touch that's hard to ignore.

Creative exercise

Using media like paint, pencils or cut paper, create playful lettering. Combine differently drawn letters to form words, pushing the boundaries of recognition. Your brain will fill in the gaps.

Creative inspiration

The work of Paula Scher and Stefan Sagmeister.

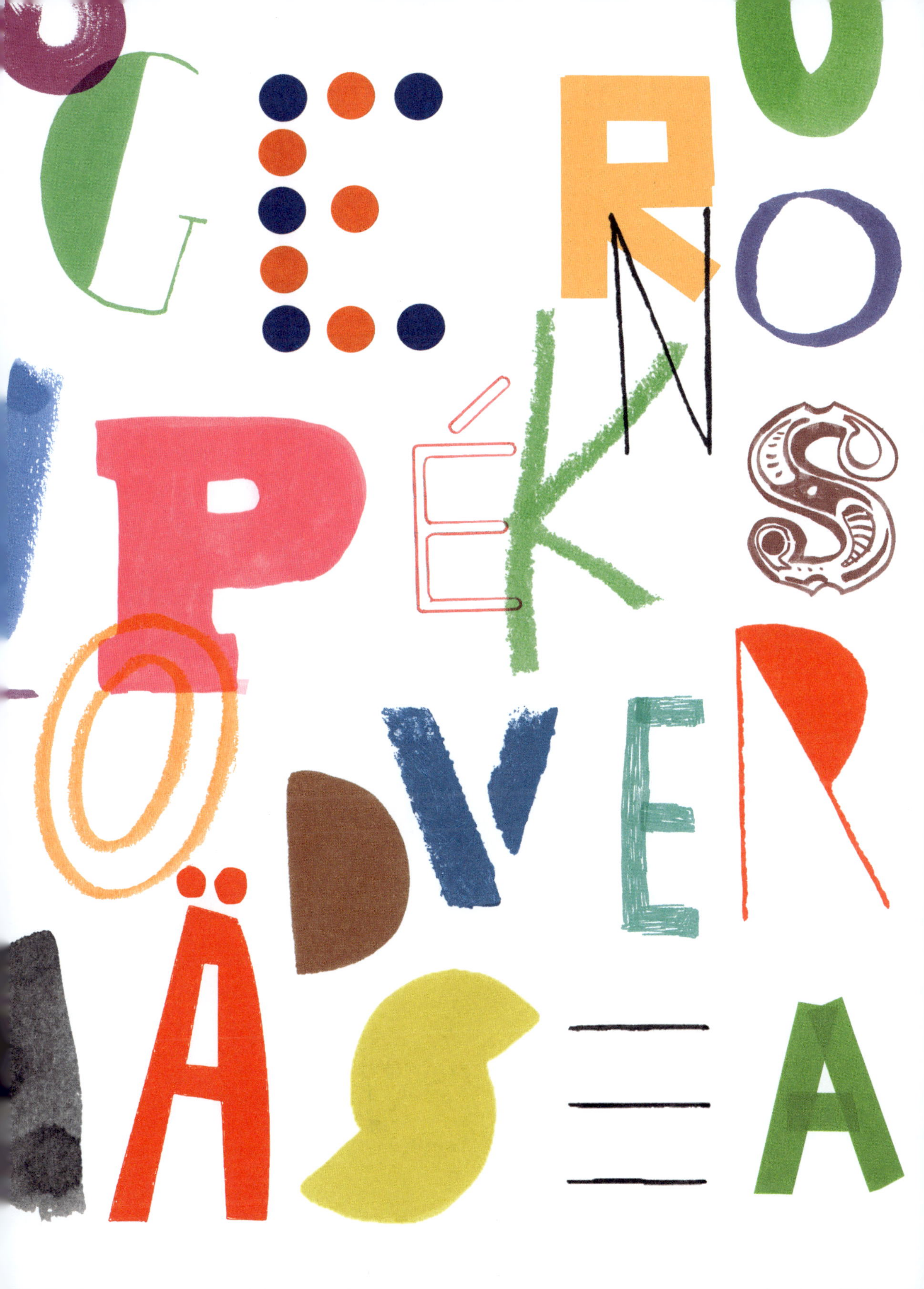

Aa Bb Cc Dd
Ee Ff Gg Hh
Ii Jj Kk Ll
Mm Nn Oo Pp

Lettering based on Copperplate script.

NARRATIVE OF FREDERICK DOUGLASS, AN FN AMERICAN SLAVE

Alphabet copied from Ben Shahn.

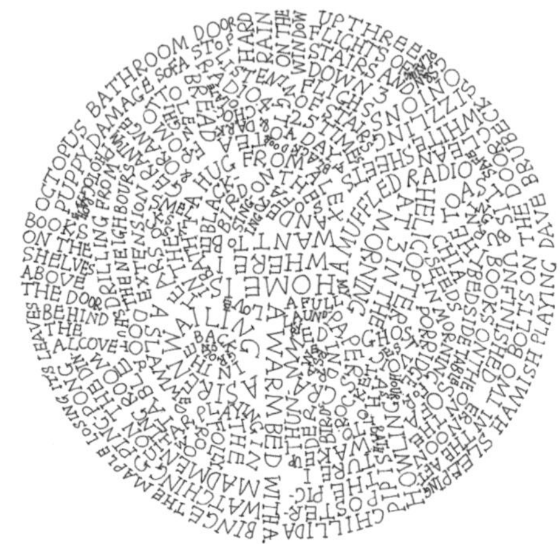

Lettering made for a plate design.

CREATE ERSTELLEN CRÉER

Lettering with crayon on a rough surface.

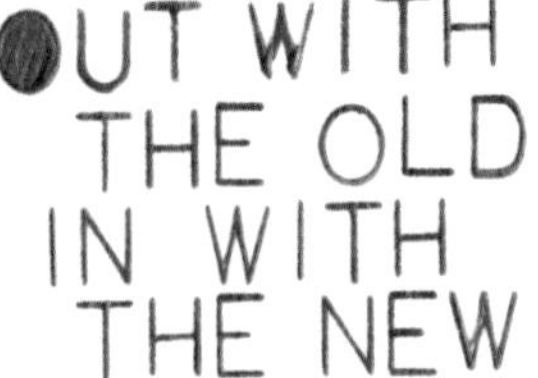

Brush hand lettering in a free style.

HACER UNA LETRA ÚNICA. JEAN-MICHEL BASQUIAT UTILIZÓ UN DISTINTIVO E

Lettering with one unique or distorted letter. Jean-Michel Basquiat wrote with a distinctive letter E.

OUT WITH THE OLD IN WITH THE NEW

Stencil lettering with pen.

QUIRKY ALPHABETS

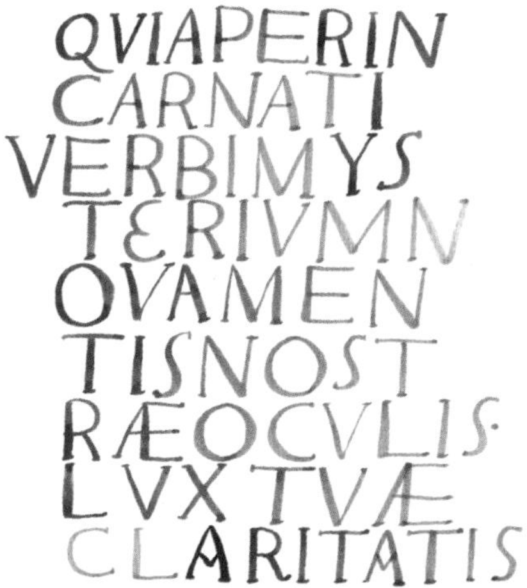

Copied lettering inspired by Roman
lettering by David Jones.

Can YOU WRITE
IN THIS aLPHaBeT
WHeRe aLL THe
LeTTeRS aRE
caPiTaLS exCePT
THe LeTTeRS 'amen'
WHICH are aLL in
LOWeR case.

Lettering inspired by artist, nun
and teacher Corita Kent.

CREATE YOUR OWN FONT

Each of us has our own unique signature.
Many artists have very distinctive hand
lettering. See if you can develop your own.
Copy some alphabets, from Anglo Saxon
to Roman. Copy artists' lettering or use
stencils. Just having one unique way of
drawing a letter can make your lettering
highly individual and recognizable: take
a look at Jean-Michel Basquiat's way of
drawing the letter E.

Creative exercise

Many alphabets are categorized as serif
or sans serif. In this context, you can
think of the word 'serif' as 'feet', and the
word 'sans' means 'without'. So letters
either have feet (serif) or no feet (sans
serif). Look at examples of each and copy
them. Example of serif typefaces include
Times New Roman and Garamond. Sans
serif: Helvetica and Gill.

Creative inspiration

The hand lettering of Alan Fletcher and
Jessica Hische.

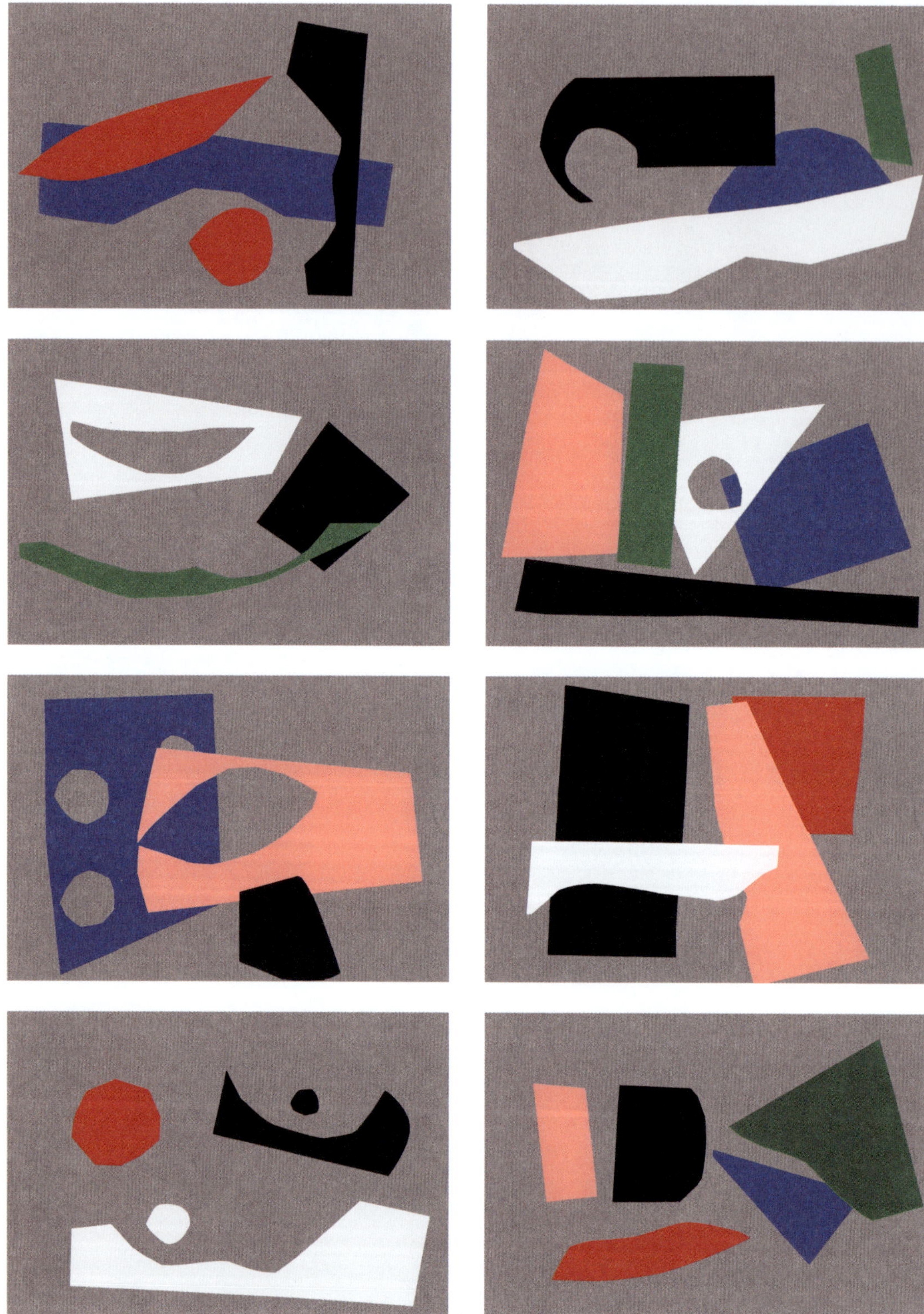

OFFCUTS

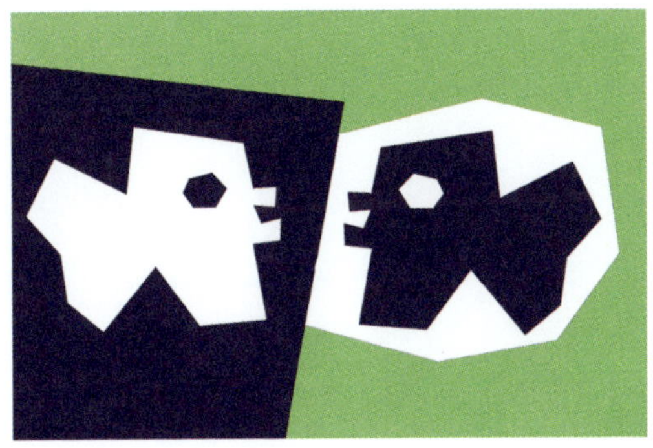

NO-WASTE COLLAGES

I'm inspired by the paper cuts of artists like Matisse and the handmade books of the Russian avant-garde of the early twentieth century. Their work looks effortless and free. In these images opposite I used discarded pieces of coloured paper from other projects to make some collages. I tried to emulate the spontaneity of those artists and their playfulness.

Creative exercise

Collect some coloured paper, discarded or otherwise. Cut up into random shapes. Cut up six rectangles of the same colour. Now playfully arrange the cut-up paper on to those rectangles until you're happy with your compositions.

Creative inspiration

The paper cuts of Matisse and books by Russian avant-garde artists like Natalia Goncharova and Aleksandr Rodchenko.

Enjoy the PROCESS

Creativity is more about the journey than the end
result, yet we often become fixated on the final
product. I've always loved the process of creating,
playing and experimenting without being attached
to any particular outcome. As the writer and
artist Lynda Barry beautifully observed,
'When we were kids … we used paper as if it were
a place, rather than a thing.' For children, paper
represents a world of possibilities to go to,
and that is something we can all be inspired by.

MARVELLOUS MARBLING

EXPERIMENT WITH OIL AND WATER

Paper marbling, historically used for bookbinding, creates unique patterns on paper using oil-based inks. It's great fun and can be used on many craft projects. Be warned, it's also addictive!

Creative exercise

Make your own marbled paper. You'll need a tray, oil-based inks, water, paper and a toothpick or brush.

Creative inspiration

Look in second-hand bookshops to see examples of marbling in old books.

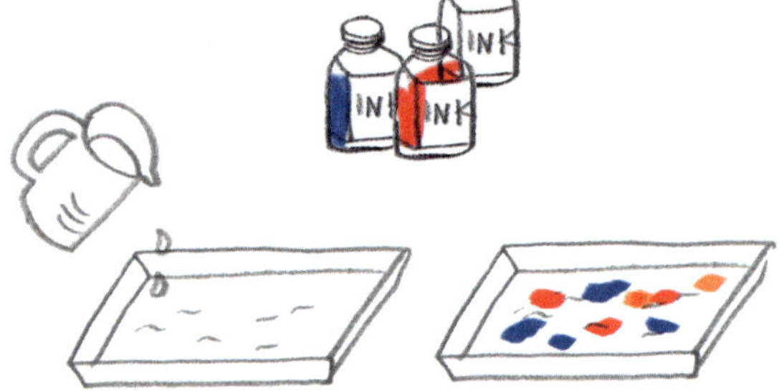

1. Add about 2cm (¾in) of water to a tray.

2. Drop some ink onto the surface of the water.

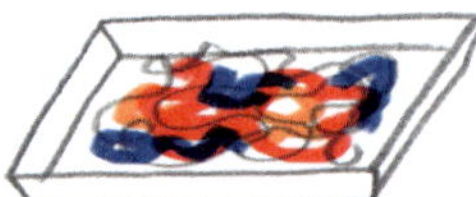

3. Swirl the colours with a toothpick or brush.

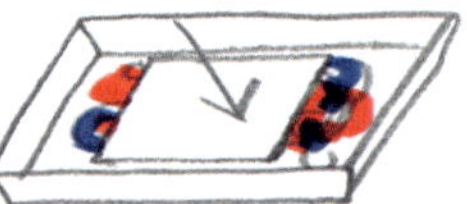

4. Lay a sheet of paper gently on the water and remove it quickly.

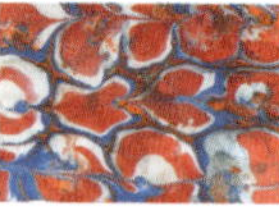

5. Let it dry.

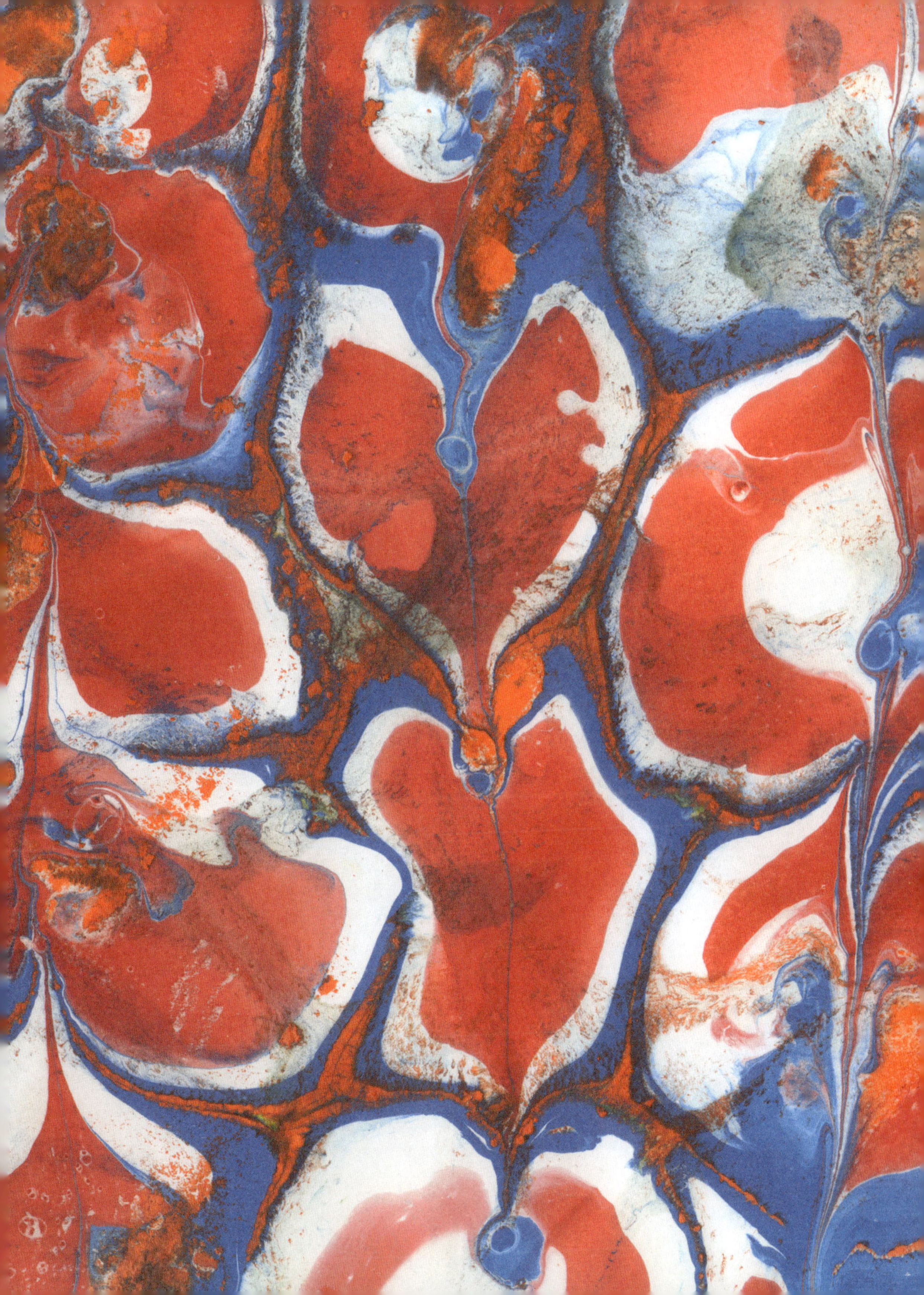

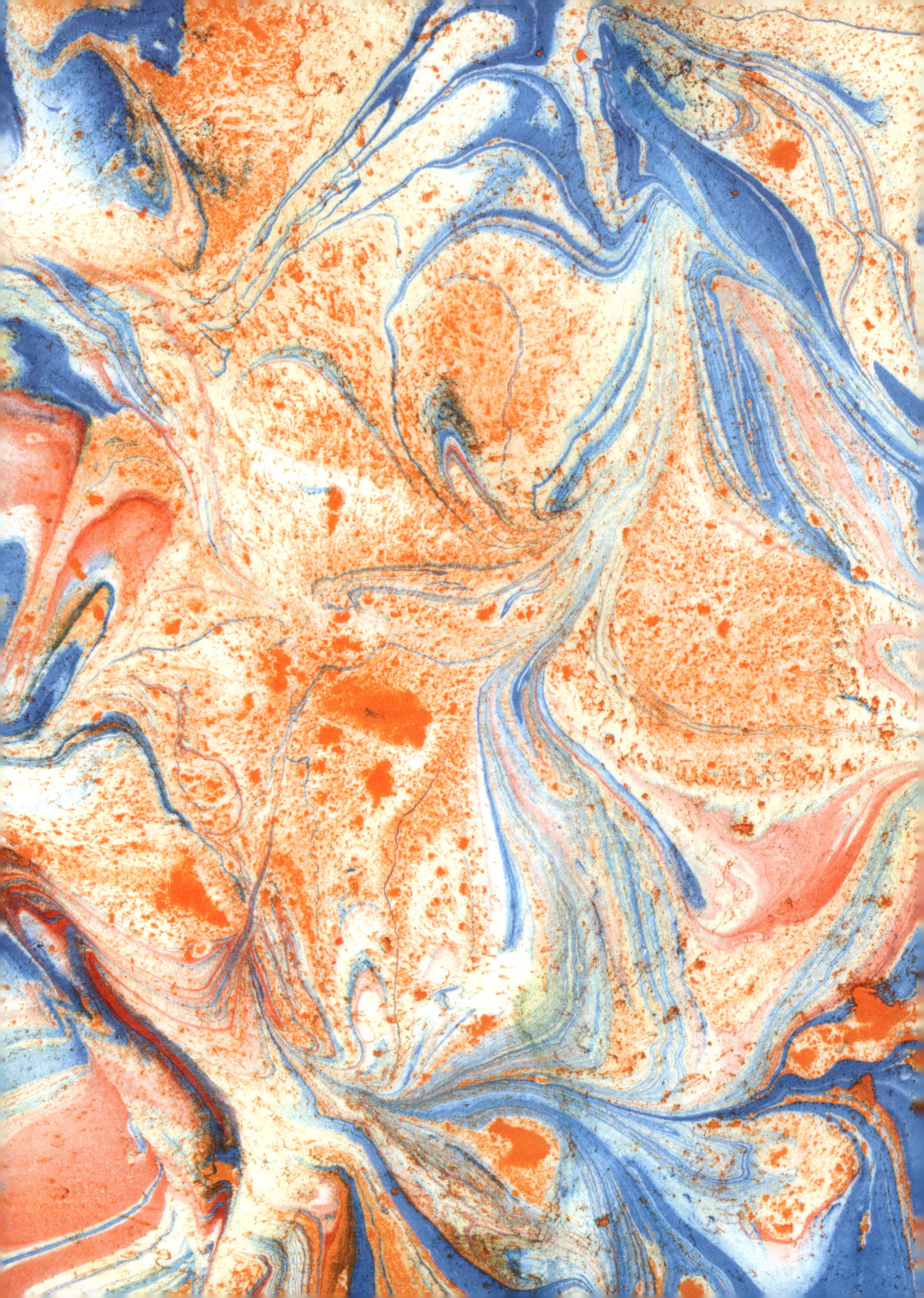

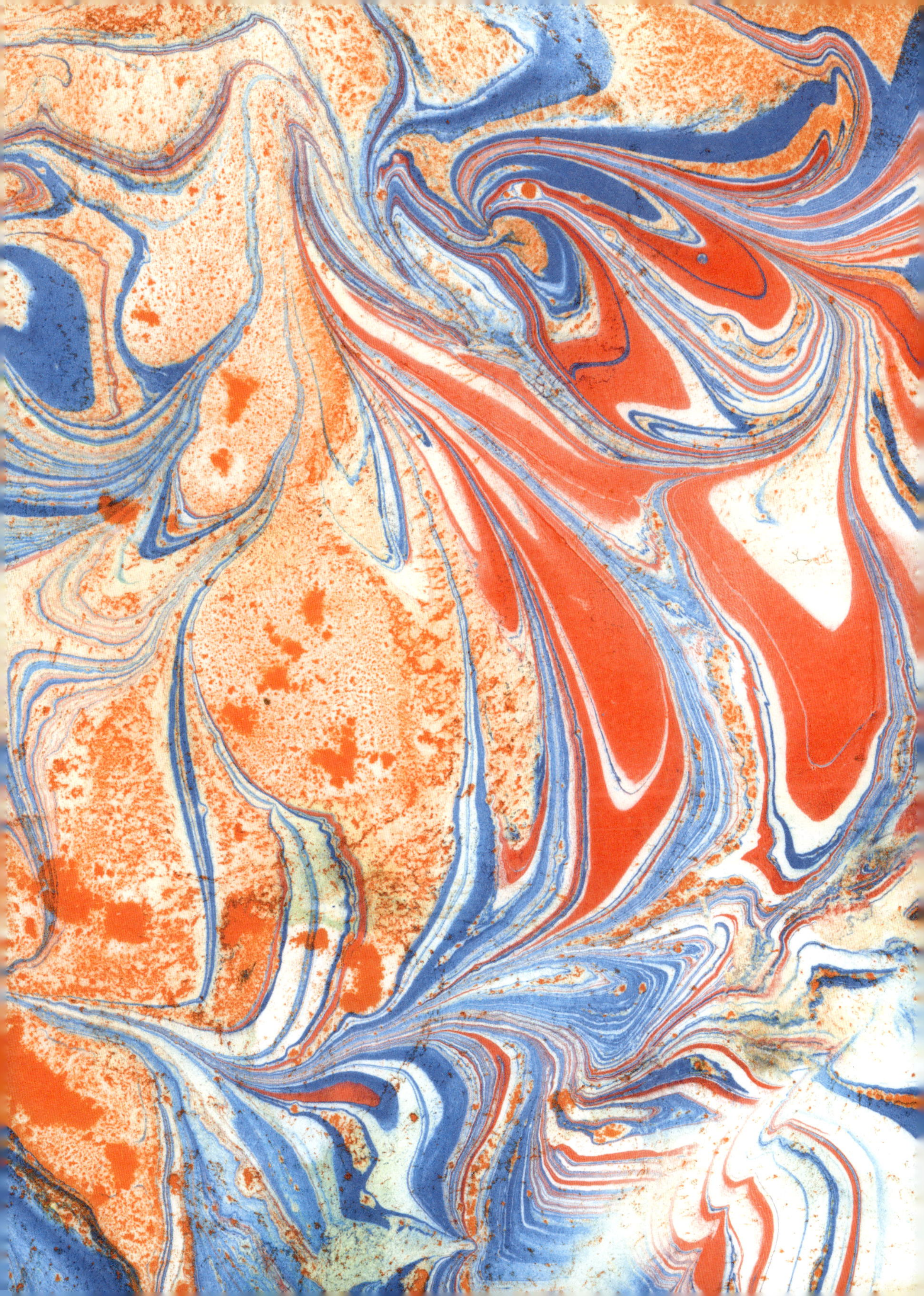

STAMP IT

HOMEMADE STAMPS

You can create stamps from a variety of materials: erasers, pencil lids, staples and sticky tack or clay. With just paper and coloured ink pads, you can print unique patterns and artworks. I love just picking up odd things from my desk, inking them and printing it! Marks made this way possess a one-of-a-kind charm, each print slightly different.

Creative exercise

Start by cutting or carving shapes into an eraser with a craft knife, then ink it, and press it firmly on to white paper to create stamp patterns. As you gain confidence, expand to printing on T-shirts, cloth or tote bags. The possibilities are limitless.

Creative inspiration

The rubber stamps of Saul Steinberg and the printmaker Stephen Fowler.

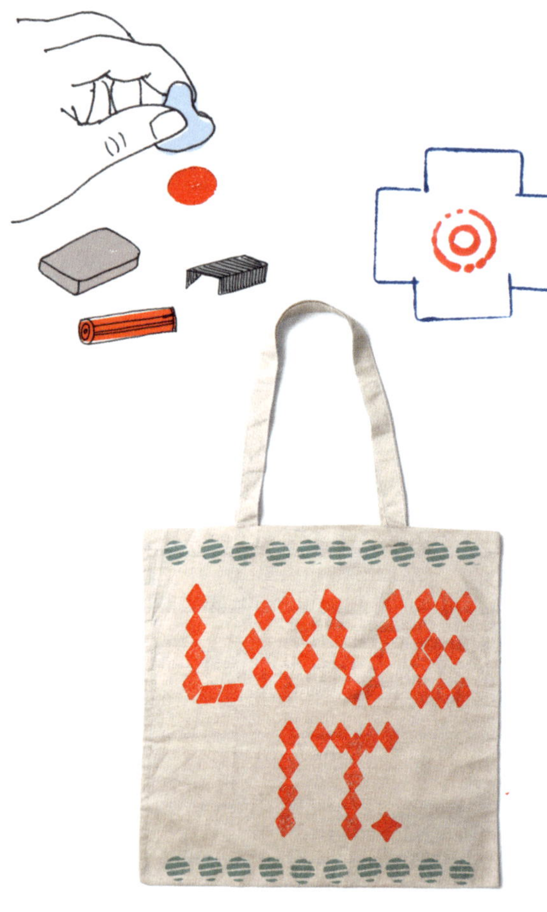

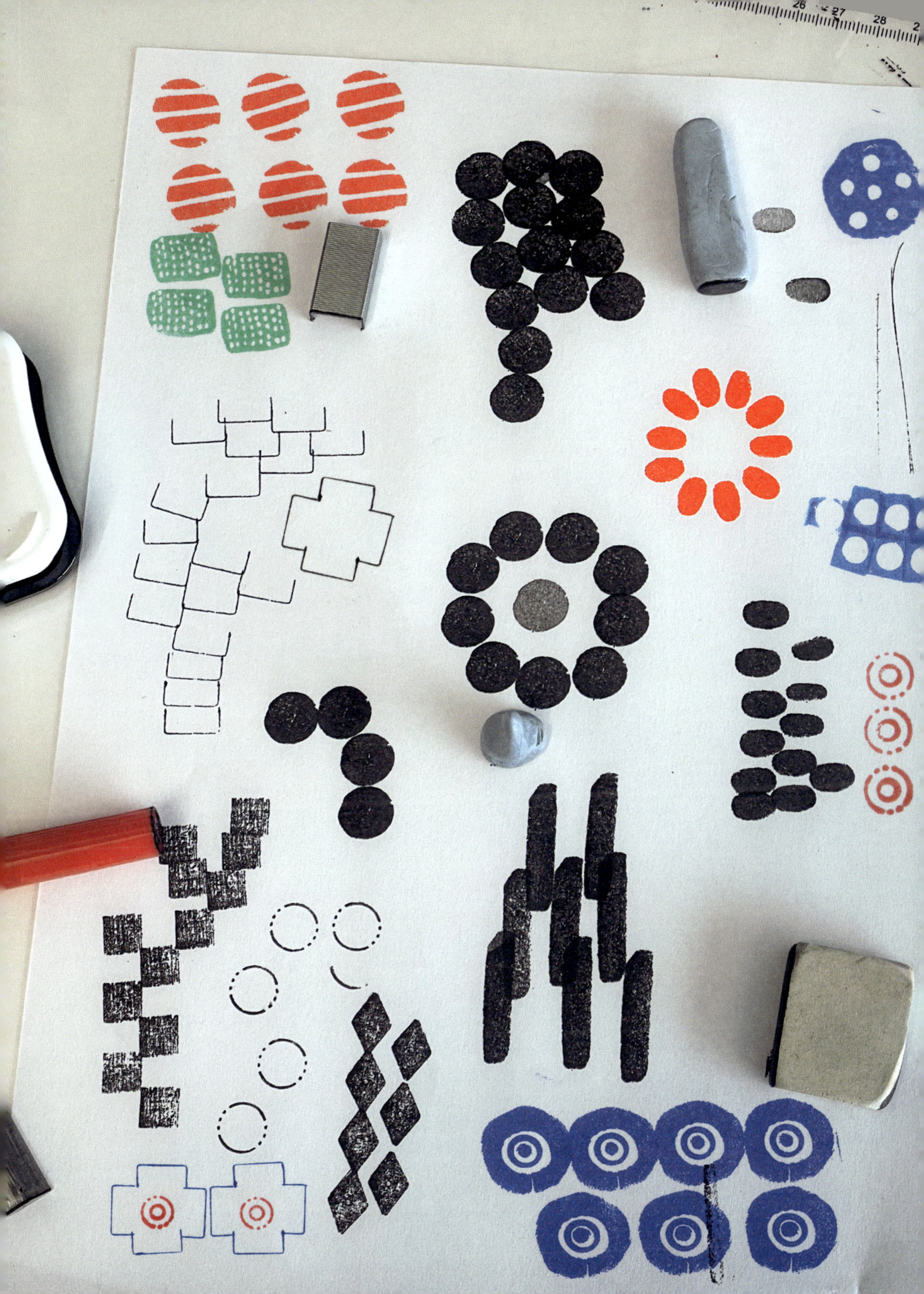

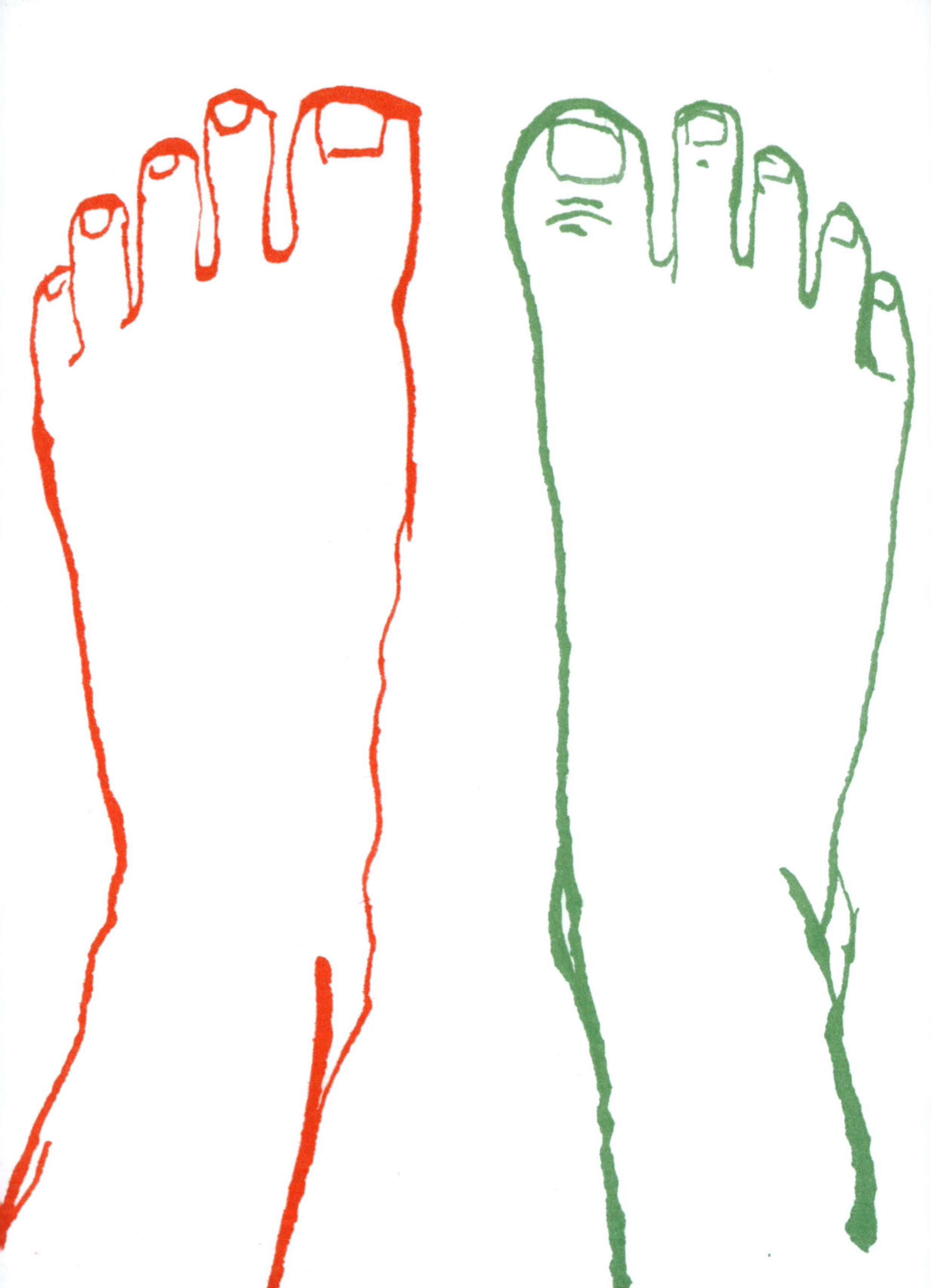

SELECTIVE COLOURS

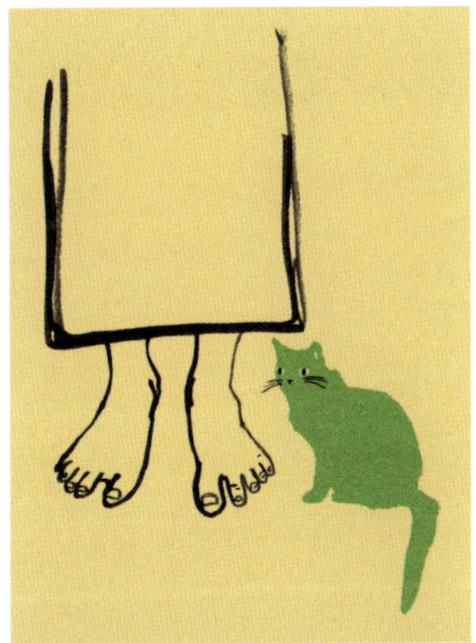

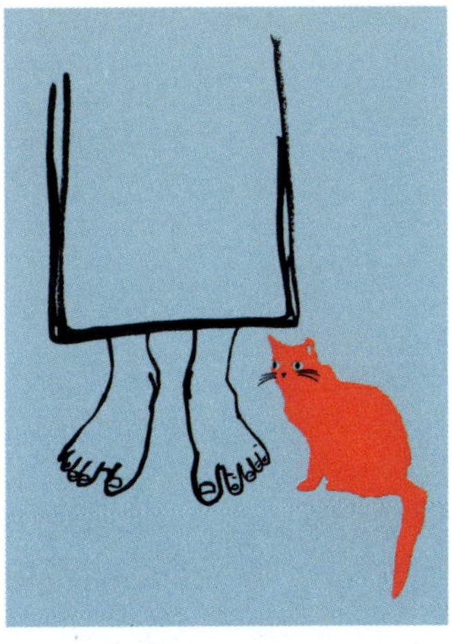

LIMIT YOUR PALETTE

Working with a limited colour palette can be both a challenging and rewarding experience. At first glance, restrictions like a two-colour-plus-black scheme might seem limiting, but they can actually inspire creativity and innovative problem-solving. I have designed many book covers where this restriction was in place and it helped me to produce some bold images.

Creative exercise

Try making some images with these restrictions:

1. Black plus one colour
2. Black plus two colours
3. Two colours only

Once you have your image, try changing the colour arrangement. You can do this exercise with conventional materials or digitally.

Creative inspiration

Research the Zorn Palette, a palette that uses four colours to create a multitude of others.

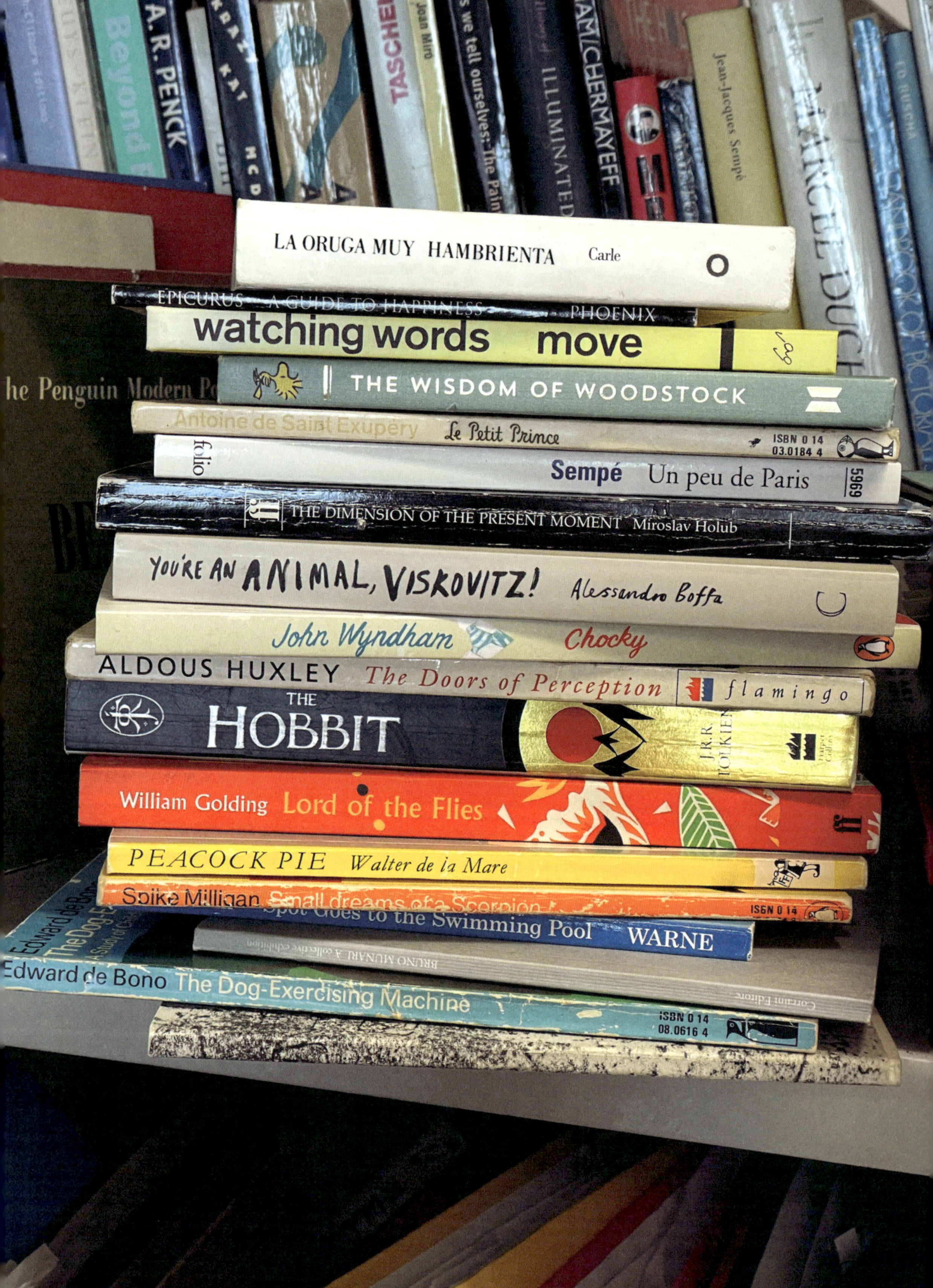
A. R. PENCK
Beyond
TASCHEN
ILLUMINATED
Jean-Jacques Sempé
MARCEL DUC
LA ORUGA MUY HAMBRIENTA   Carle
EPICURUS - A GUIDE TO HAPPINESS   PHOENIX
watching words   move
THE WISDOM OF WOODSTOCK
Antoine de Saint Exupéry   Le Petit Prince   ISBN 0 14 03.0184 4
folio   Sempé   Un peu de Paris   5969
THE DIMENSION OF THE PRESENT MOMENT   Miroslav Holub
YOU'RE AN ANIMAL, VISKOVITZ!   Alessandro Boffa
John Wyndham   Chocky
ALDOUS HUXLEY   The Doors of Perception   flamingo
THE HOBBIT   J.R.R. Tolkien   HarperCollins
William Golding   Lord of the Flies
PEACOCK PIE   Walter de la Mare
Spike Milligan   Small dreams of a Scorpion
Spot Goes to the Swimming Pool   WARNE
BRUNO MUNARI A collective exhibition
Edward de Bono   The Dog-Exercising Machine
ISBN 0 14 08.0616 4

MY LIFE AS A BOOK

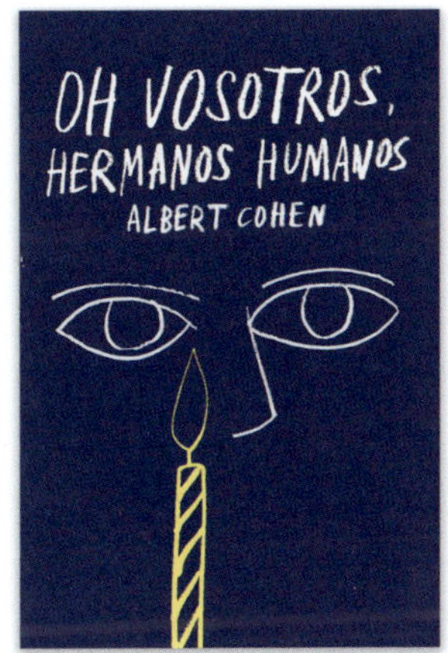

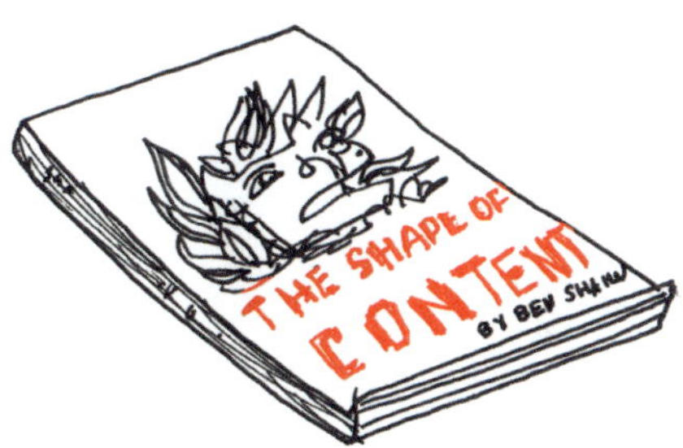

CHOOSE A FAVOURITE BOOK

For me, reading fiction and non-fiction alike always sparks ideas for my work. Can you recall a favourite book, whether for adults or children, fiction or non-fiction? Remember where you read it? Describe the surroundings, smells and sounds. Reflect on your feelings and on the events in your life then. Note or sketch a memorable character, place or emotion from the story. Or take a character from your favourite book and have an imaginary conversation with them. Can you offer some insights or guidance from your own time and perspective?

Creative exercise

Make an image for the cover of your favourite book. It can be drawn, painted, photographic, mixed media or digitally created.

Creative inspiration

The cover designs of Paul Rand, David Pearson and Coralie Bickford-Smith.

GRAPH PAPER

MINDFUL DRAWING

I find drawing a straight line quite challenging, but using a ruler and graph paper makes it easy. Different graph papers offer various grids, from squares to axonometric shapes, that are ideal for creating intricate patterns, angles and 3D shapes. I've spent hours mindfully colouring in multicoloured boxes, exploring endless possibilities for shapes and patterns. It takes me back to maths class when I used to doodle instead of working.

Creative exercise

Explore creativity with various types of graph paper. Colour patterns spontaneously. Use coloured pencils or pens.

Creative quickie

Try making pixel art, creating images one square at a time, like this crab, for example.

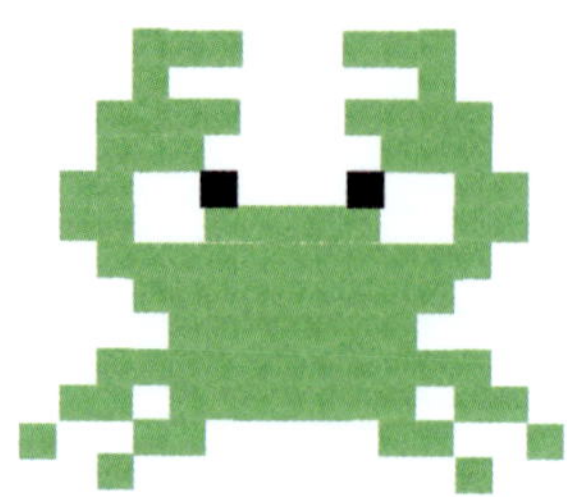

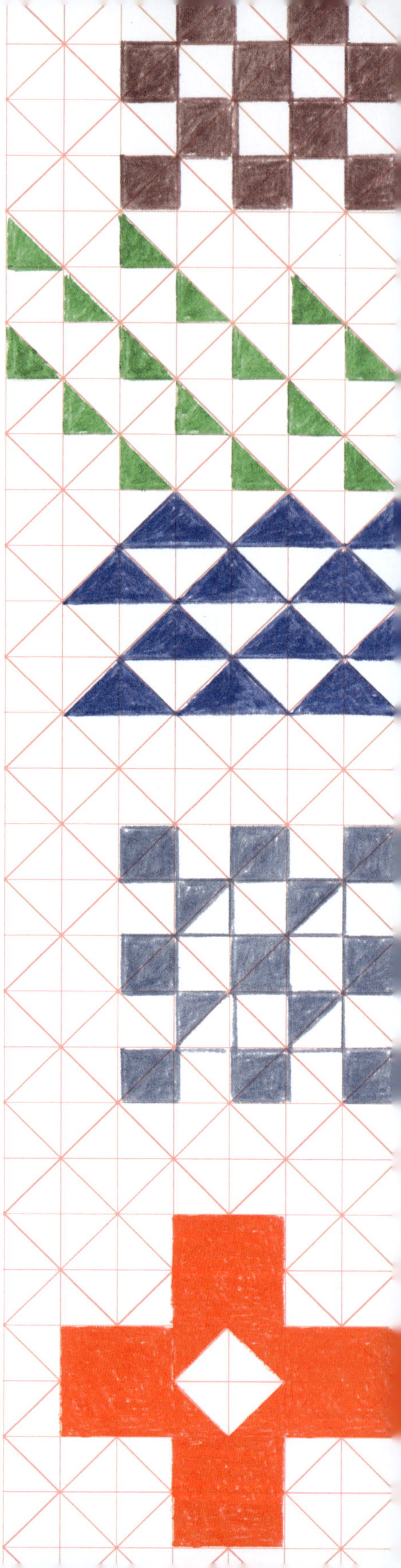

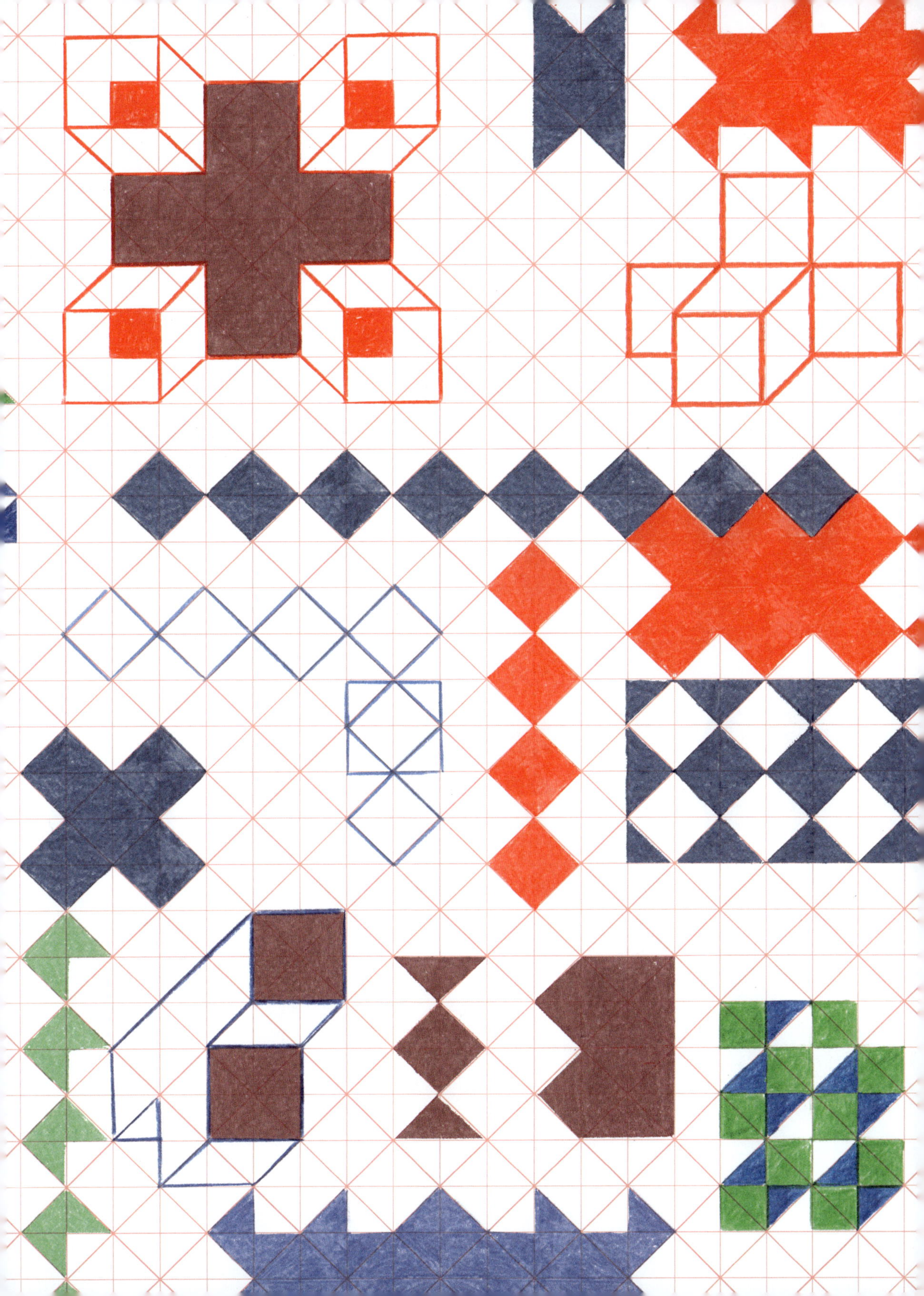

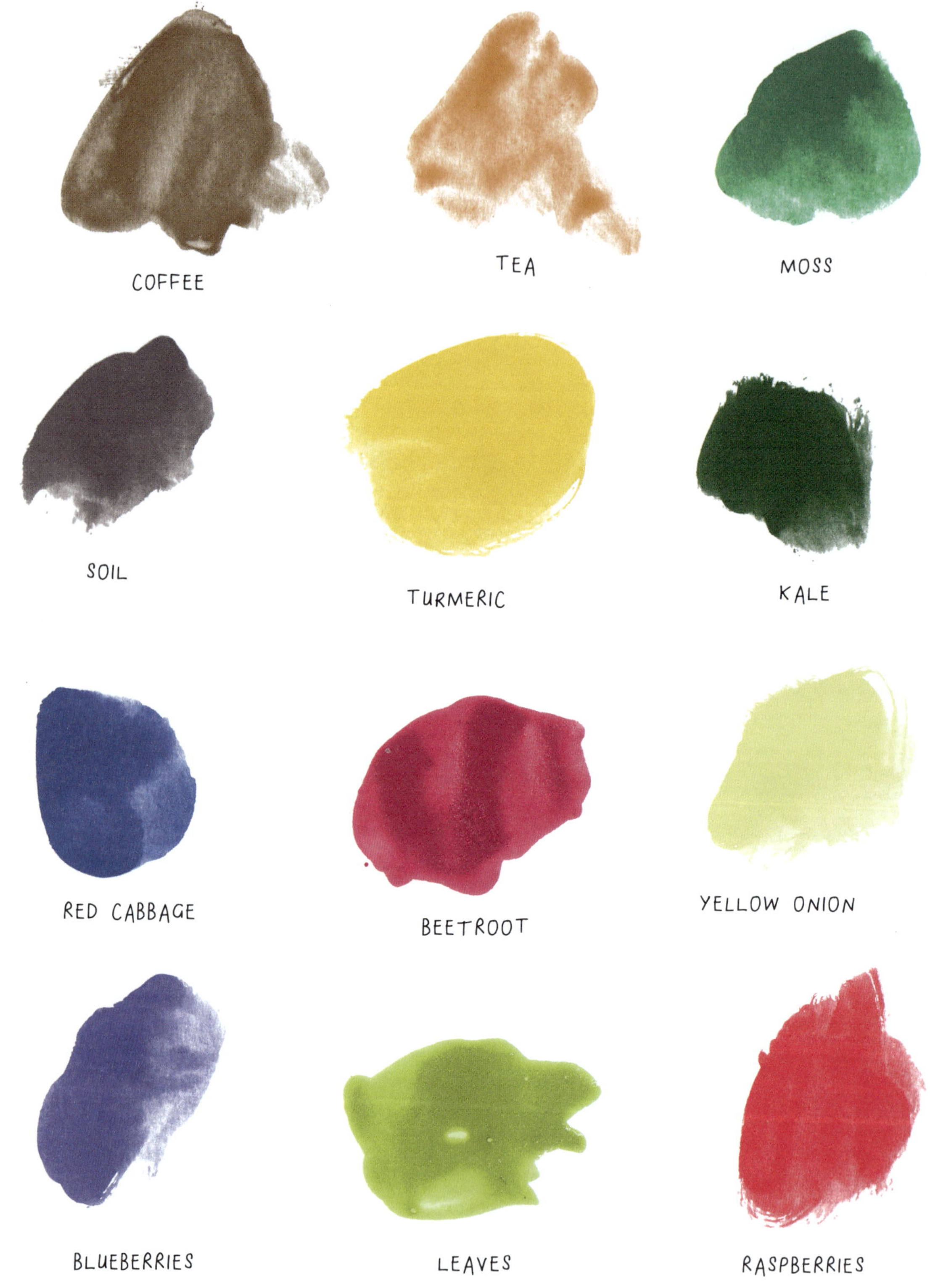

COFFEE
TEA
MOSS
SOIL
TURMERIC
KALE
RED CABBAGE
BEETROOT
YELLOW ONION
BLUEBERRIES
LEAVES
RASPBERRIES

NATURAL INKS

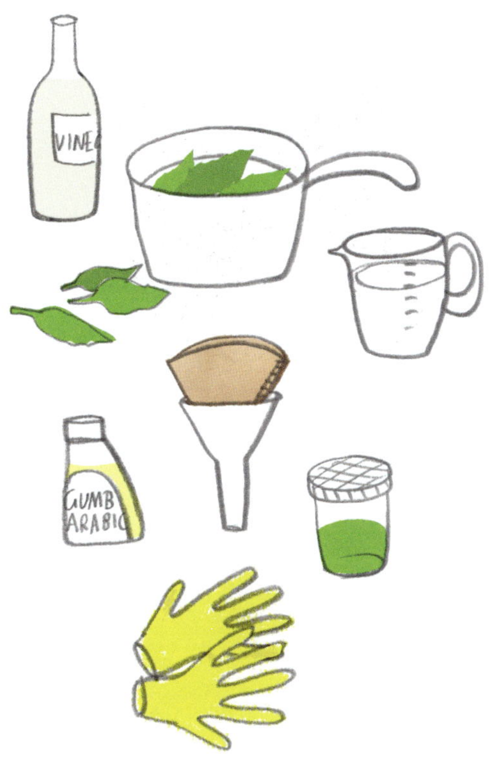

MAKE YOUR OWN COLOURS

You can make your own natural ink using household or outdoor items like fruits, vegetables, flowers or soil. You need an old pot, white vinegar, gum arabic, salt, a coffee filter, a funnel and some glass jars with lids. To make the ink, simmer your item in water with a teaspoon of vinegar and a teaspoon of salt for approximately one hour or until the consistency and colour feels right. Filter the mixture through a coffee filter into a glass jar. Add gum arabic to the ink at a 1:10 ratio. You're ready to draw with your own ink!

Creative exercise

Spend some time looking for materials to make ink within a few miles of where you live. Use these inks to draw a personal piece of artwork that reflects your home or sense of place.

Creative inspiration

Jason Logan's book *Make Ink*, and prints made with food and household products by Ed Ruscha.

DRAW WITH ANYTHING

MAKE PICTURES WITH FOUND OBJECTS

While on holiday in Spain I found these carob seed pods falling to the ground. I experimented with their varied shapes – curly, straight and bent – to create drawings and patterns on both large and small scales. I encourage you to explore your surroundings and use natural materials like stones, leaves, twigs, pinecones, driftwood, seeds, sand or mud to inspire your own art.

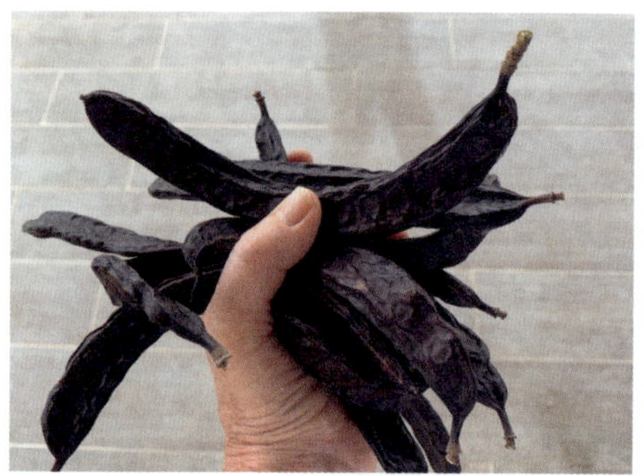

Creative exercise

Try to 'draw' using items found around the house, like pasta, tools, paper clips, staples and kitchen implements. You will be surprised what images you can make from them!

Creative inspiration

The work of Choi Jeong-Hwa, and Caitlin Easterby and Simon Pascoe's art collective, Red Earth.

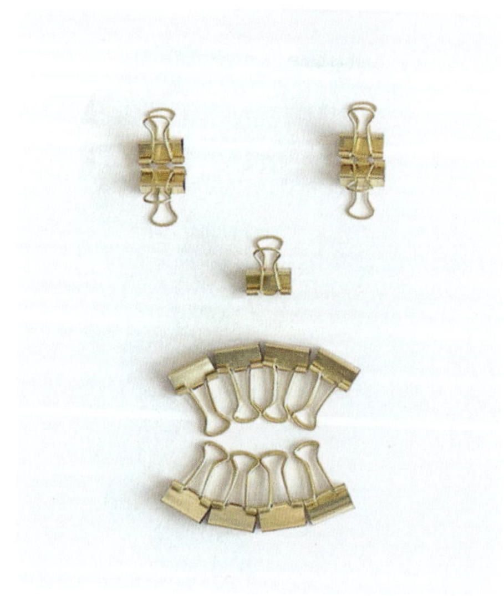

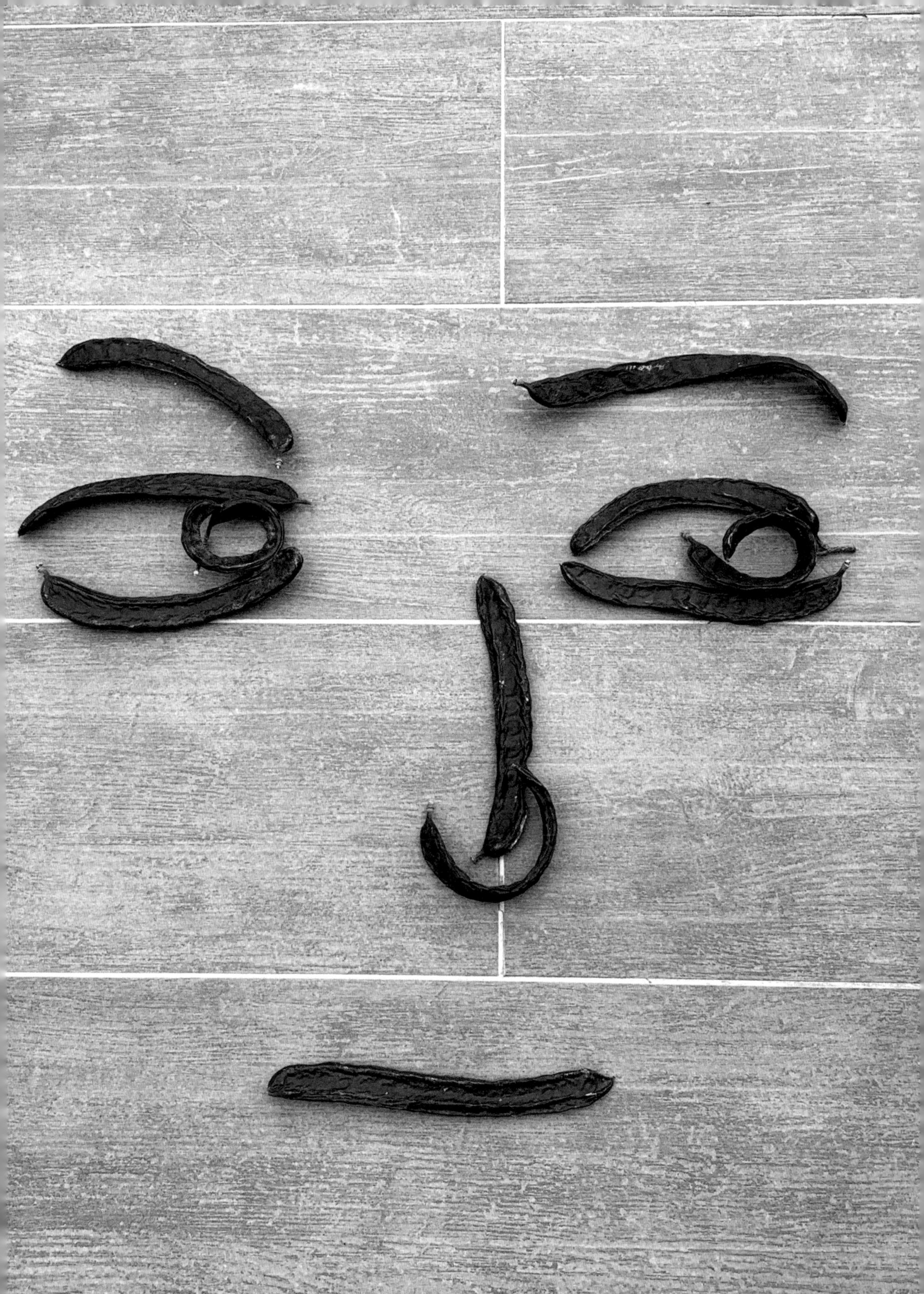

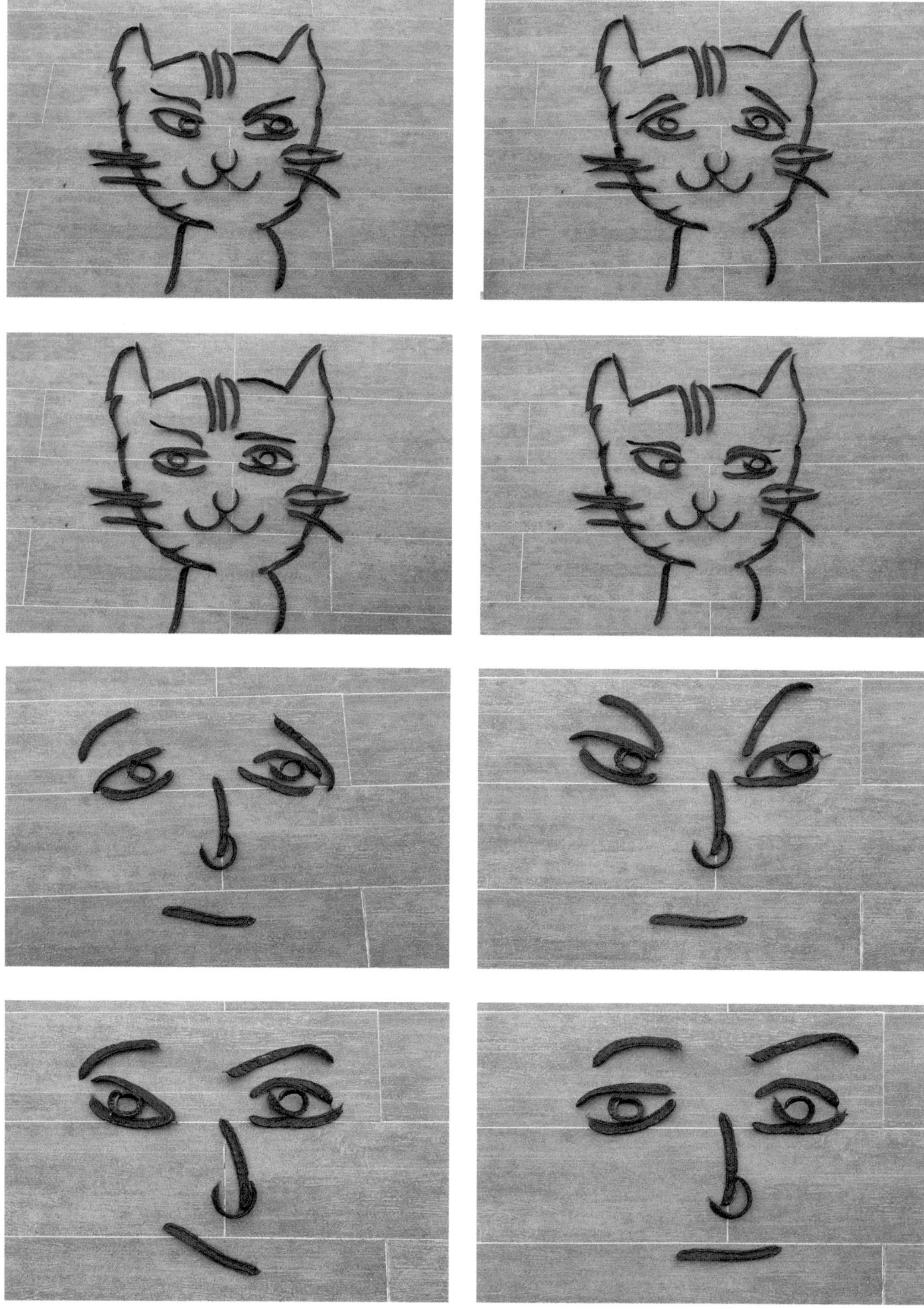

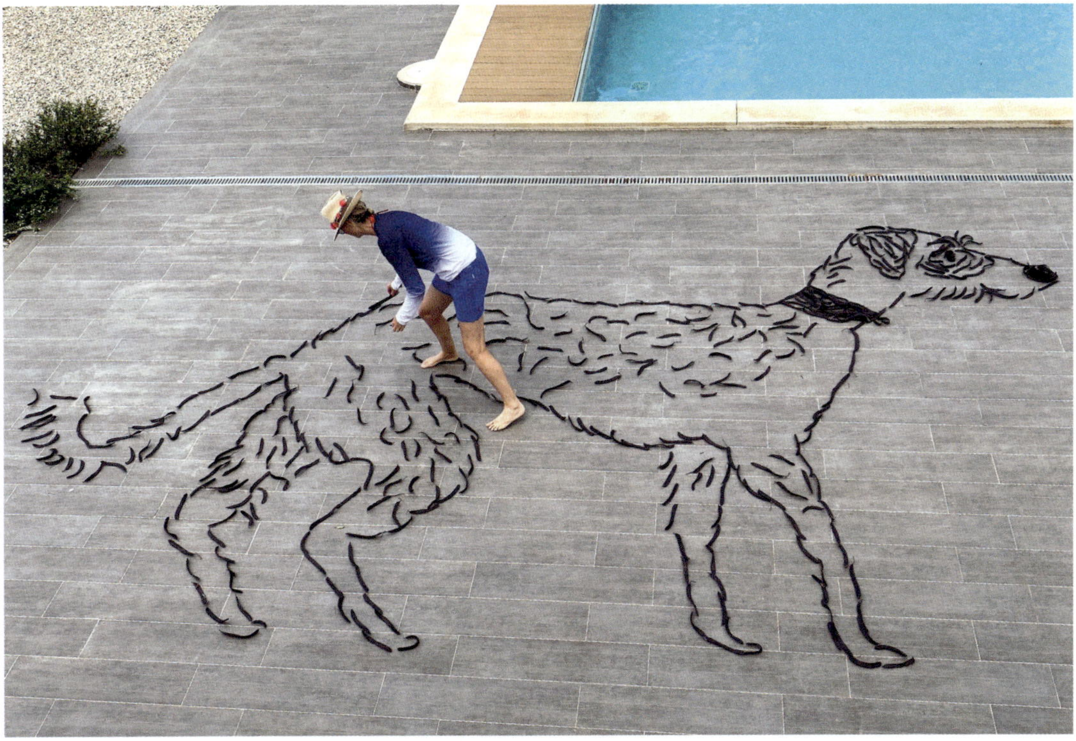

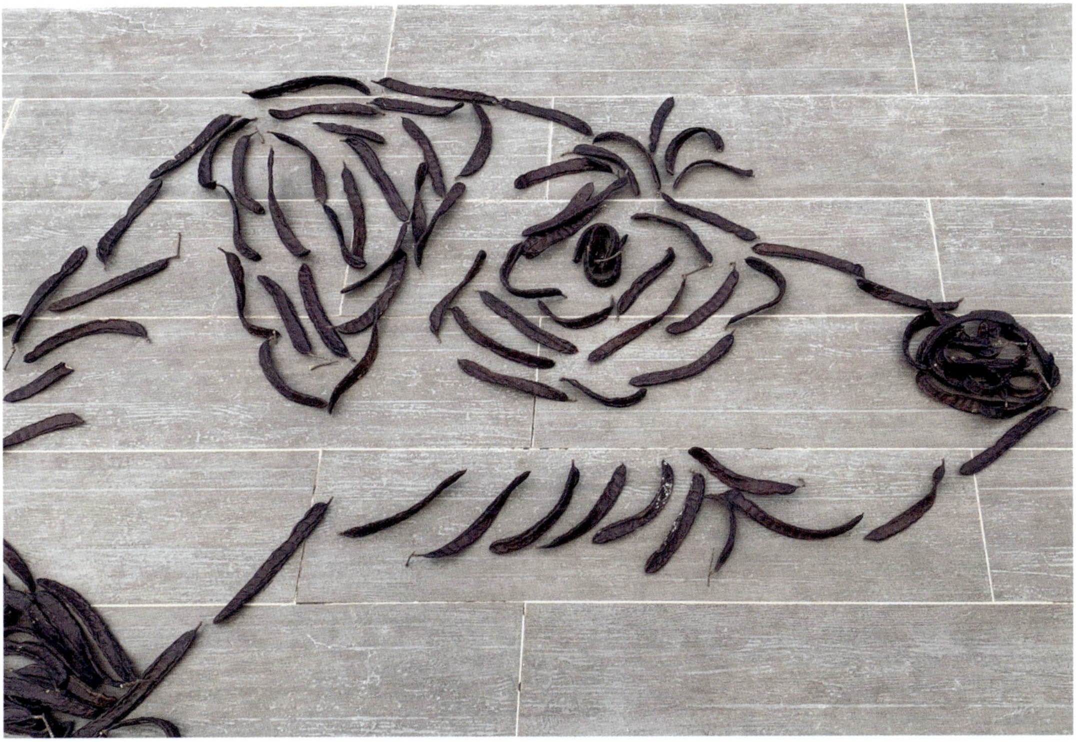

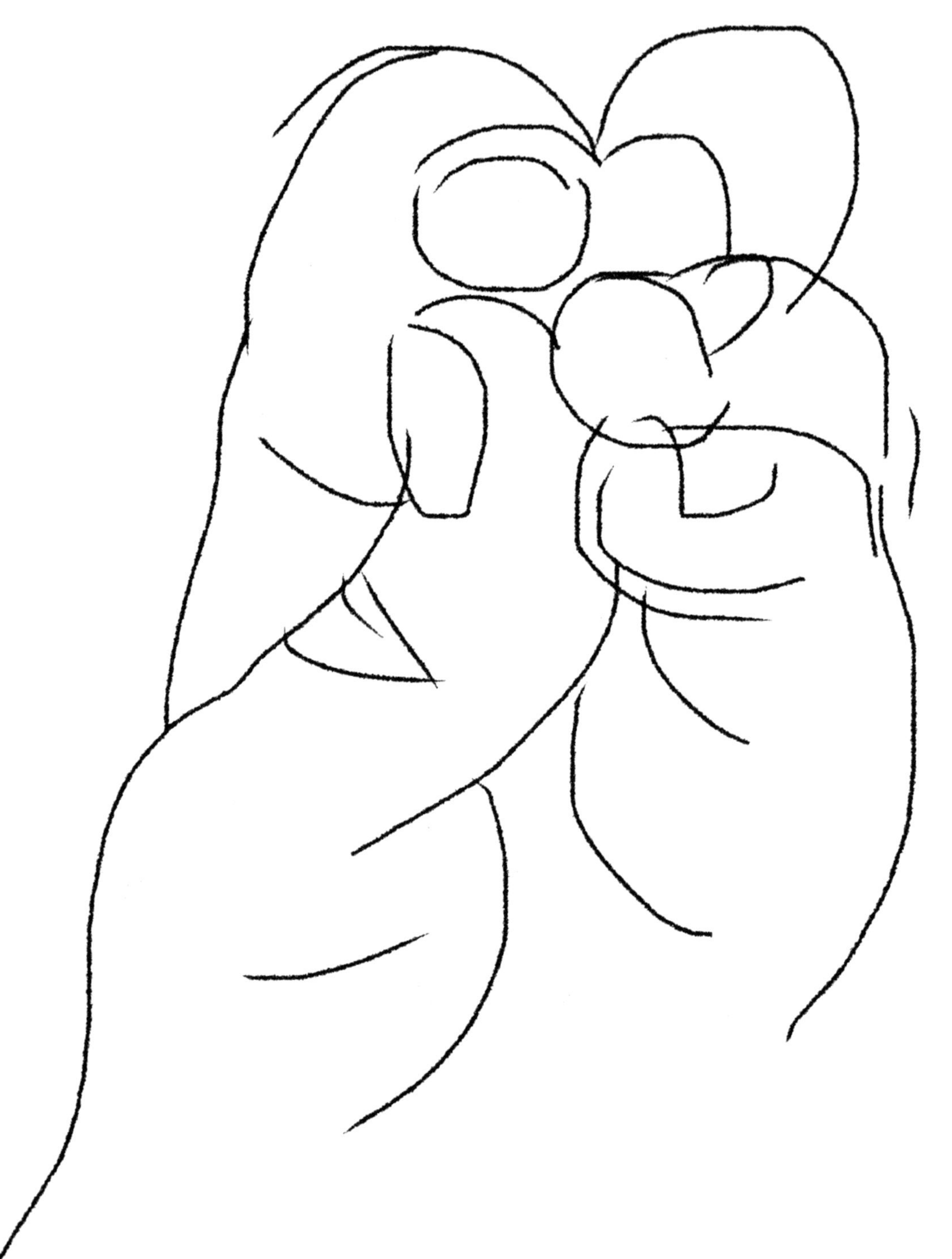

STOPWATCH DRAWINGS

DRAWING FAST

Drawing with a timer is a great discipline to help stop overthinking and fear.
It pushes you to focus and make quick decisions about what's essential in your artwork. This not only improves how you look at things, which is really what most drawing is about, but also helps develop spontaneity and liveliness.

Creative exercise

Using a stopwatch, get ready to draw your opposite hand, your foot or your face. Do the first drawing in one minute, then draw for two minutes and finally five minutes. Now compare the three drawings.

Creative inspiration

The line drawings of Quentin Blake and Louise Bourgeois.

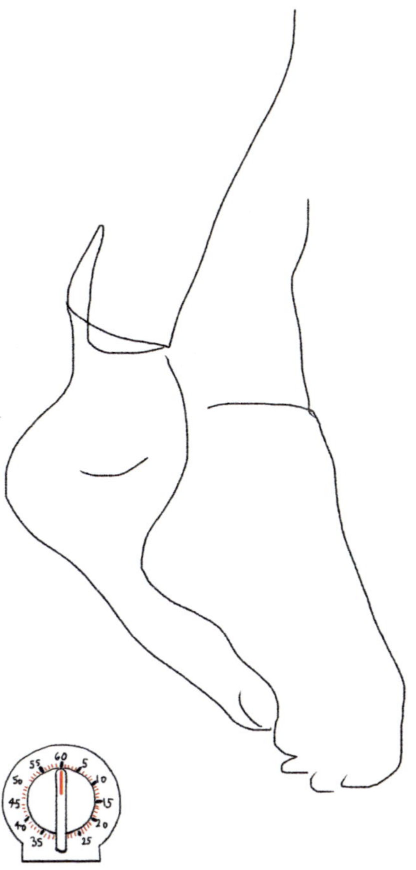

A one-minute iPad drawing of my son's feet.

POSTCARD PAINTING

AVOID THE BLANK PAGE

Starting a painting can be intimidating, but using a postcard or photo as a base can ease that anxiety by eliminating the daunting blank canvas. Here I've used acrylic gouache to paint over postcards and photos, but you can use any paint or paint pen. For glossy surfaces, use a transparent primer layer before painting.

Creative exercise

1. Paint freehand on a postcard, without overthinking what to cover or reveal.

2. On another card, use masking techniques as demonstrated on the opposite page.

3. On a third image, apply low-tack tape to create shapes, paint over it, and remove once dry.

Creative inspiration

The work of John Baldessari and the overpainted photographs of Gerhard Richter.

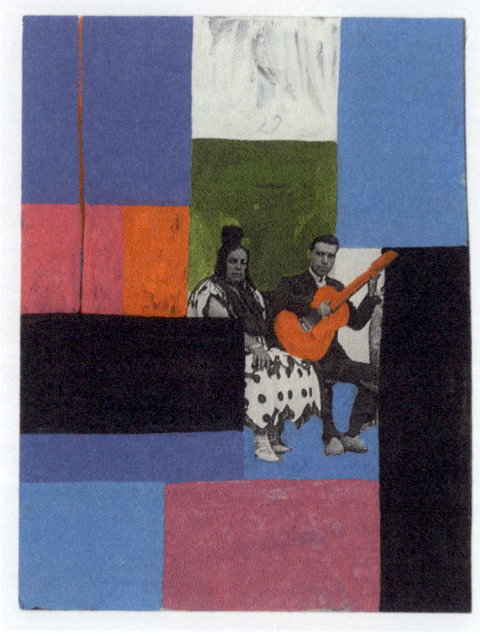

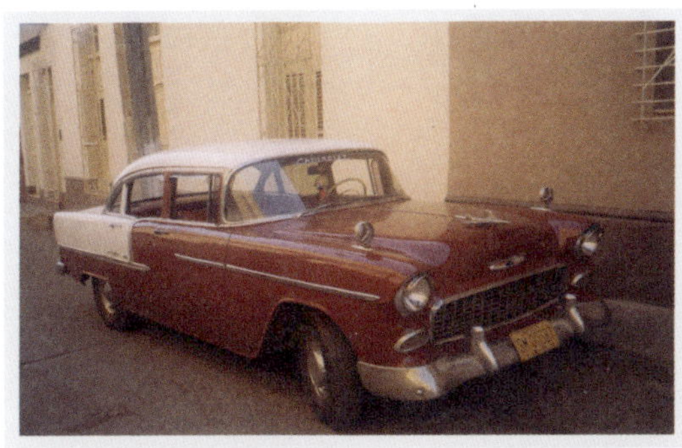
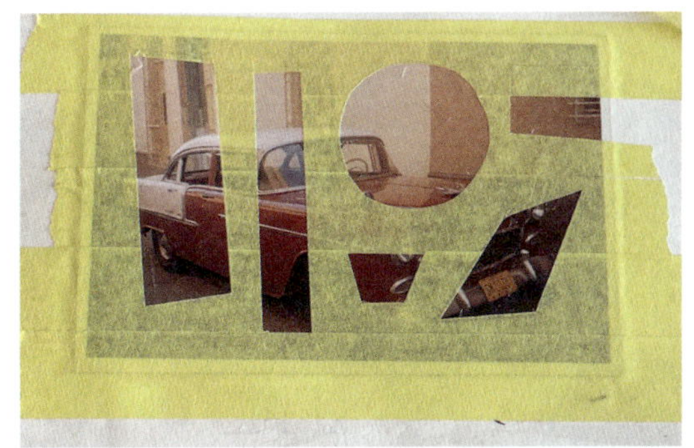
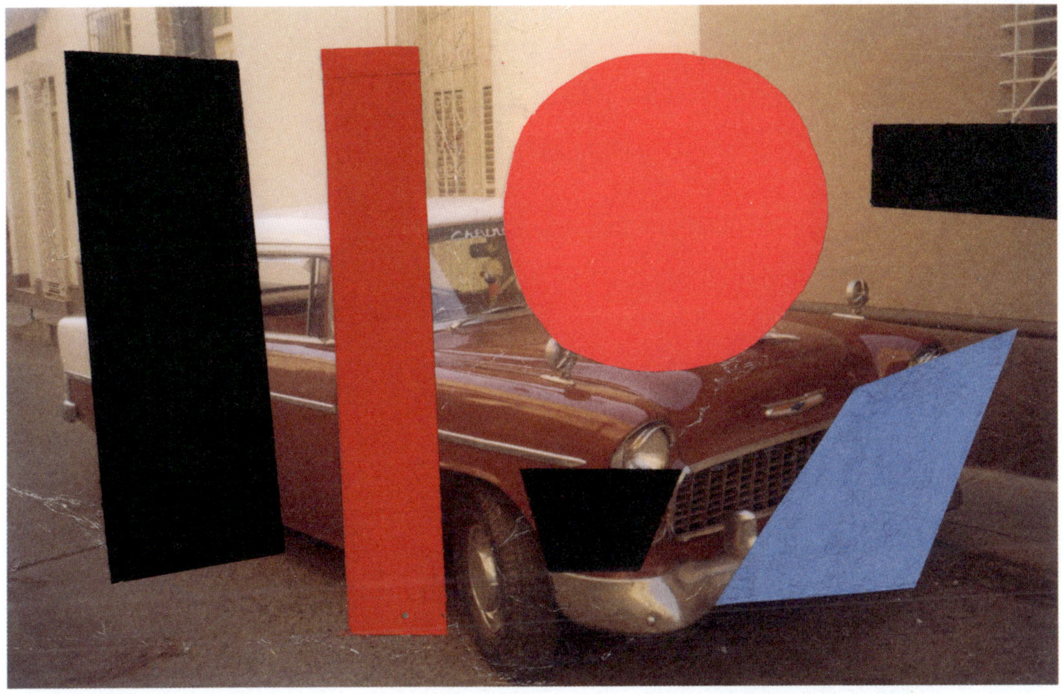
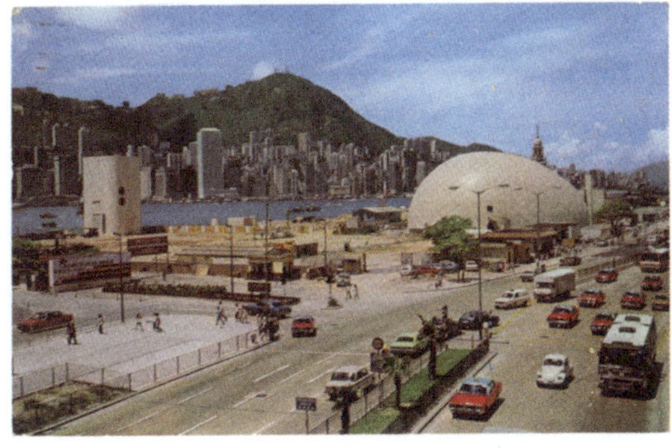
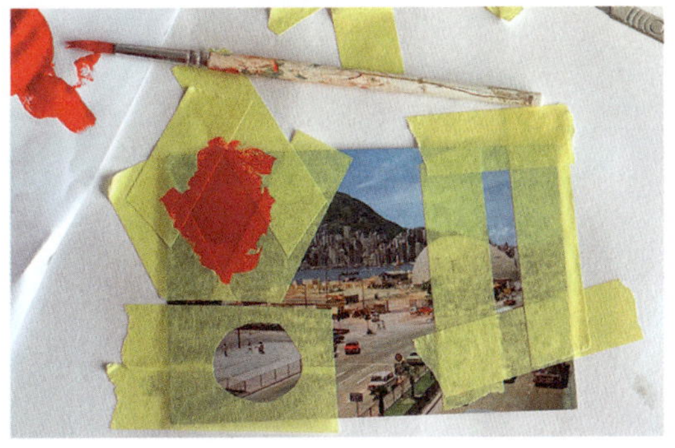

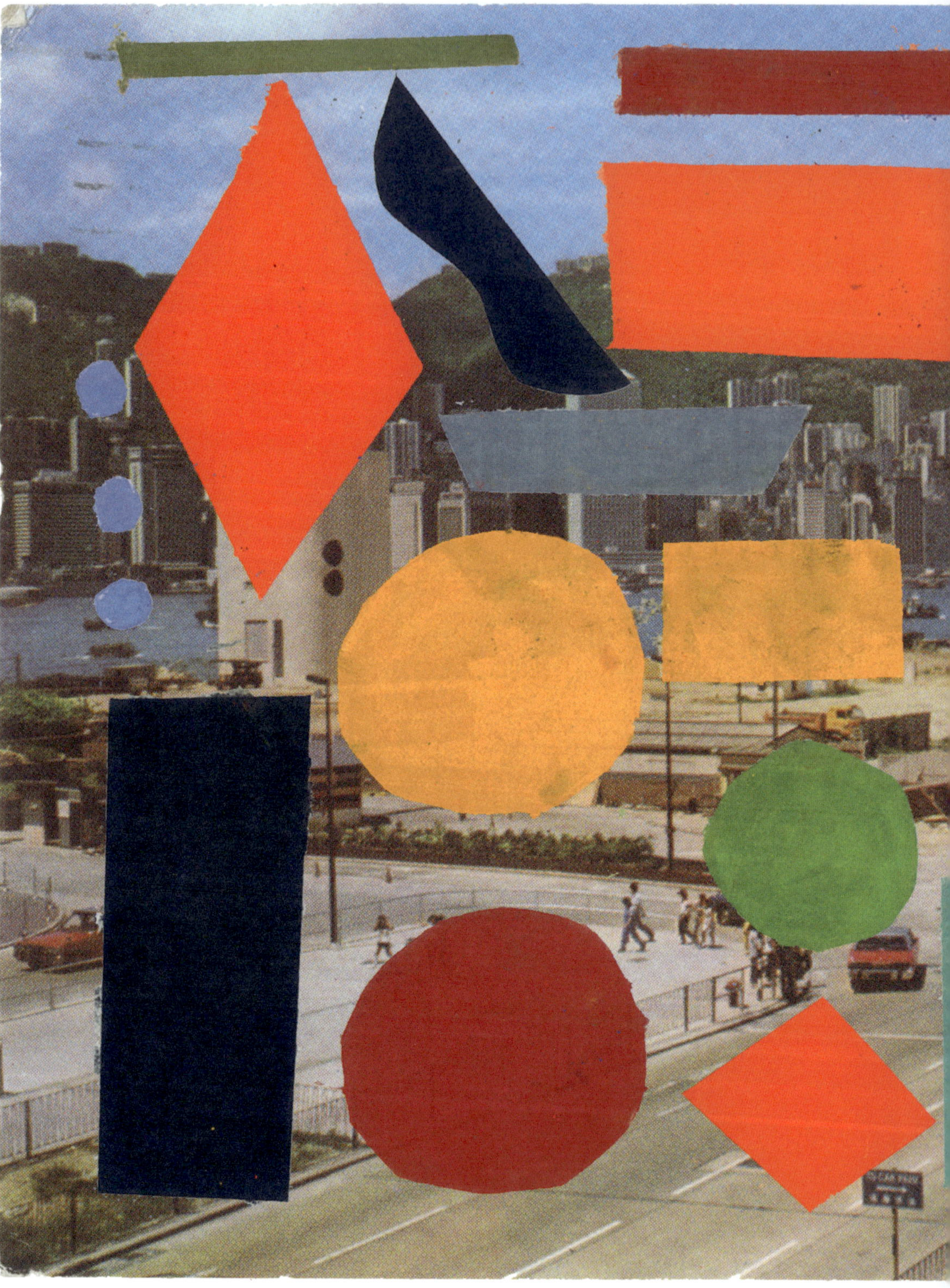

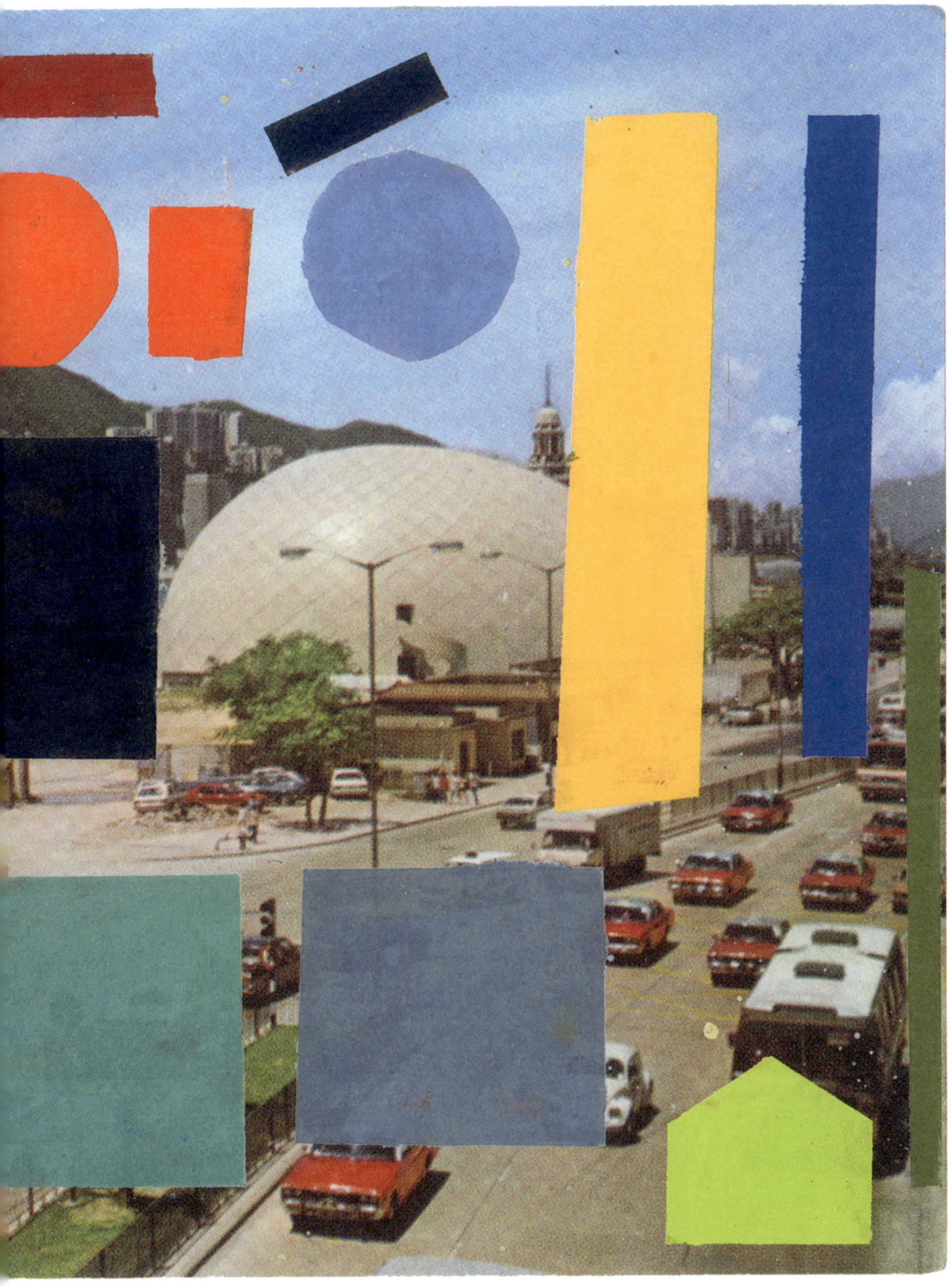

Make a DEADLINE

The toughest part of engaging in a creative act is often just getting started. Distractions and excuses are always lurking. I always find something to divert my attention, whether it's checking email or tidying my desk. The best thing to do when procrastination takes hold is to simply begin: do something, no matter what.

This is when a deadline can really help your self-discipline. This could be something modest, like committing to draw or engage in a creative activity once a week. Alternatively, you could commit to spending ten minutes a day taking a mindful walk, sketching or simply looking up at the sky. When I'm particularly unfocused, I sometimes use a kitchen timer to help me concentrate. A deadline gives us something to work towards, and having some boundaries can really help.

MIND MAP ME

VISUAL DIAGRAM TO ORGANIZE IDEAS

Mind maps are a very useful tool to help you organize information and ideas. They are a way to visualize imagination and association, and they help you use both sides of your brain to generate new thoughts and connections. You can use a mind map for anything, from planning a book to organizing a birthday party, and all you need is paper and pens or coloured pencils.

Creative exercise

Make a mind map on a single sheet of paper or sketchbook. Start with your main subject in the middle of the page and let your thoughts and ideas grow from it, the words spreading out radially from the central idea. Connect the words with lines, like branches of a tree.

Creative inspiration

Look up the educator Tony Buzan, who originated mind maps in the 1970s, to see all the different types.

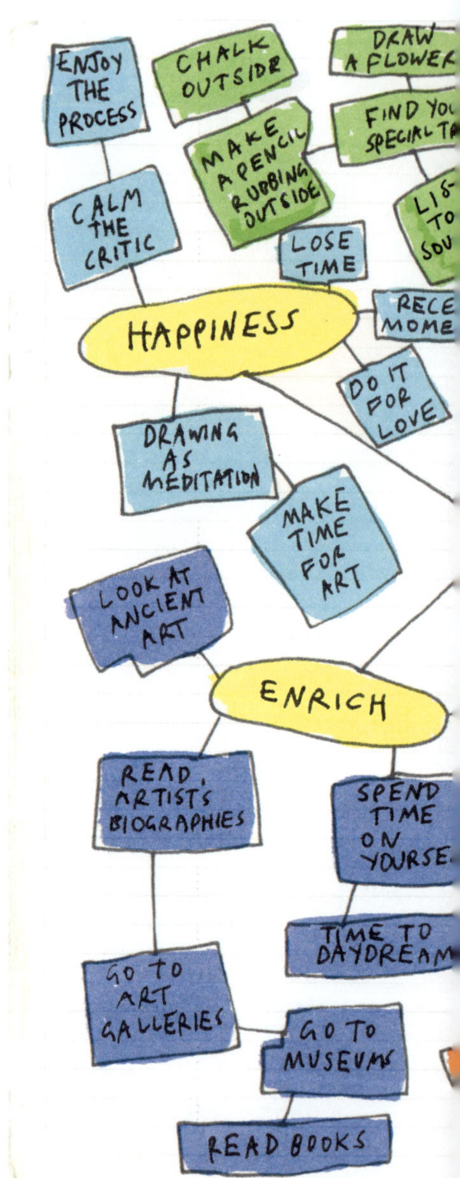

LLECT
LEAVES

LOOK AT THE GROUND

LOOK FOR 'AWE'

DAILY WALK

APPRECIATE THINGS AROUND YOU

LOOK AT SHADOWS

LOOK UP

E Y DAY TIVE

MAKE A SKETCHBOOK

PLAY

BE INSPIRED

MAKE A PAPER BOAT

STEAL COLOURS

DRAW FROM TV

JOIN A CLASS

CHANGE SCALE

MAKE A RUBBER STAMP

THROW A POT

DRAW A SLEEPING DOG

SEW A BUTTON

COLLAGE FROM A MAGAZINE

MAKE A SUN PRINT

MAKE SOMETHING YOU'VE NEVER MADE BEFORE

MAKE A SPACE FOR ART

USE COLOURS YOU NEVER NORMALLY USE

MAKE YOUR OWN ALPHABET

DONT WAIT FOR THE BIG IDEA

GIVE YOURSELF A DEADLINE

COPY SOMETHING

LEARN SOMETHING NEW

GO TO ART EXHIBITIONS

PLAY VISUAL CONSEQUENCES

REPEAT A PATTERN

MAKE A PLAY DESK

DRAW WITH WATER AND A MOP

USE FOUND OBJECTS

PAINT WITH YOUR FINGERS

GET YOUR HANDS DIRTY

MAKE MISTAKES

CUT IT UP

DRAW FAST

DRAW WHILST WALKING

DRAW SLOW

INK BLOTS

DRAW UPSIDE DOWN

DRAW WITH YOUR EYES CLOSED

DRAW OUTSIDE

MAKE YOUR OWN INK

DRAW WITH YOUR OPPOSITE HAND

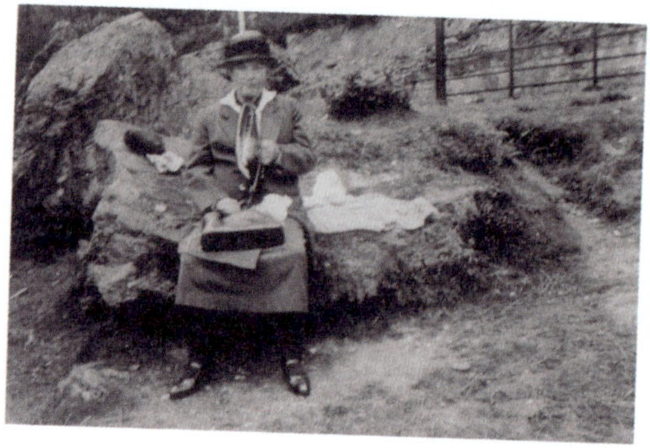

THE LAST THING ON JEAN'S MIND THAT HOT, LAZY AFTERNOON ... WAS MURDER.

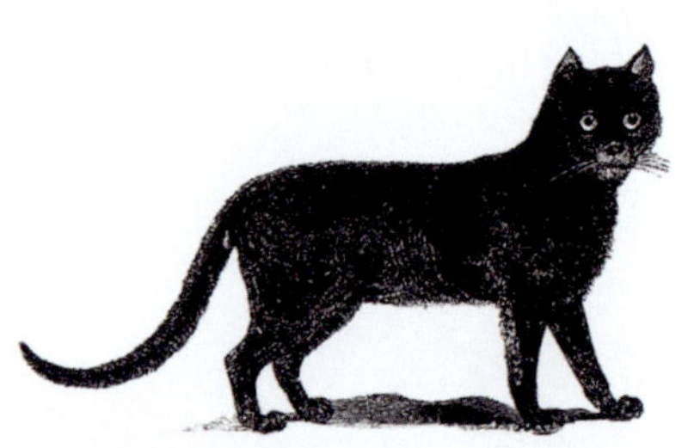

OSCAR NEVER FELT COMFORTABLE AS A CAT, IN HIS HEAD HE WAS 100% RABBIT.

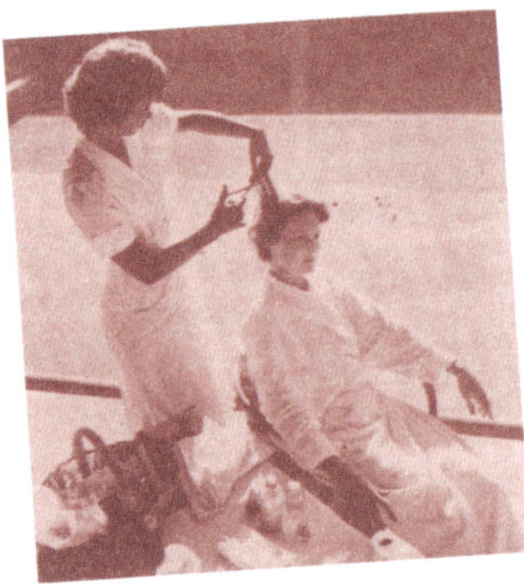

NO ONE WAS ALLOWED TO JOIN THE EXCLUSIVE TRINITY CLUB WITHOUT ELIZABETH FIRST TAKING A HAIR SNIPPET FOR HER COLLECTION.

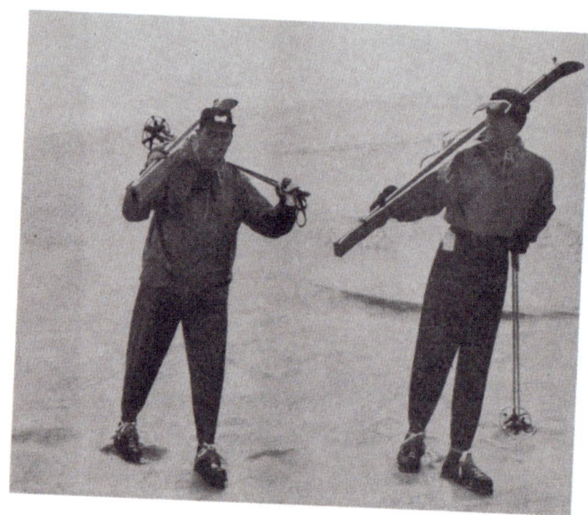

SOMETHING UNDER THE ICE WAS SLOWLY MAKING ITS WAY TOWARDS DINNER.

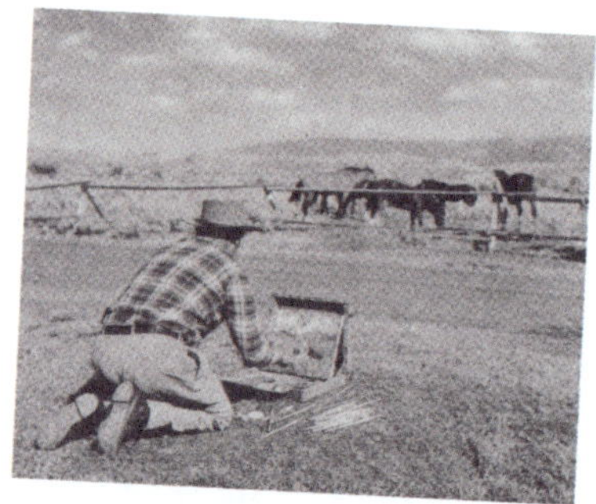

HE HAD FOUND AN INGENIOUS WAY TO CONTROL THE HORSES FROM MOVING AROUND TOO MUCH: A SLOW, LOW-PITCHED WHISTLE THAT MADE THEM FREEZE TO THE SPOT.

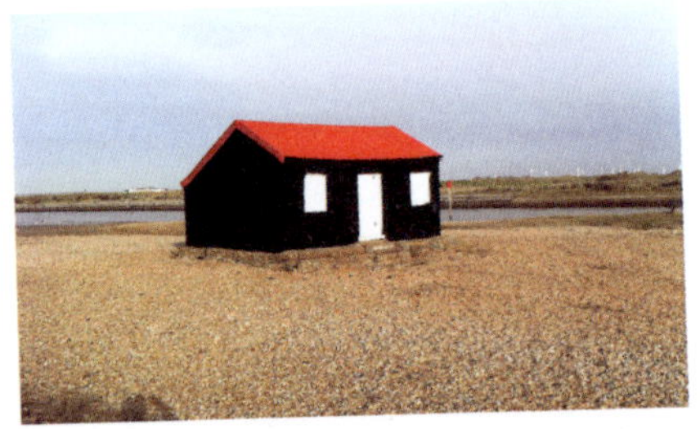

JOE ONLY CAME OUT OF HIS RED-ROOFED HOUSE ON TUESDAYS.

TELL A STORY

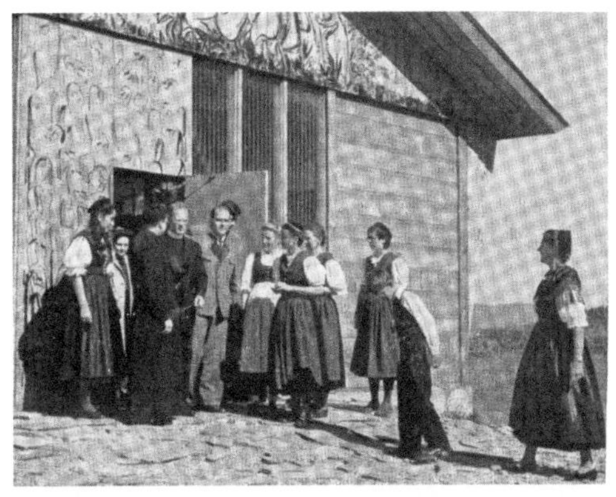

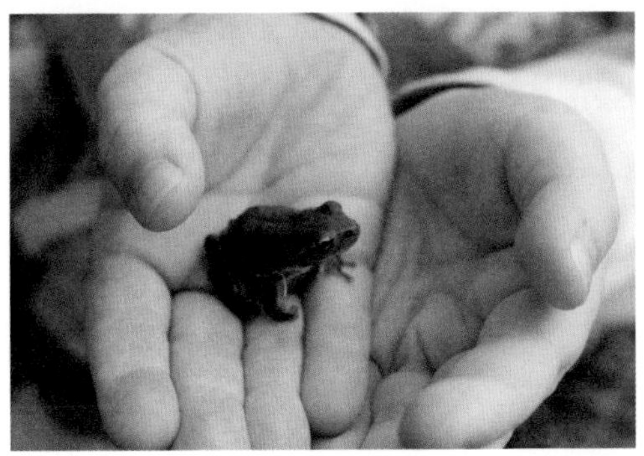

START WITH AN IMAGE

A single photo, or a mix of them, can spark vivid stories or art. As an art student, I was given a very simple but enigmatic black-and-white picture to inspire a body of work. This constraint pushes you to dig deeper into limited material. Examine the photos opposite: in one, an elderly lady may appear innocent but could be sinister – what's in her bag? In another, a cat might have identity issues, or it could be someone in a costume. Limits like these help unlock your creative imagination.

Creative exercise

In a writing course led by Lou Kuenzler, we were tasked with creating book titles inspired by random photos and drawings. Try this exercise using the two photos shown, or use some of your own.

Creative inspiration

The work of Andrzej Klimowski and Anne Howeson, and John Berger's book *Ways of Seeing*.

STEAL COLOURS

FIND A NEW PALETTE

Creating a balanced colour palette can be daunting, leading us to stick with old favourites. The solution? Borrow colours from other artists or diverse sources. For this example, I drew inspiration from a vintage Japanese toy catalogue, appreciating its unique, subdued palette. Try copying and mixing these colours in paint; they don't need to be exact. It's quite an effort to mix unusual colours and this exercise alone is very beneficial.

Ilona Came Floating Up Through the Waves, Jay van Everen, 1922.

Creative exercise

Choose at least two or three reference images to copy palettes from. The *Madonna* postcard here is a good example of a small and limited palette that will be challenging to mix and use.

Creative inspiration

The 'Homage to the Square' series of paintings by Josef Albers, and the book *The History of Colour* by Neil Parkinson.

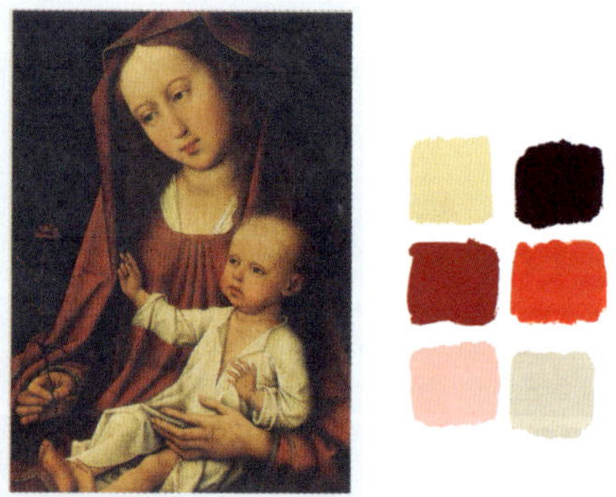

The Madonna of the Carnation, circle of Rogier van der Weyden, *c.* 1480.

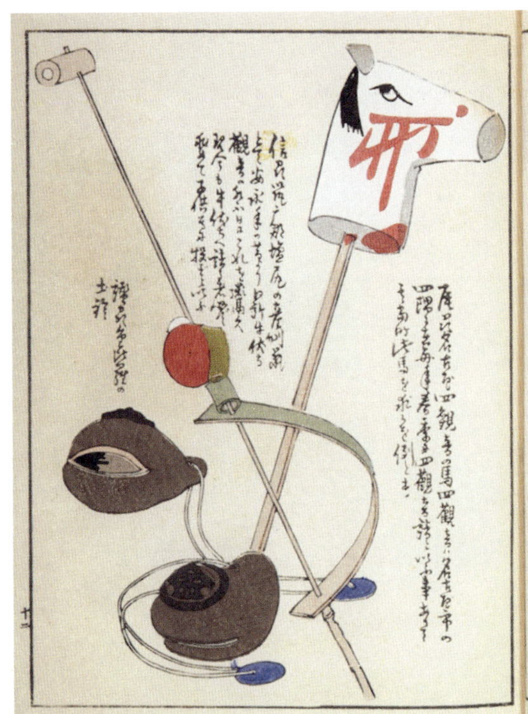
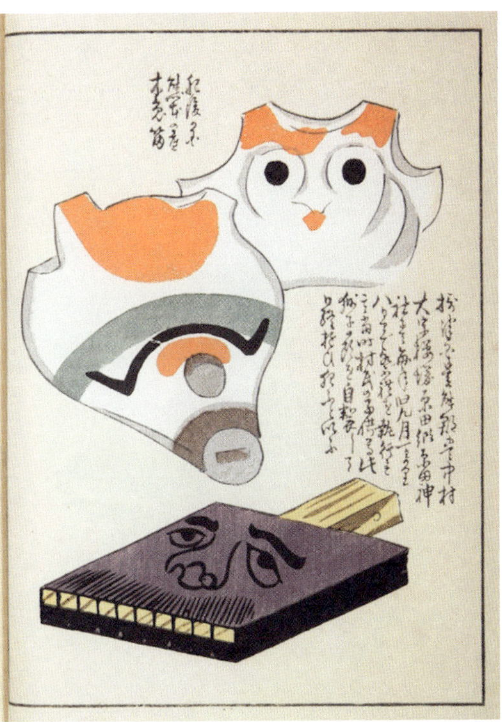

Pages from a Japanese toy catalogue, 1891.

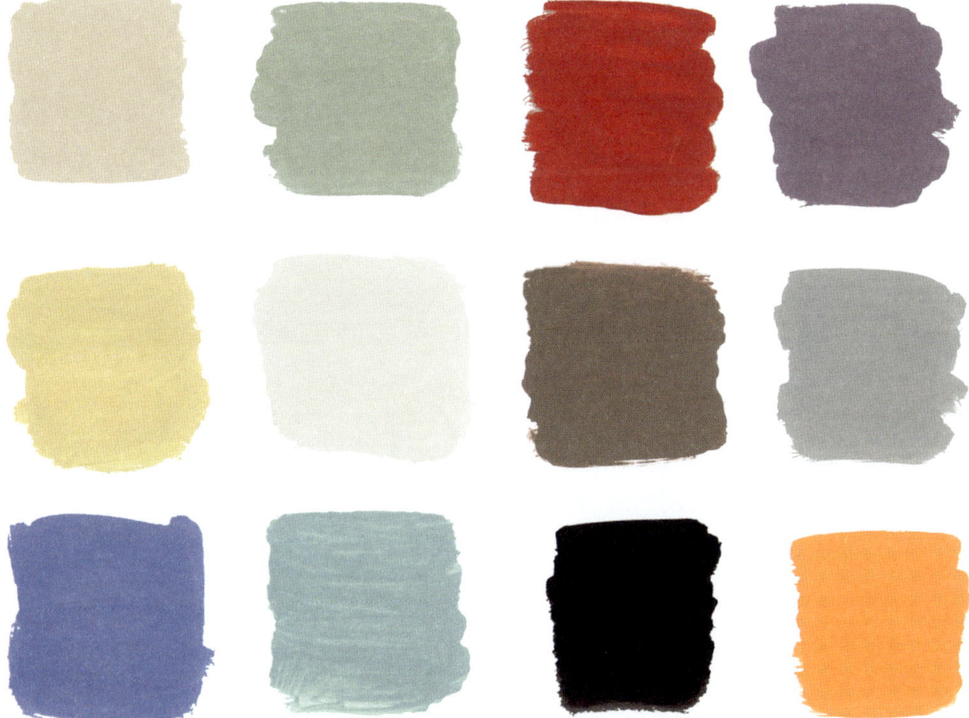

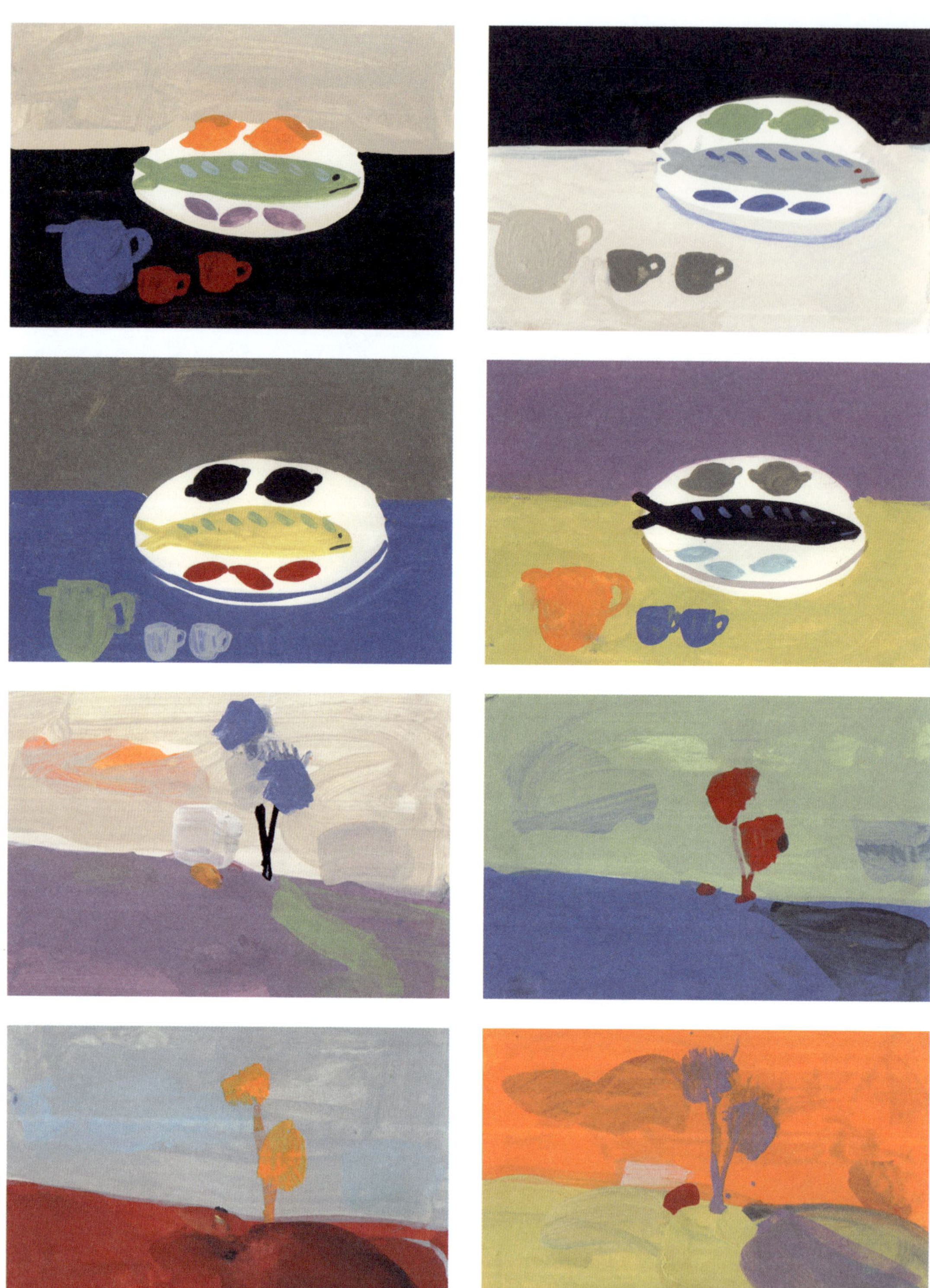

COMBINING COLOURS

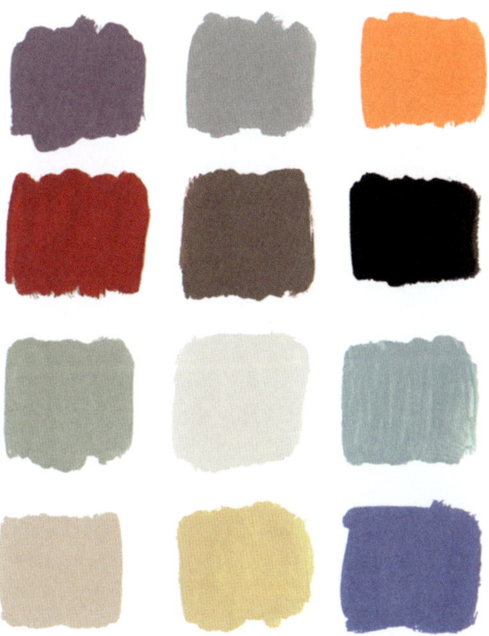

Palette from a vintage Japanese toy catalogue.

USE YOUR NEW PALETTE

This exercise builds on the concept of stealing colours shown on the previous page. After mixing a new palette, I created still life and landscape colour studies to showcase it. In the subsequent pages, you'll see birds I've painted using these colours too. The possibilities for using the same palette in varied configurations are endless. Note how colours shift in perception based on adjacent hues; some may appear brighter or duller.

Creative exercise

Paint your own still life or landscape and aim to create as many different colour versions of the same scene as possible, using your new palette. This will help you understand colour relationships and yield unexpected results.

Creative inspiration

Explore the Zorn Palette, a technique using just four colours – yellow ochre, cadmium red, ivory black and white – to create a wide range of hues.

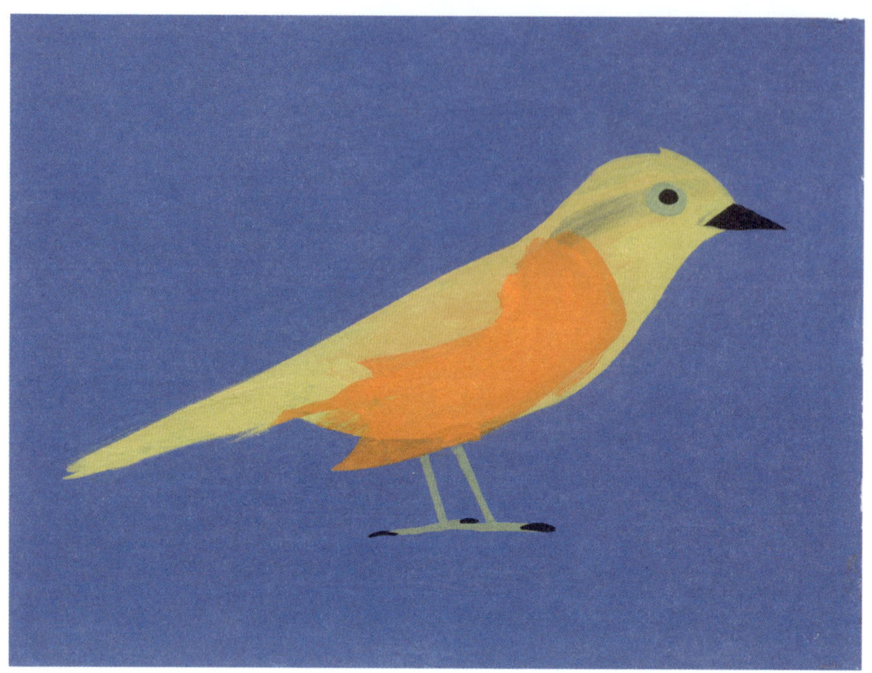

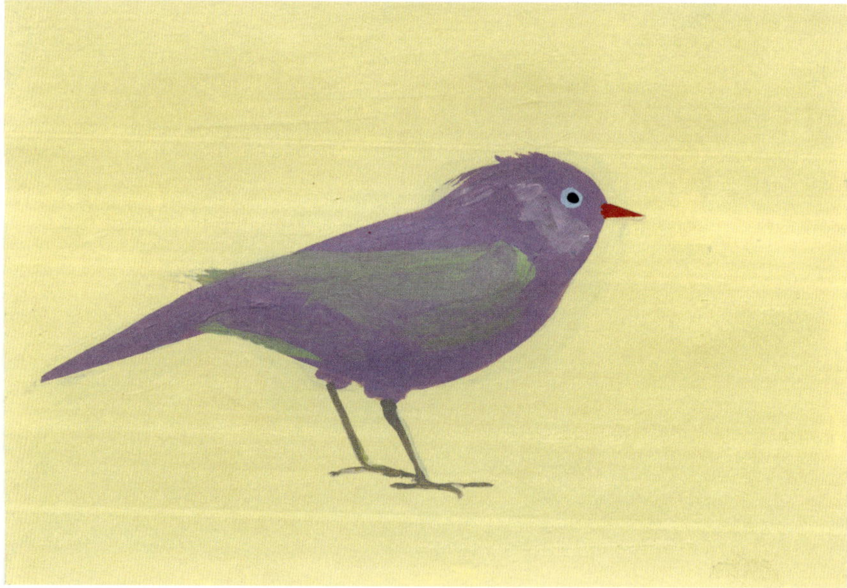

Birds painted using the palette from
a vintage Japanese toy catalogue.

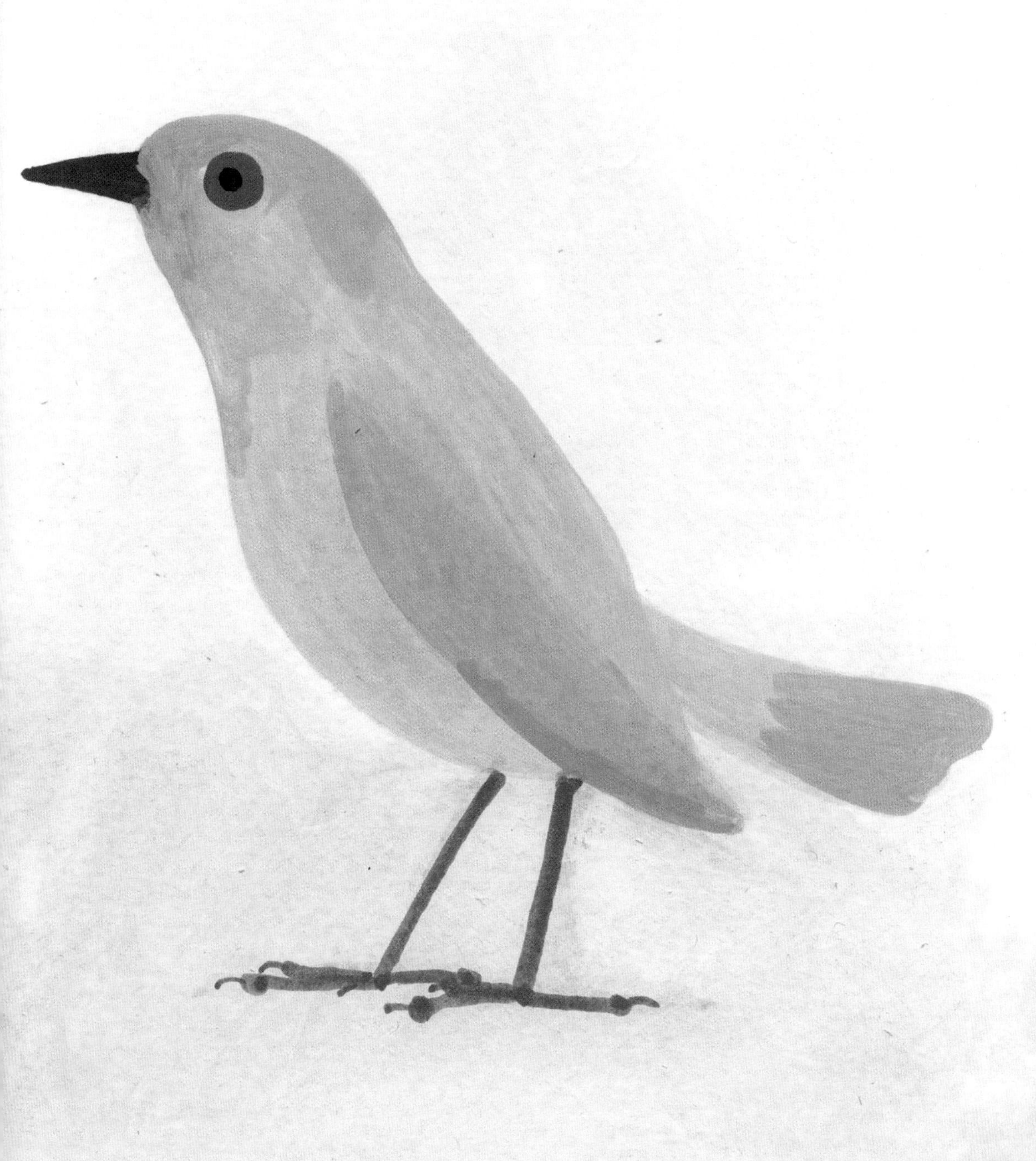

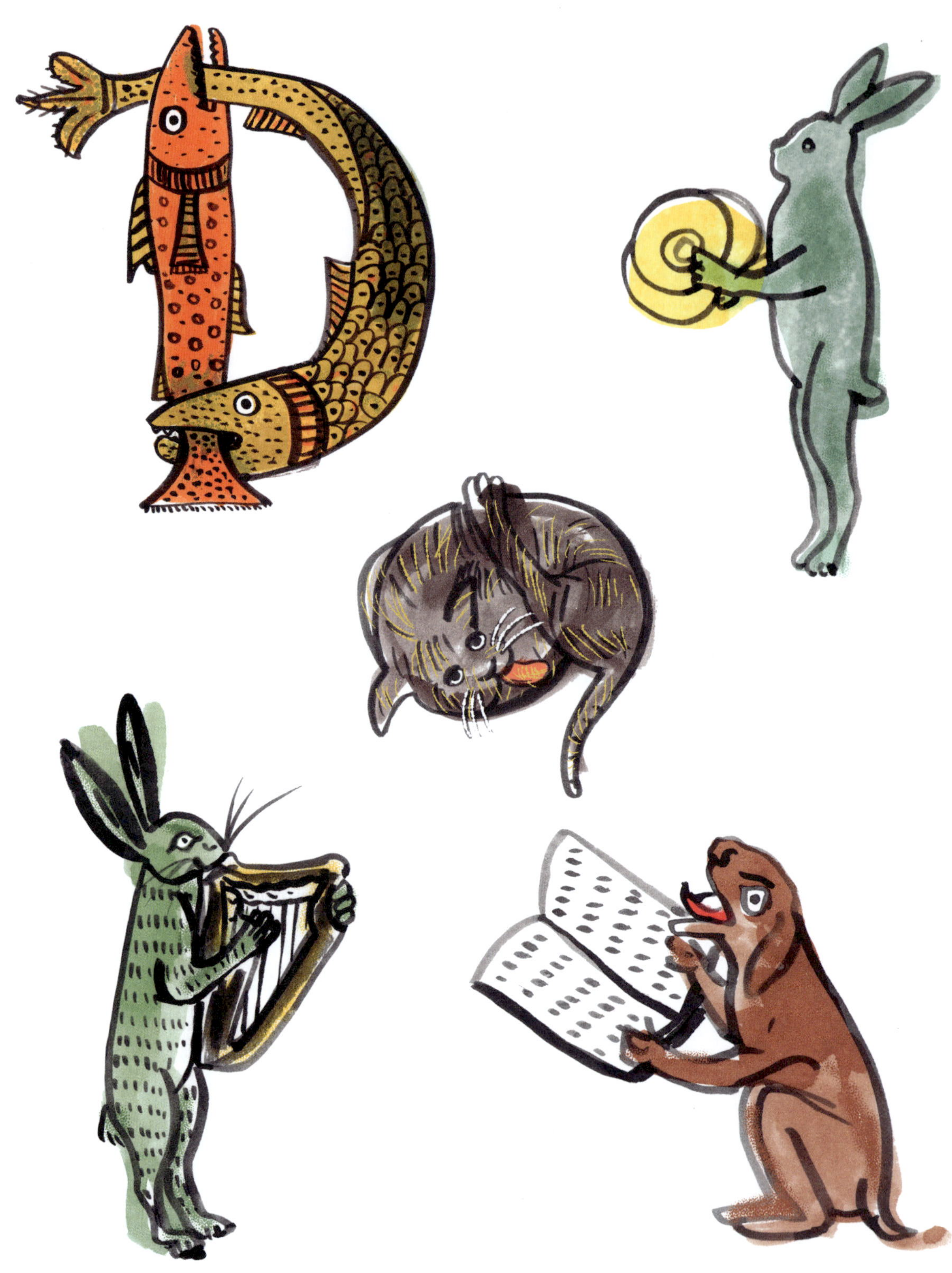

ILLUMINATE ME

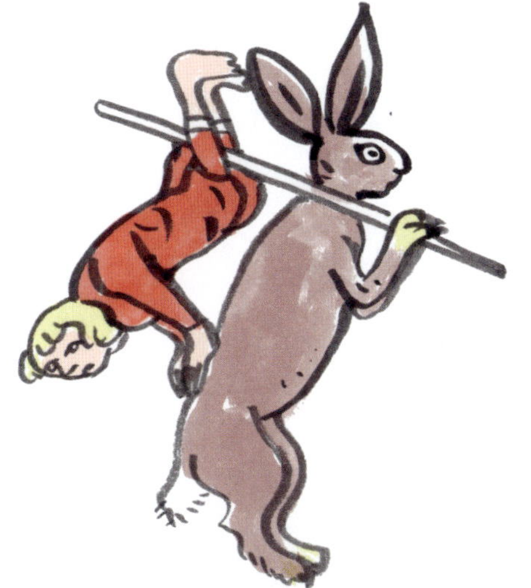

ILLUSTRATED CHARACTERS

Major libraries, like the British Library, have extensive collections of illuminated (illustrated) manuscripts, both in physical form and online. These manuscripts often have symbolic and allegorical animals or strange creatures in the embellished initials and margins. Animals are often depicted doing human activities in order to reflect the 'topsy turvy' nature of the world. I'm always searching for unique inspiration and this is a treasure trove.

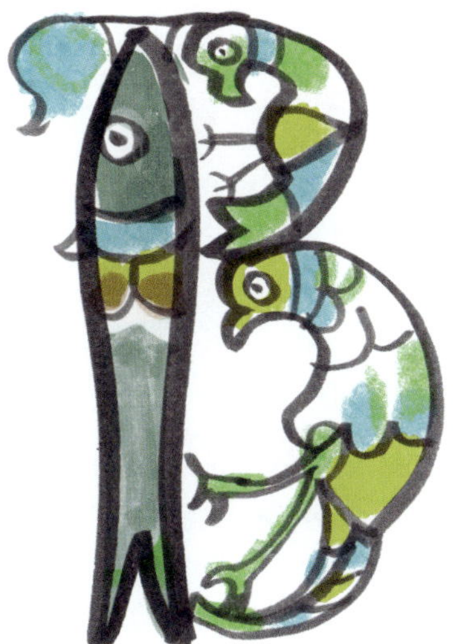

Creative exercise

Illuminated initials in manuscripts often feature zoomorphic or foliate designs, where animals or flowers conform to the shape of the letter. Make your own initials this way.

Creative quickie

Look up these two famous illuminated manuscripts: *The Book of Kells* and the *Lindisfarne Gospels*.

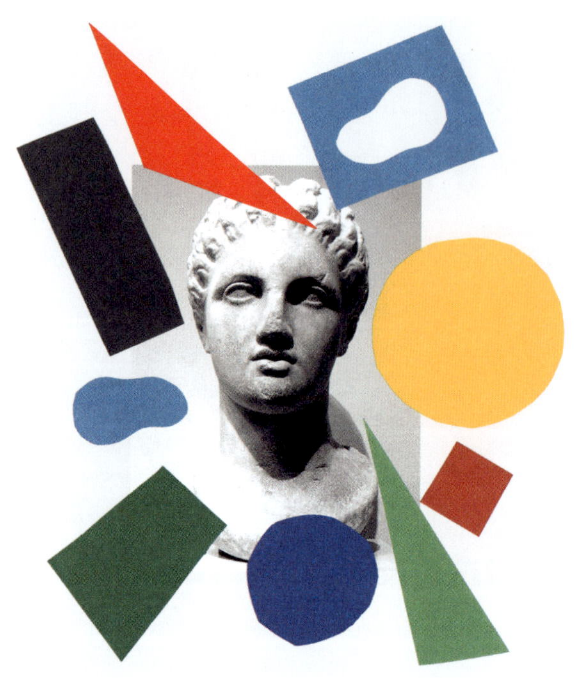
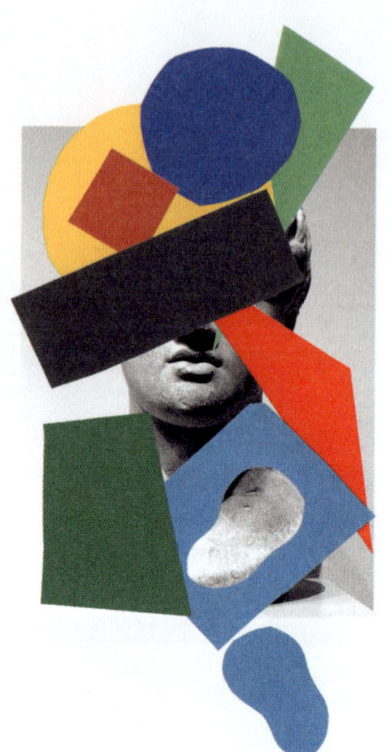
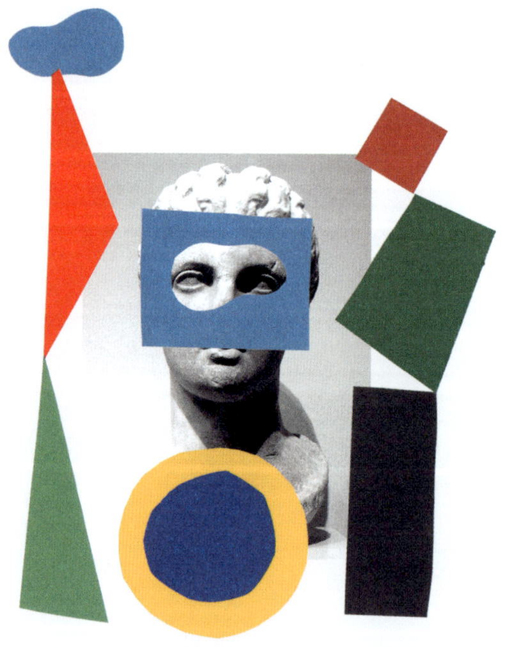
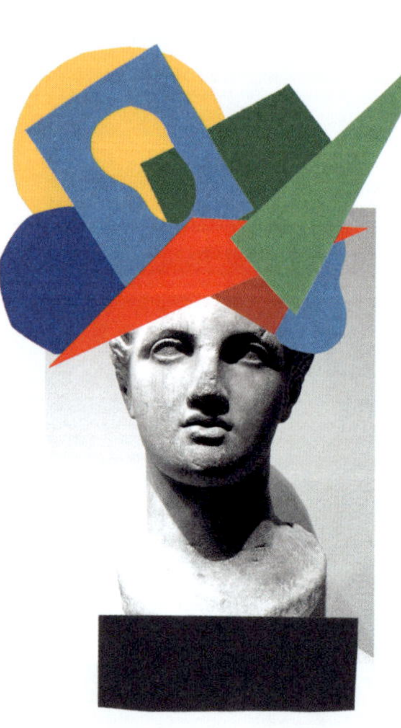

COMPOSITION SHAKE-UP

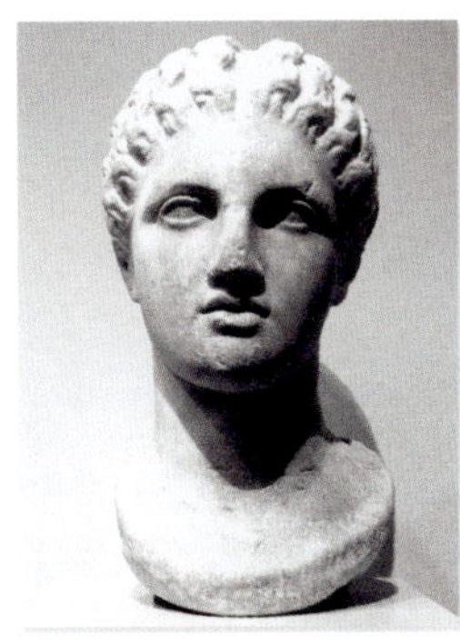

VARIATIONS IN DESIGN

Using the same elements, I mixed collage and photography to create unexpected, dynamic variations. I juxtaposed a black-and-white photo of a classical statue with simple shapes cut from coloured paper. You can arrange the shapes randomly or carefully; the key is the tactile process of placement and experimentation.

Creative exercise

Try this exercise with a photograph of a human head, contemporary or ancient. You can make your own coloured paper by painting sheets in gouache or acrylic paint.

Creative inspiration

The work of Peter Blake, Henri Matisse's paper cut-outs and the multimedia work of Lorna Simpson.

STICKS!

PAINTING STICKS

Collect some sticks from a park or from the countryside. Using acrylic paint pens or paint, begin decorating them with black and white patterns to focus on design. As you gain confidence, introduce more colours to add vibrancy. This activity offers a meaningful connection to ancestral traditions, evoking images of people throughout history engaging in similar artistic expression.

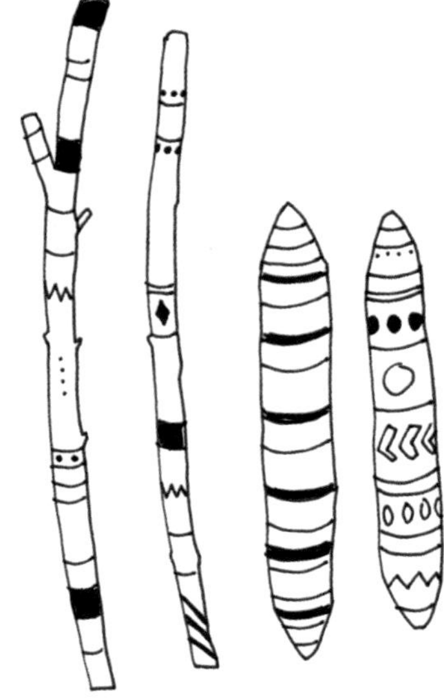

Creative exercise

Add a functional element to your sticks. Collect slightly thicker sticks that are about 15cm (6in) long and sharpen the ends to transform them into 'clapping sticks'. These come from indigenous Australian culture and are used to keep the beat in songs and dances. Decorate them in bright colours.

Creative inspiration

Indigenous Australian clapping sticks and American sculptor Sally Russell's ceramic totems.

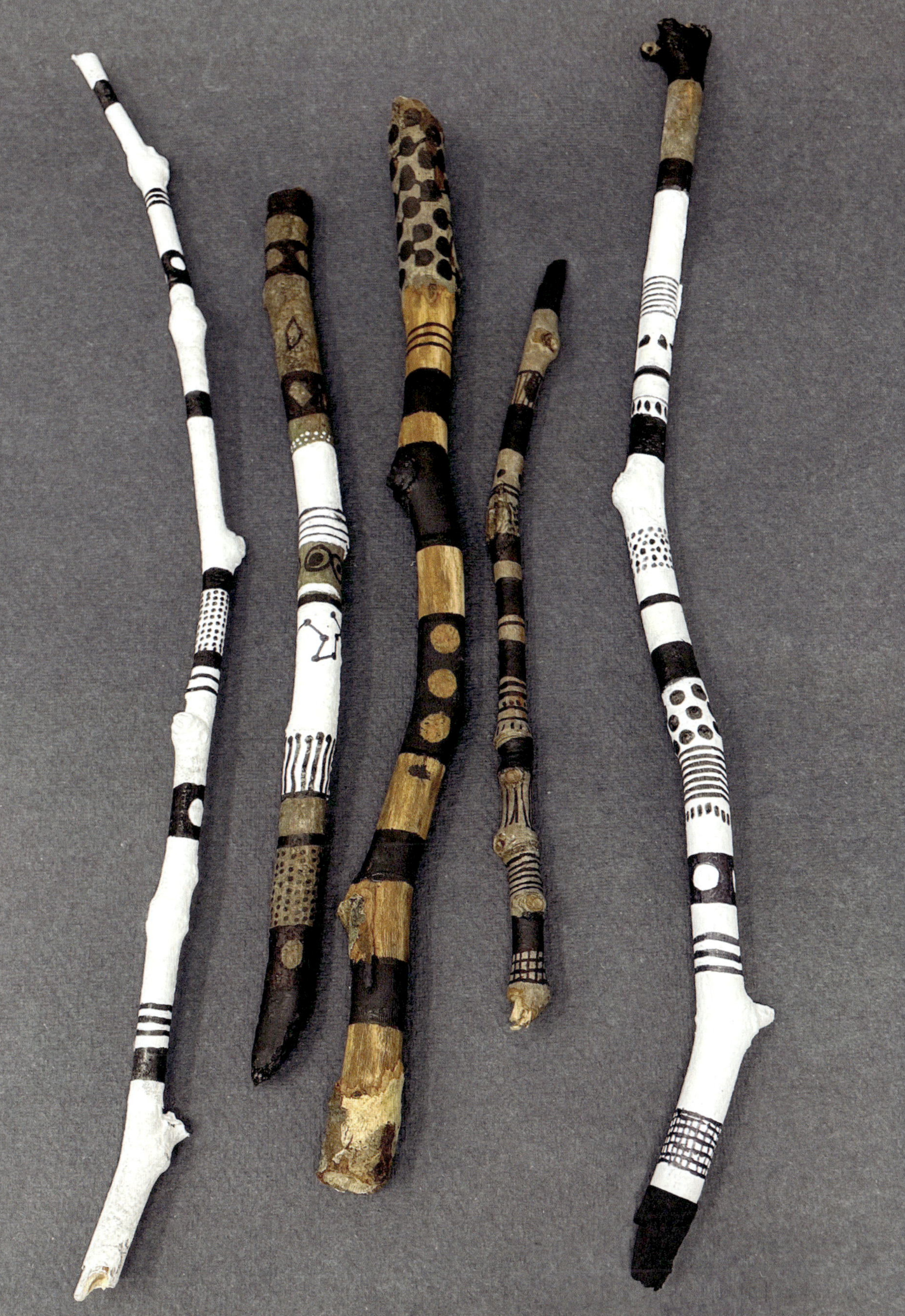

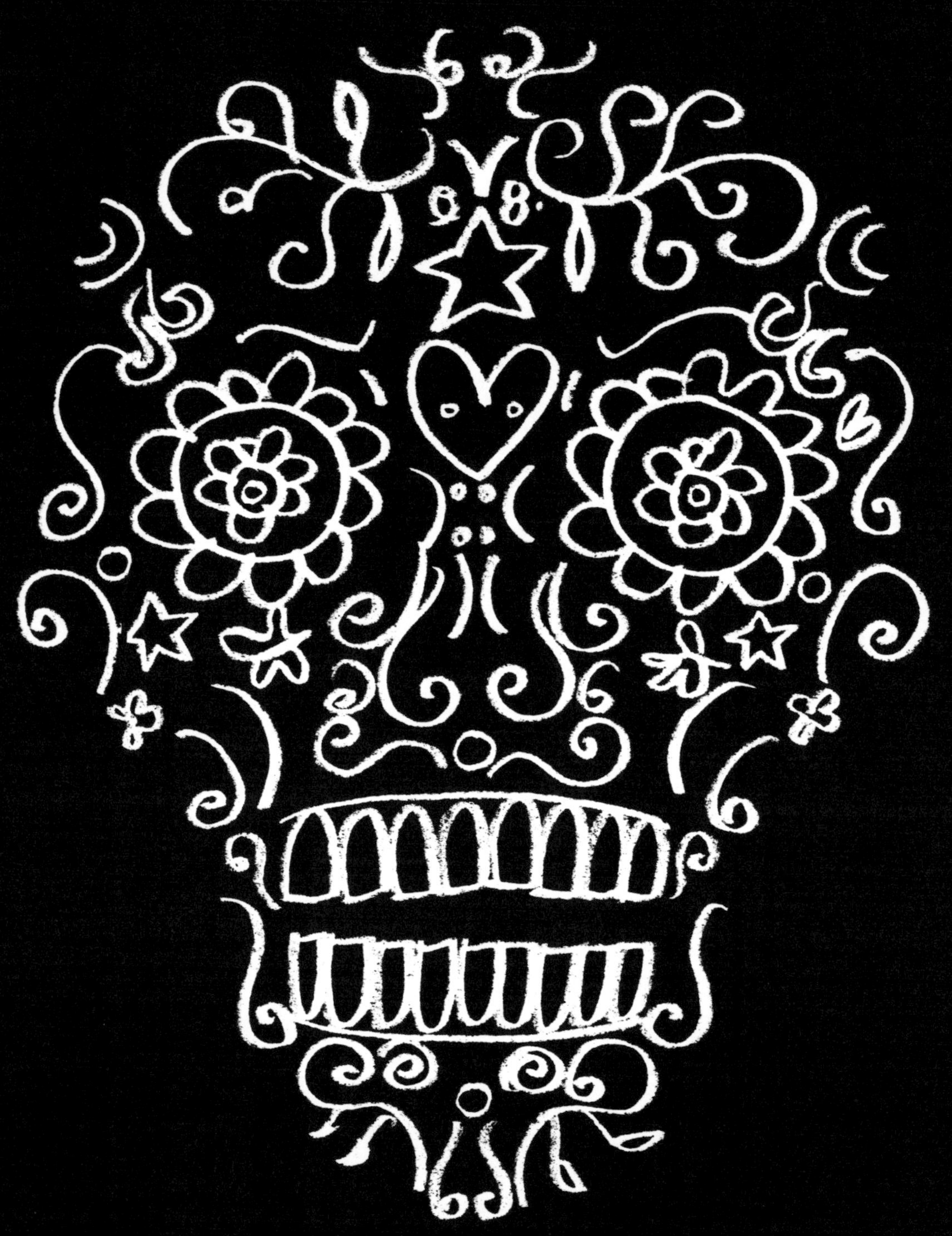

WHITE ON BLACK

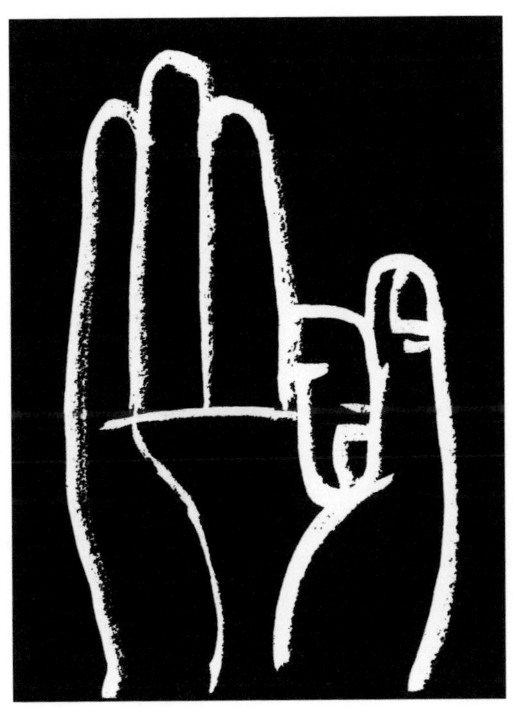

DRAWING IN NEGATIVE

I often use this technique because it challenges and surprises me. Working with white media on black paper makes you rethink traditional shading and layering techniques. This approach is especially effective for creating strong, simple, linear images. It encourages a bolder, more minimal style, as the black paper naturally becomes part of the negative space. Here, I've drawn a skull inspired by the Mexican Day of the Dead festival, as well as a graphic hand inspired by medieval manuscripts.

Creative exercise

Choose a subject to draw. It can be anything familiar, such as cats, faces or leaves. Draw with white paint, ink, chalk or acrylic paint pens on black matt paper. Draw quickly and boldly to begin with, aiming to produce a series of drawings to free you up.

Creative inspiration

The work of Keith Haring and Aubrey Beardsley.

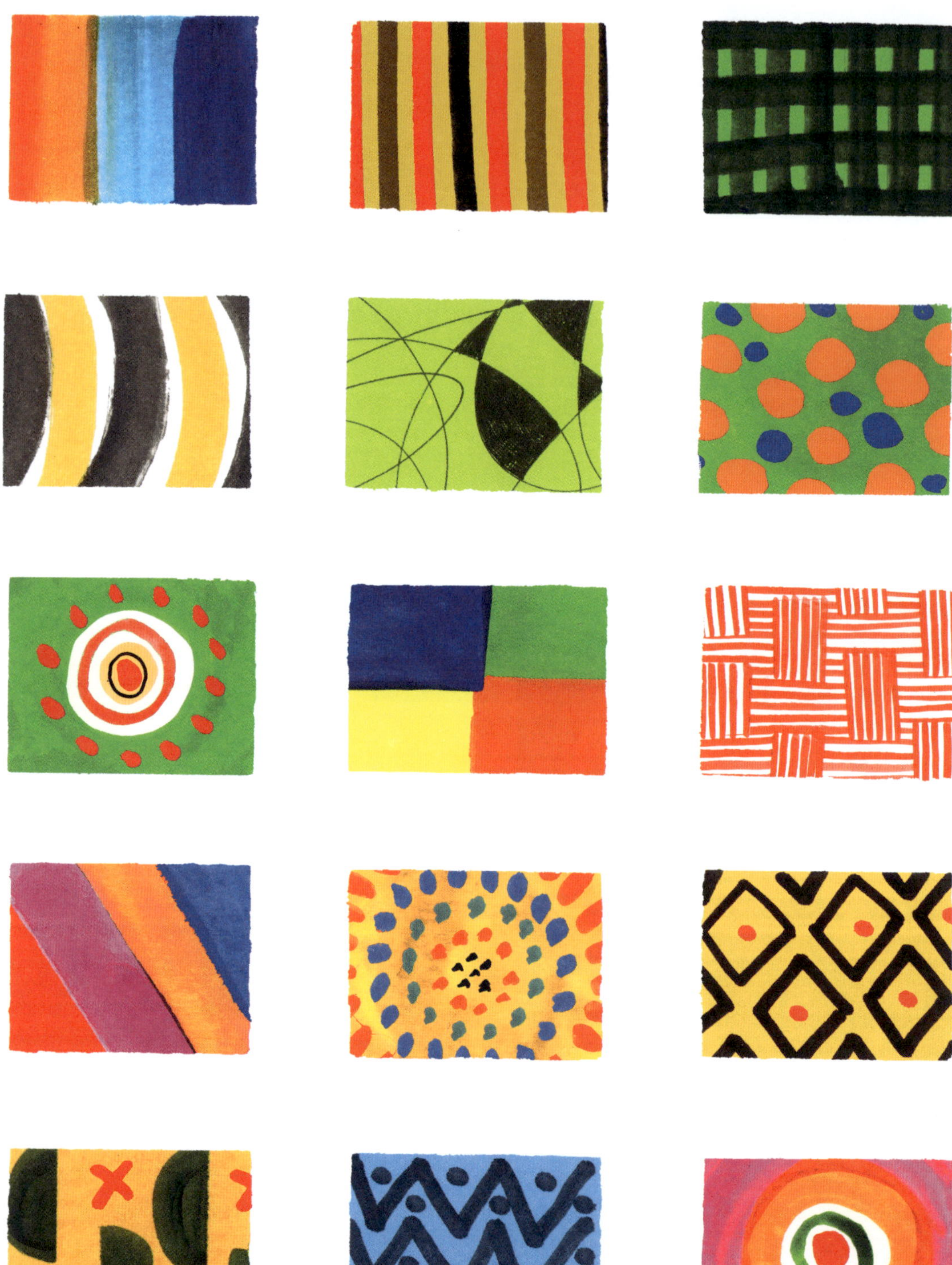

ON THE GRID

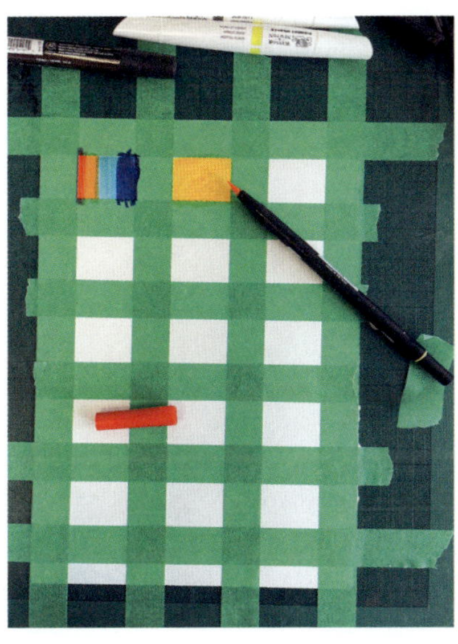

MAKING PATTERNS EVERYWHERE

Making patterns is something we can all do. It's a human inclination to look for and find patterns in everyday life. Start with doodling, then practise making patterns in different colours with pens or pencils. This can be a very meditative practice and can help you hone design skills like balance, symmetry and colour theory – all applicable to various art forms.

Creative exercise

Apply low-tack masking tape on paper to form a grid of rectangles or squares. Fill these shapes with different patterns. Once done, remove the tape to reveal a neat design of patterns. You can use this taping device to make other kinds of images – try making portraits or landscapes in the squares.

Creative inspiration

The intricate painted patterns of Australian artist Betty Chimney.

PORTABLE SCULPTURES

POST-IT!

Create your own portable art inspired by Bruno Munari's concept of travelling sculptures. Munari suggested making small, movable sculptures from paper to personalize your space while on the go. In my take on this idea, I've used sticky notes – easily accessible and versatile. You can either cut them into shapes with scissors or tear them by hand. These miniature artworks add a personal, creative and inspiring touch to your surroundings!

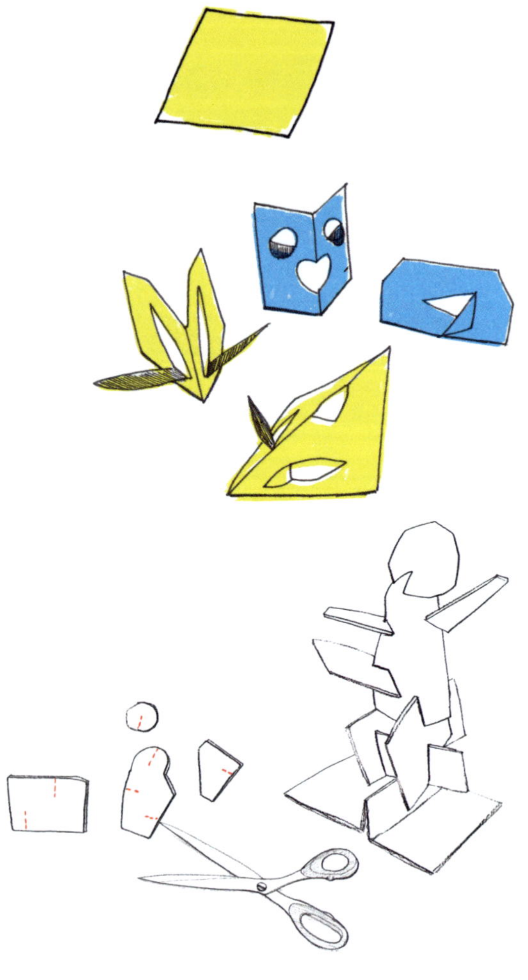

Creative exercise

Cut various shapes from card or thick paper and make a slit in each. Interlock the shapes to create a unique sculpture, a technique well-used by artists like Picasso and Miró.

Creative inspiration

The paper sculptures of Picasso, the 'stabiles' of Alexander Calder and the sculptures of Isamu Noguchi.

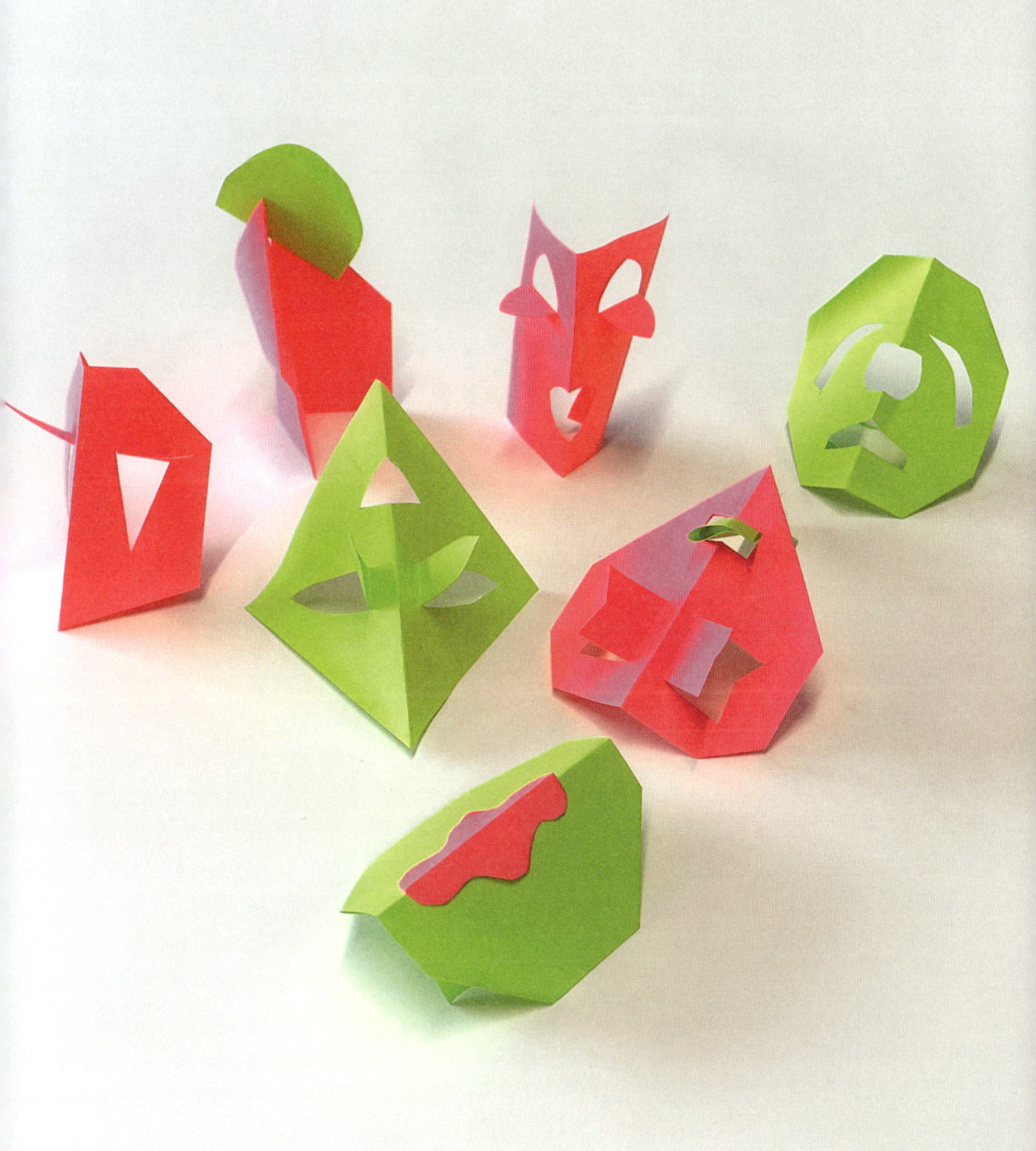

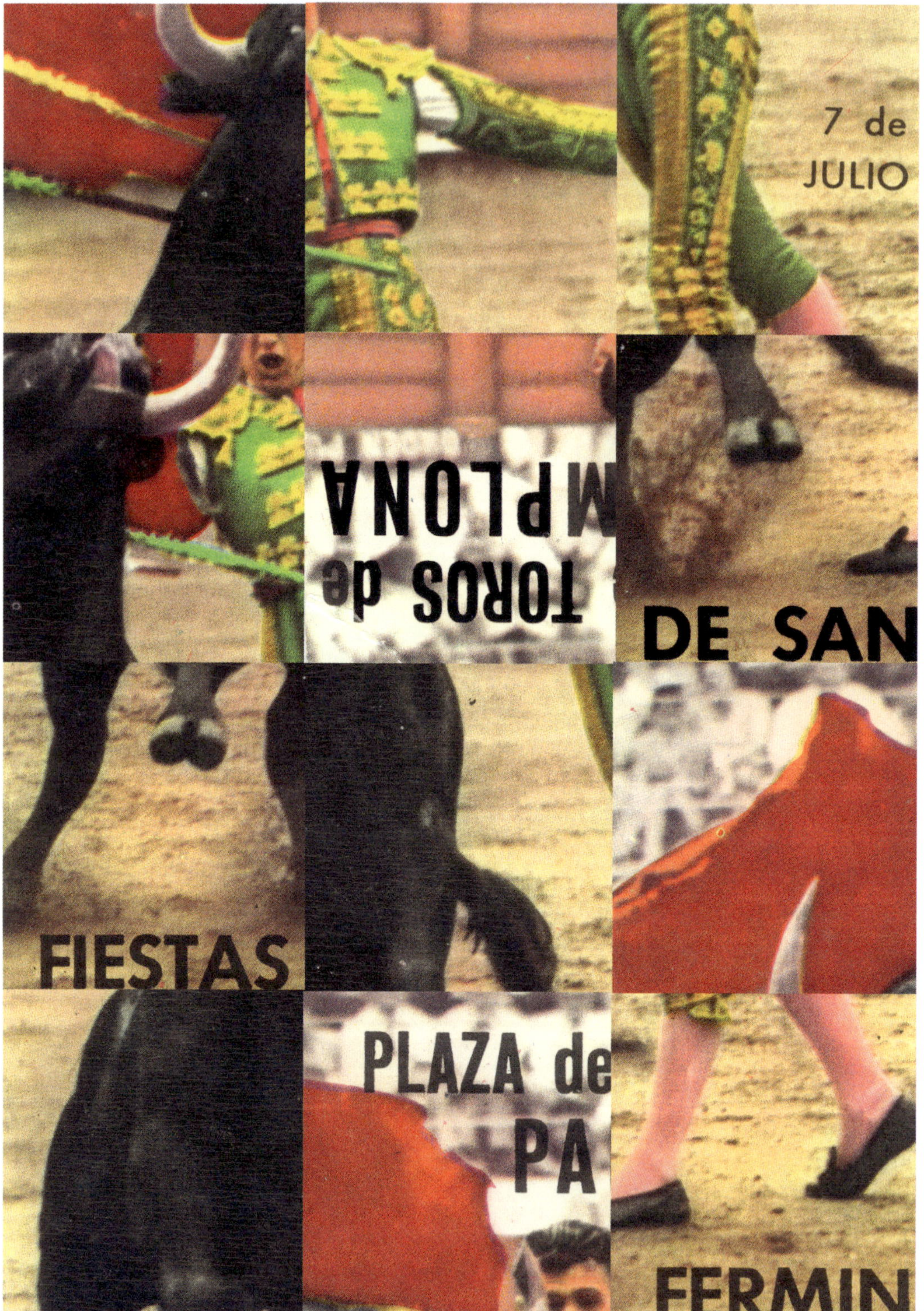

7 de JULIO
TOROS de PAMPLONA
DE SAN
FIESTAS
PLAZA de PA
FERMIN

MIX IT UP

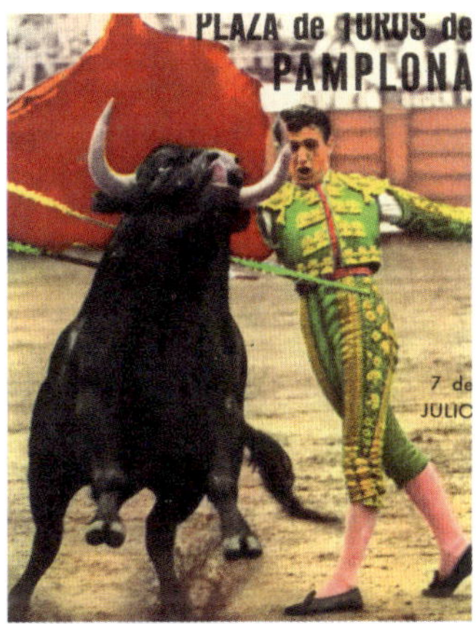

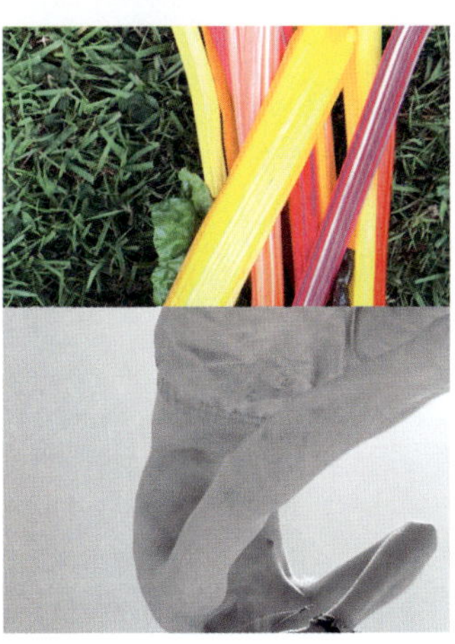

DECONSTRUCT AN IMAGE

David Hockney famously experimented with cutting up and rearranging photographs into abstract grids. I chose a vintage Spanish bullfight poster, attracted to its vibrant colours, dynamic movement and typography. After cutting it into 12 equal squares, I shuffled them until I achieved a composition that I was happy with. It's fascinating how manipulating an image can amplify its original message rather than dilute it.

Creative exercise

Select an image and divide it into 9 or 12 equal squares or rectangles. Rearrange them on a page until you're happy with the composition. Experiment with both colour and black-and-white photography or even drawings.

Creative quickie

Juxtapose two very different images. Look at the work of Man Ray or John Stezaker for inspiration.

LIE DOWN

ALTERED PERSPECTIVE

I remember, when I was young, drawing an image of myself drawing in my sketchbook. The drawing started from my sketchbook page and continued beyond to show my body down to my feet. On another occasion I tried to draw things from the level of my three-year-old child's viewing perspective. This altered perspective can make for interesting drawings. So try getting down on your knees or tummy and draw what you see from down there.

Creative exercise
Try drawing yourself from an unusual perspective or place: in the bath, lying on your tummy or your body from the head down. You can use a mirror if you like. Or draw from the perspective your dog or cat might see.

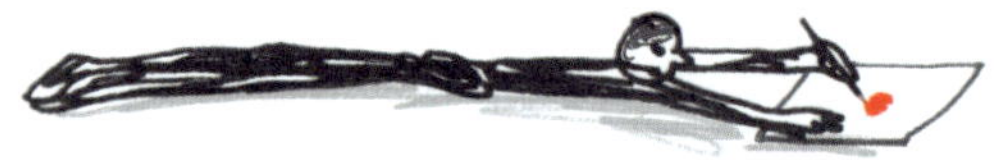

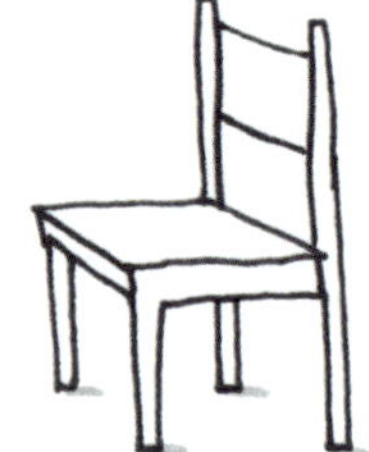

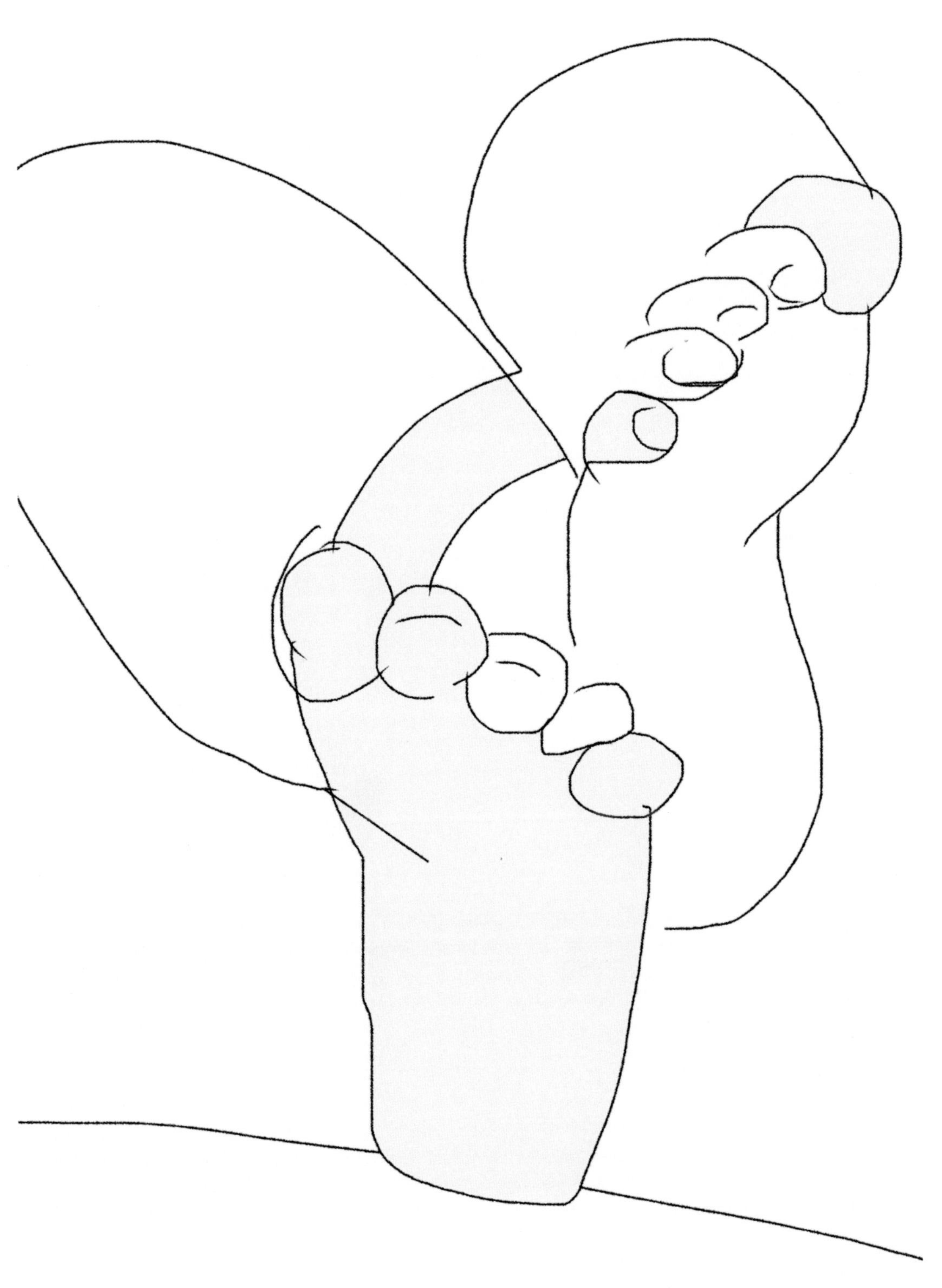

DON'T forget to DAYDREAM

As a child, I used to go on a favourite walk to a little
grassy ridge. There, I'd hang my legs over the edge
and daydream. My siblings found this an odd way to
spend an afternoon. 'What do you do up there all day?'
they would ask. It's a habit that has stayed with me.
It's like exploring a multiverse, where each
decision or idea could lead to a different outcome.
In a world where being busy is prized above all else,
I find inspiration in this 'in-between' time.

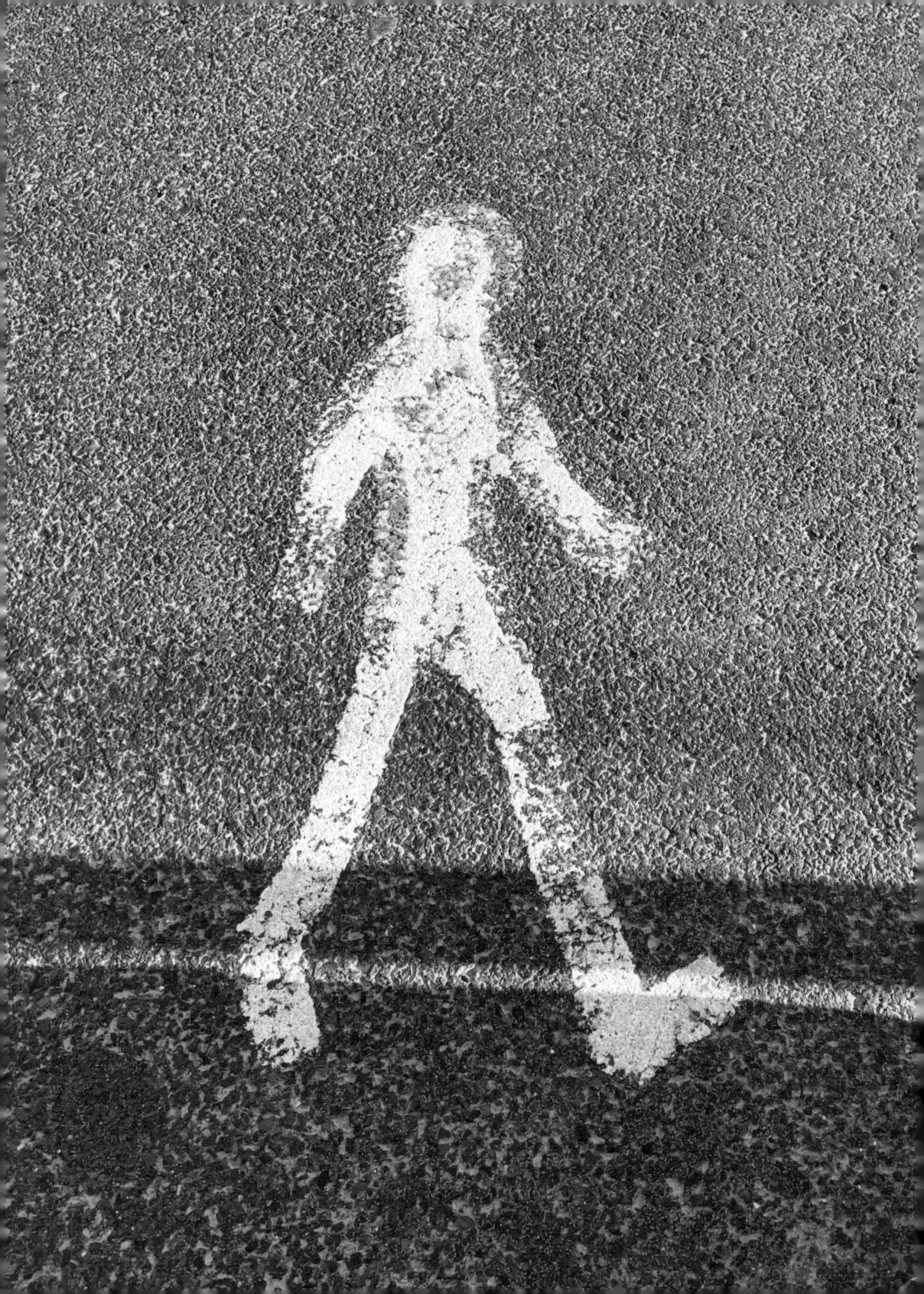

SENSORY WALK

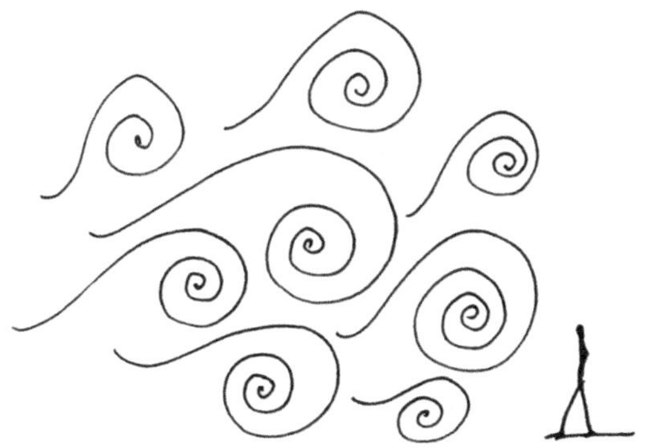

PRACTISE ENHANCED LOOKING

A good walk can be incredibly productive. Stepping away from screens and deadlines often leads to 'aha' moments. When I seek artistic inspiration, a walk usually provides the clarity I need. It releases endorphins, reduces stress and creates a mental state conducive to creativity.

Creative exercise

Pick a 30-minute walk, familiar or new. Bring a small sketchbook and pen.

1. First ten minutes: observe and jot down visual details like clouds, leaves or patterns.

2. Next ten minutes: focus on smells like wet grass, petrol or food.

3. Last ten minutes: pay attention to touch, for example tree bark, a cold lamp post or smooth metal.

Write down everything you experience and develop your jottings into drawings.

Creative quickie

The work of Richard Long and Hamish Fulton. Or try listening to a walking meditation by Tara Brach.

SHADOW WORLD

FOCUS ON LIGHT AND SHADE

'Were it not for shadows, there would be no beauty', wrote author Junichiro Tanizaki in his book, *In Praise of Shadows*. Tanizaki argued that the Japanese have a unique appreciation for shadows and darkness, which is reflected in their art, architecture and culture. Spend the day focusing purely on shadows; it completely changes how you see and appreciate your everyday surroundings. These photographs were mainly taken on my walk to work in the city of London.

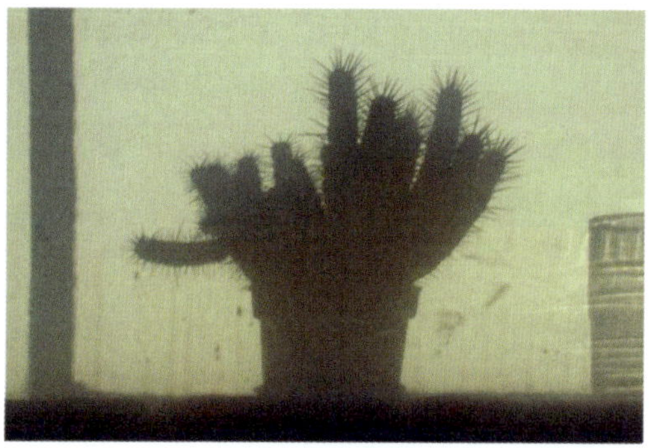

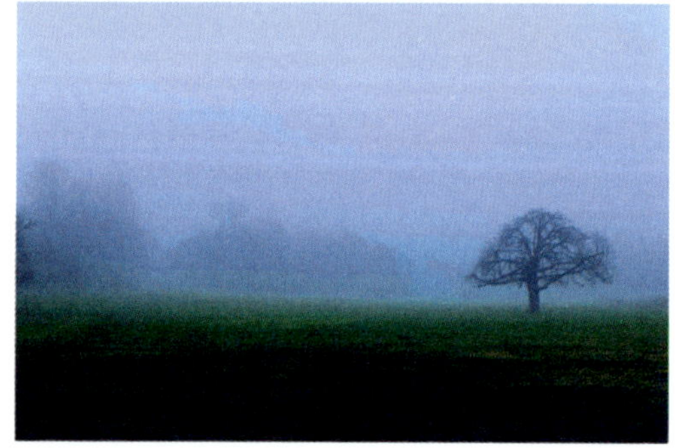

Creative exercise

Create your own art exploring the beauty of darkness. This could be anything from painting or drawing to photography or writing.

Creative quickie

Observe the shadows around you and try to write a haiku (a three-line poem with a 5/7/5 syllable pattern), capturing what you see or feel.

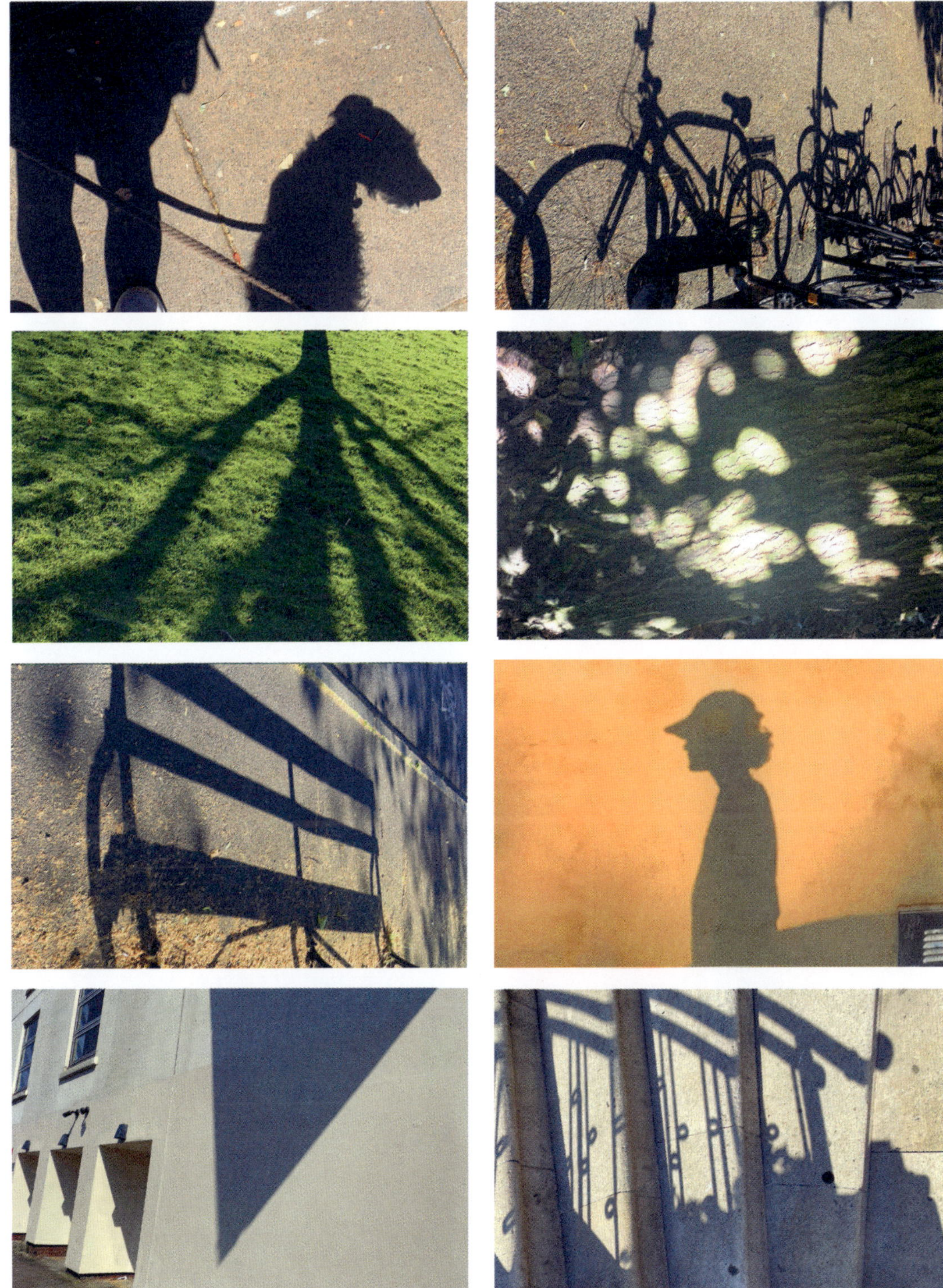

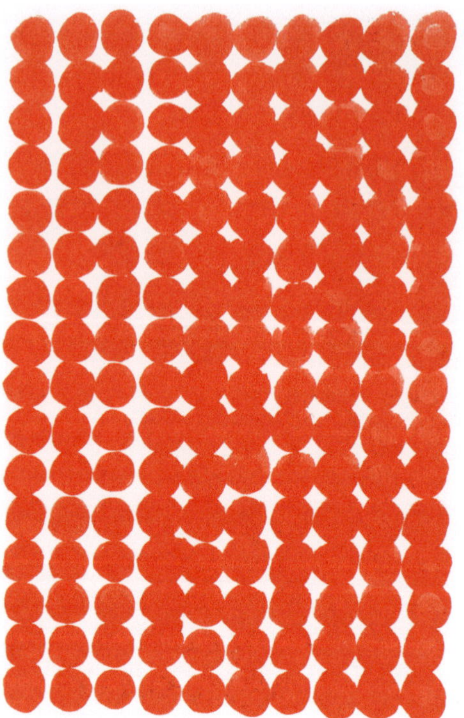
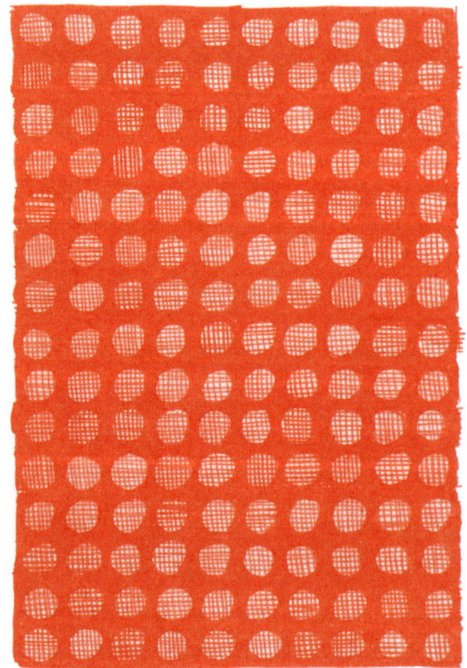
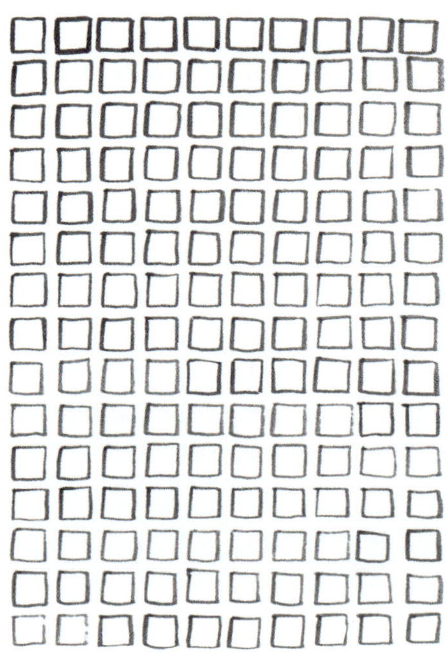

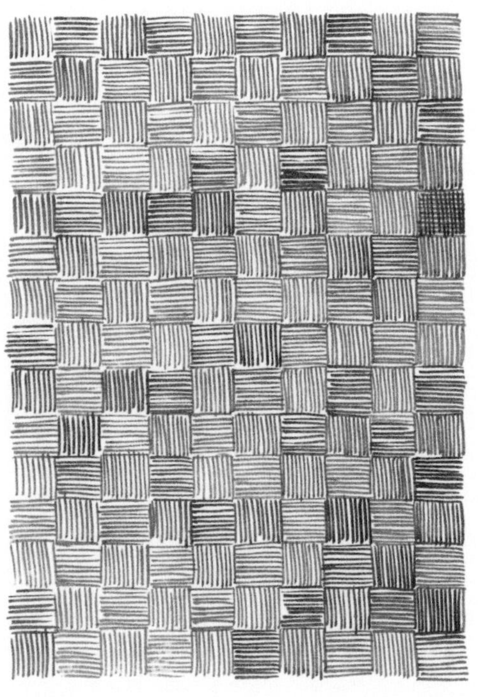

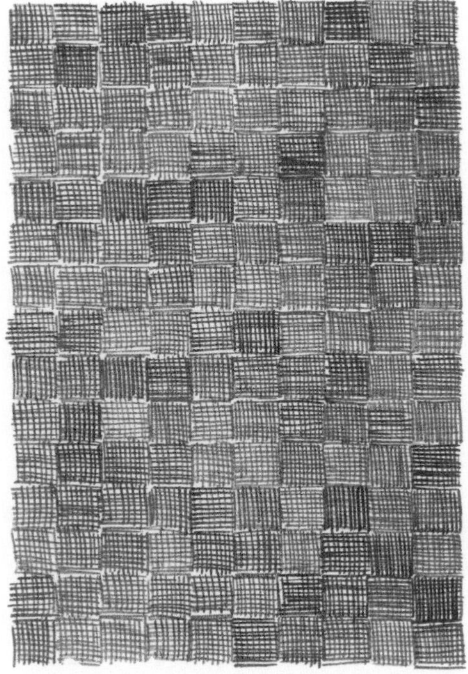

VISUAL RHYTHM

MINDFUL REPETITION

Working with a single visual element like painted dots or squares really helps you to understand the principles of minimalism and how visual rhythm works. This may seem like a doodling and playing exercise, but it's also an invitation to dig deep into the potential of simple design, pattern, repetition and placement. On a sheet of white paper, I lightly pencilled a grid to serve as a guide, and then used acrylic gouache and a fine, round brush to fill the sheet as evenly as possible.

Creative exercise

On a gridded page, select one shape, like a square or dot. Explore size, position and clustering to create a rhythmic pattern. Focus on how each dot or square influences the overall composition.

Creative inspiration

The grid drawings of Eva Hesse and Sol LeWitt.

STENCIL IT

PLAY WITH SPRAY

Stencilling as an art form gained widespread attention through artists like Banksy, but it has deeper roots that extend from street graffiti to activist posters. These simple stencils were made using cut paper and a spray can. If you don't have a spray can try using a bottle of ink and an ink diffuser, which are sold at most art stores. This gives you a more splattered effect, but it's equally interesting.

Creative exercise

Make your own protest poster. It can be on any subject and can include words or be pictures only. Keep the image simple with no delicate bits. If you're using paper you may not get many repeat uses from the stencil, but it will be much easier to cut than card.

Creative inspiration

The work of Banksy and Miss. Tic, and Patrick Thomas's book *Protest Stencil Toolkit*.

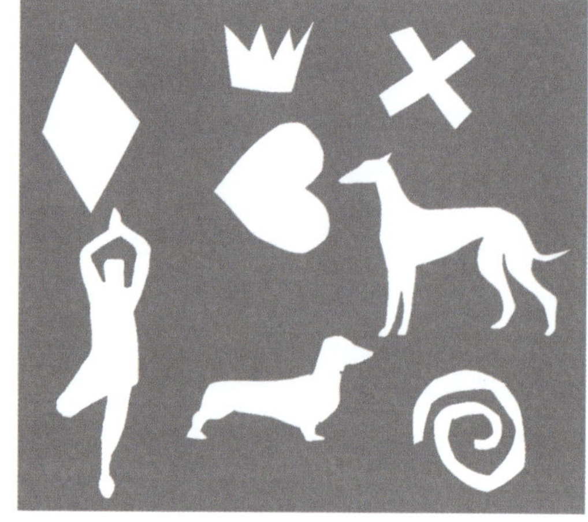

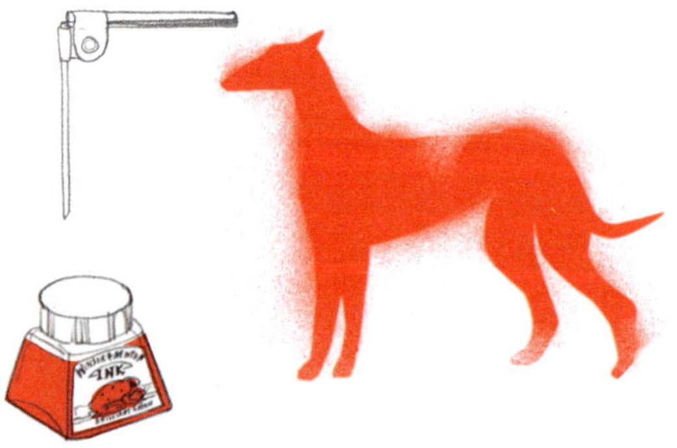

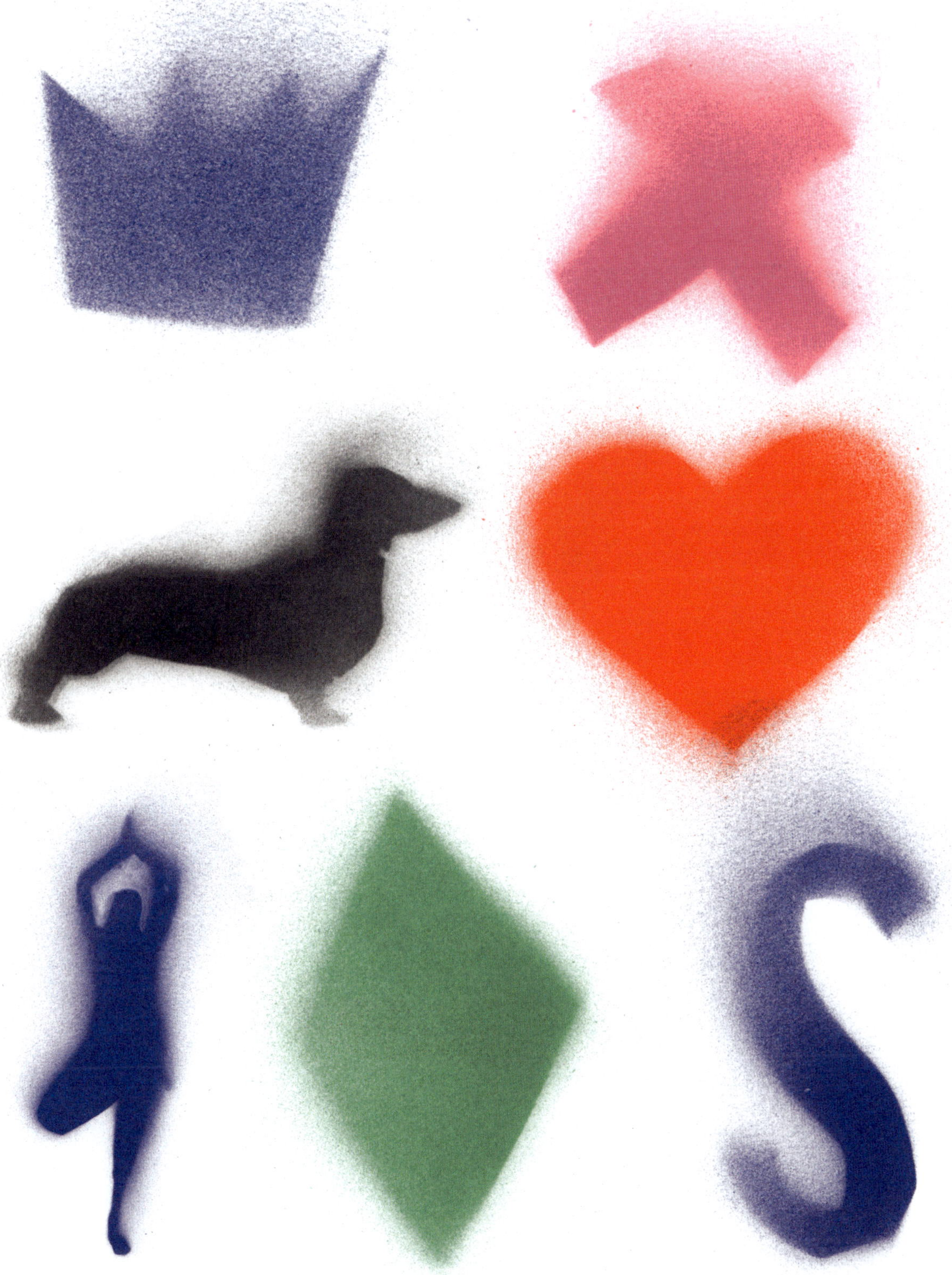

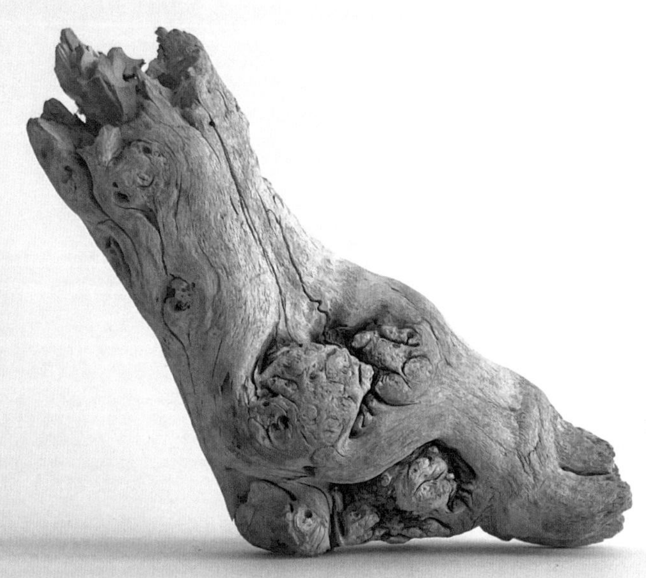

OUT OF SCALE

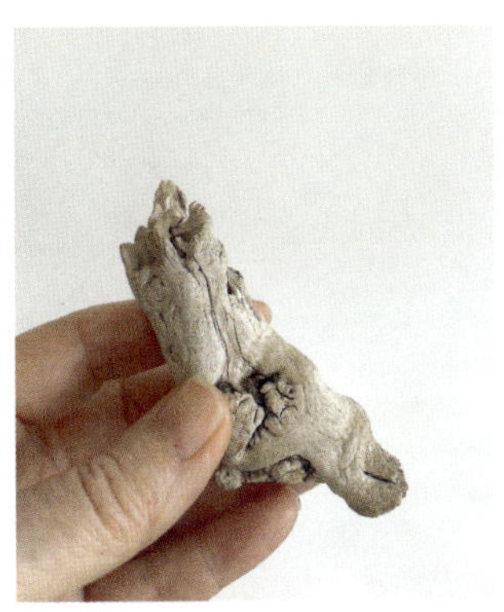

PLAYING WITH PERCEPTION

Photographing objects and manipulating scale and perception is great fun way to make intriguing images. Here I've photographed a piece of driftwood against a white backdrop and then used computer graphics to add the small dog to the image. You can also print the image and manually draw on it to achieve a similar effect.

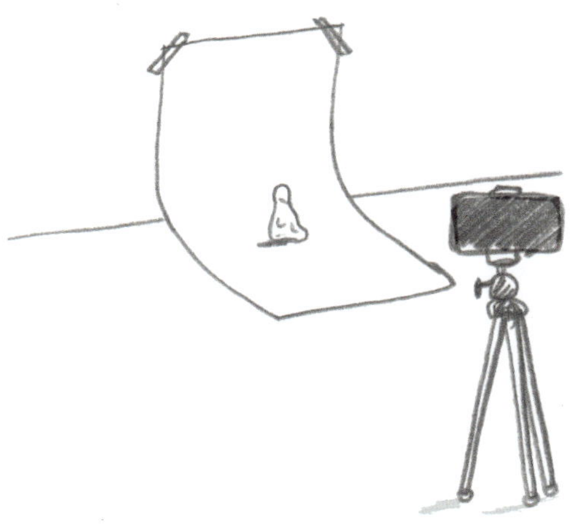

Creative exercise

Collect some items to photograph and try to create your own intriguing image. A useful tip for photographing items is to hang a large sheet of white or grey paper on the wall, letting the bottom half rest on a desk or floor. This isolates the object in both time and space.

Creative inspiration

The work of Leonora Carrington and Kansuke Yamamoto.

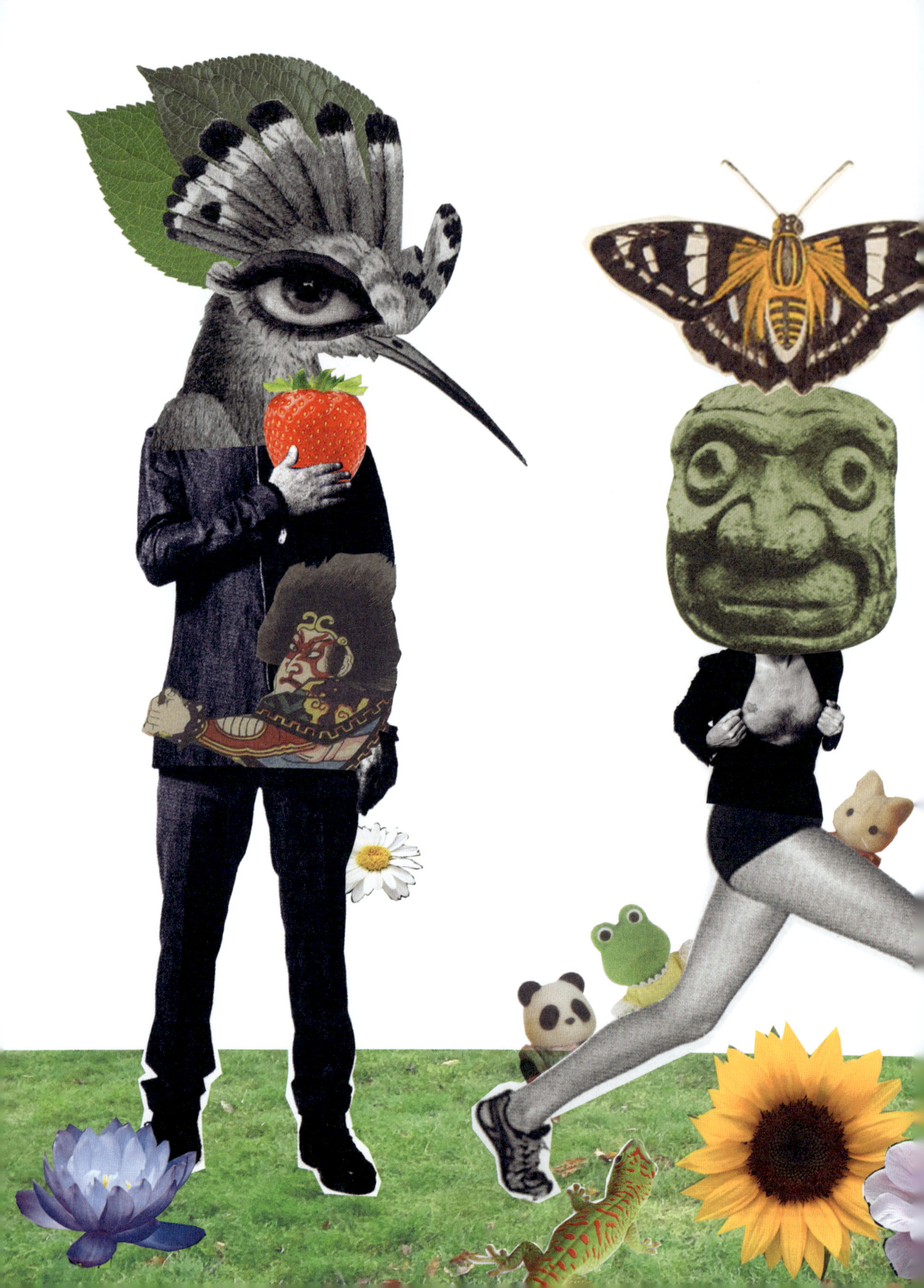

SO SURREAL

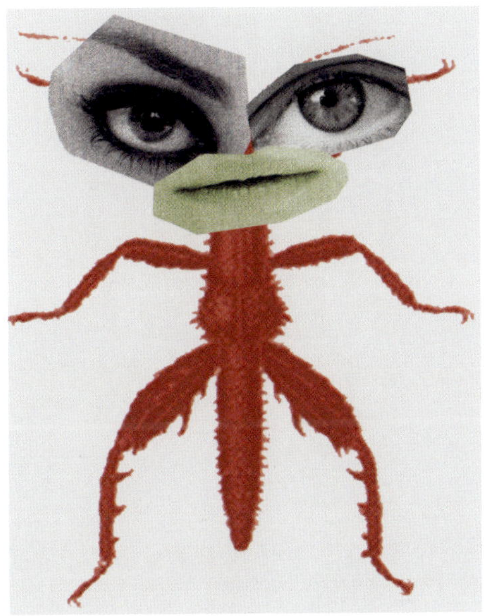

COLLAGE WITH PHOTOGRAPHS

Hannah Höch, a key figure in the Dada and Surrealist movements, is widely credited with popularizing photomontage. In today's digital age, making such montages has become easier than ever, and the mass of available printed materials is practically endless. Though the examples I've made here are quite crudely done, the odd juxtapositions make for strong, unusual imagery.

Creative exercise

Collect materials from magazines and online, and experiment with unconventional juxtapositions and unusual compositions. Remix images to form alternative narratives. Work on a single sheet or in a sketchbook. Think about writing character narratives to deepen your project.

Creative inspiration

The work of Hannah Höch, Martha Rosler and Lorna Simpson.

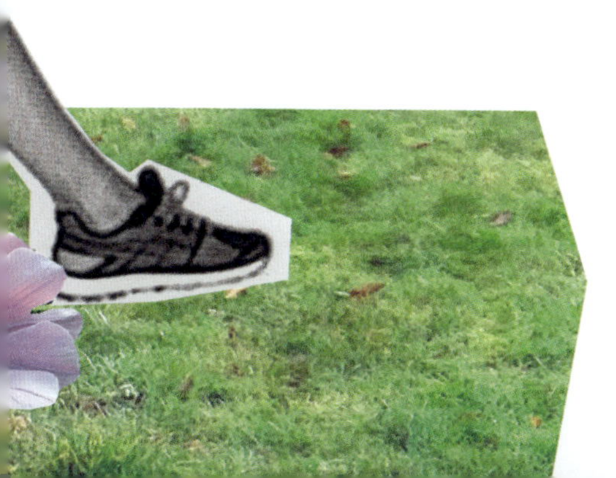

TAPE IT

TYPOGRAPHY WITH TAPE

You can make different styles of lettering using materials like tape, round or square stickers and cut paper. In these examples I made an alphabet using masking tape and a sharp knife and a ruler. I made it quickly without much deliberation. Below, in colour, the letters ABCD were made by tearing coloured masking tape and sticking it down.

Creative exercise

Using coloured masking tape, make your own poster featuring tape or sticker typography. Select a quote or create your own, aiming for a harmonious layout on your paper. The handmade aesthetic will enhance its charm and immediacy.

Creative inspiration

The cut-outs of Rob Ryan and the experimental typography of Sarah Boris.

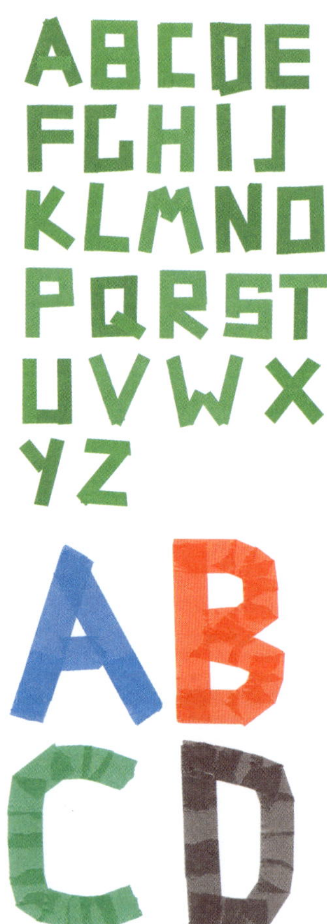

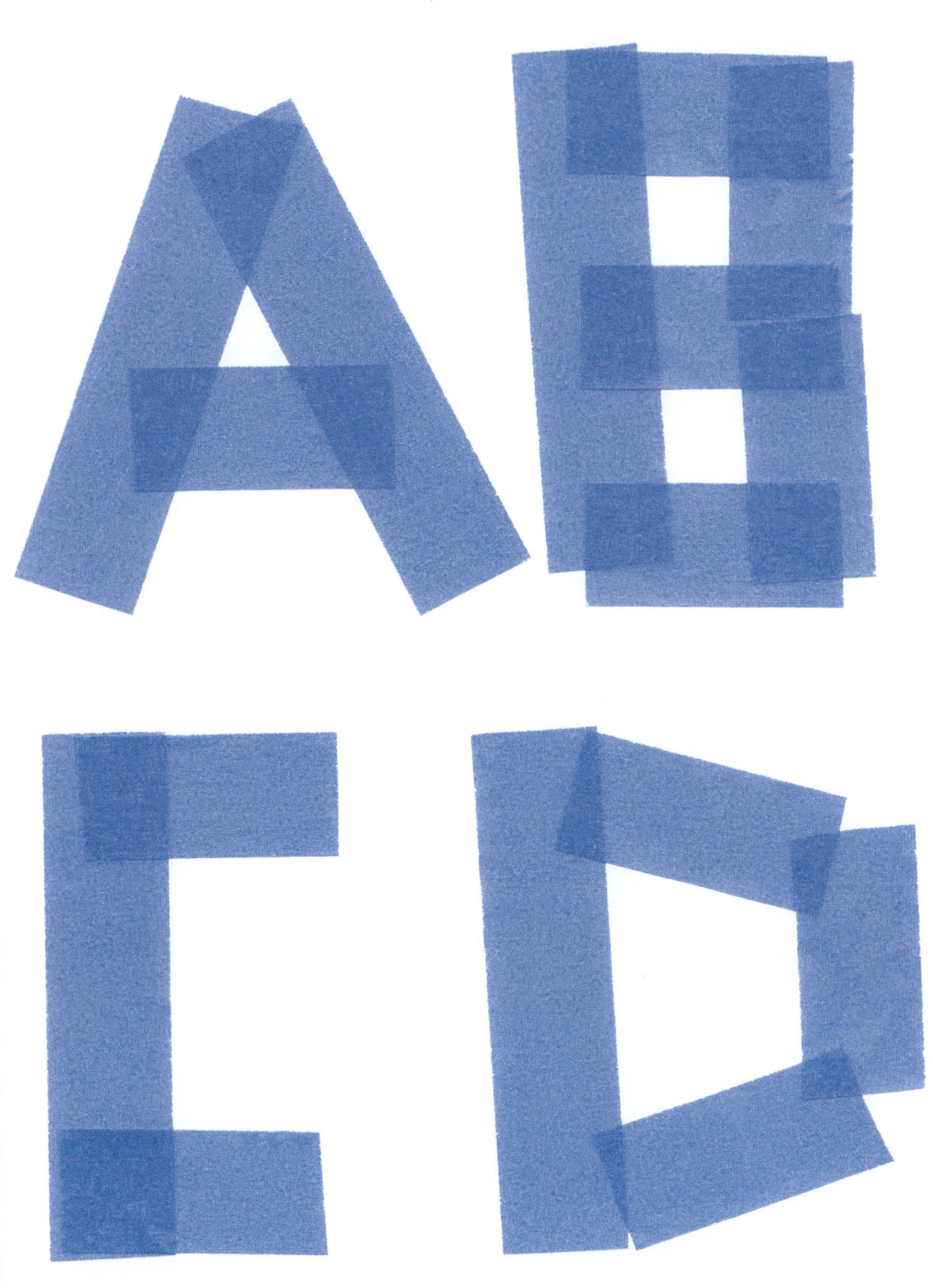

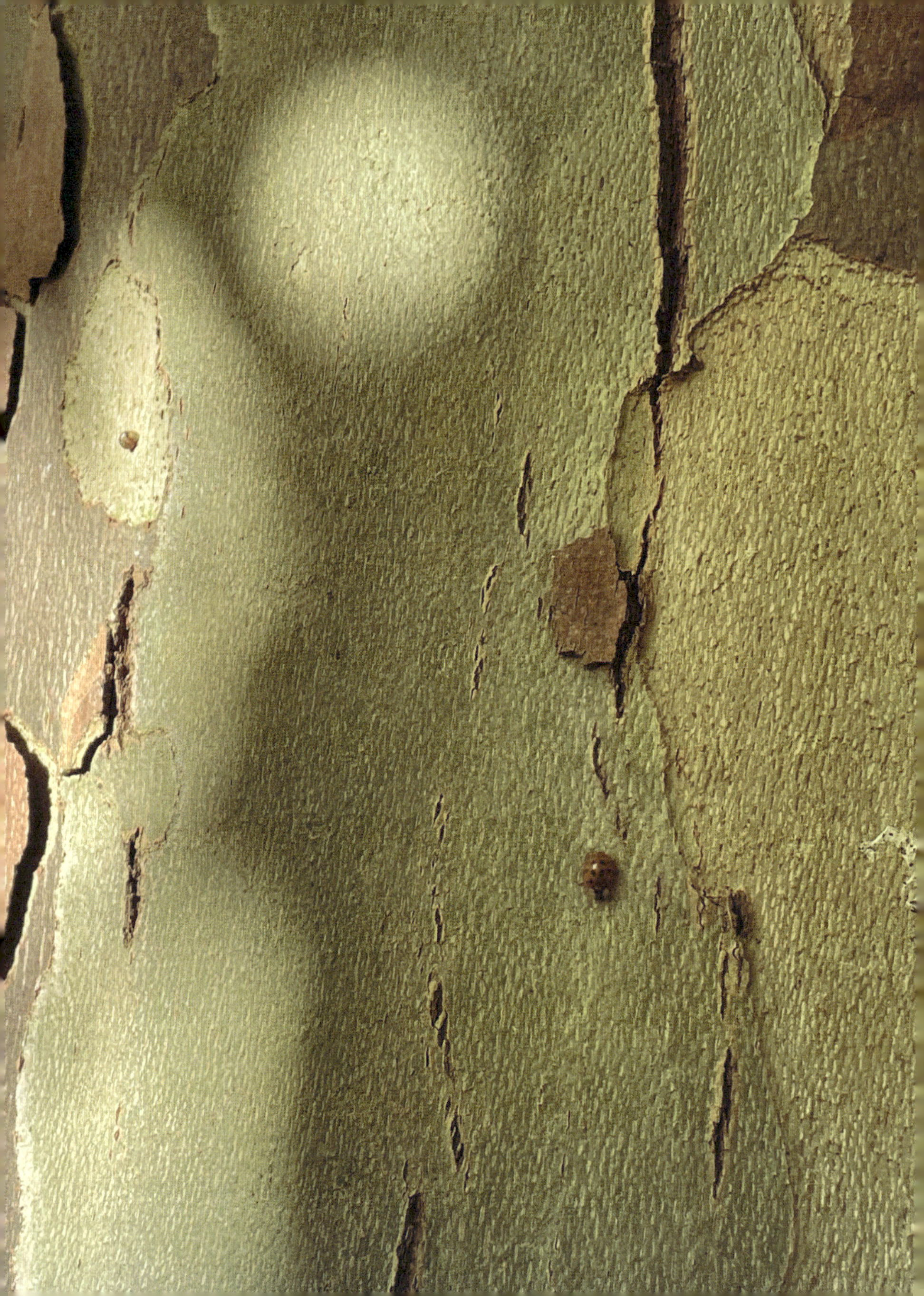

DAILY TREE

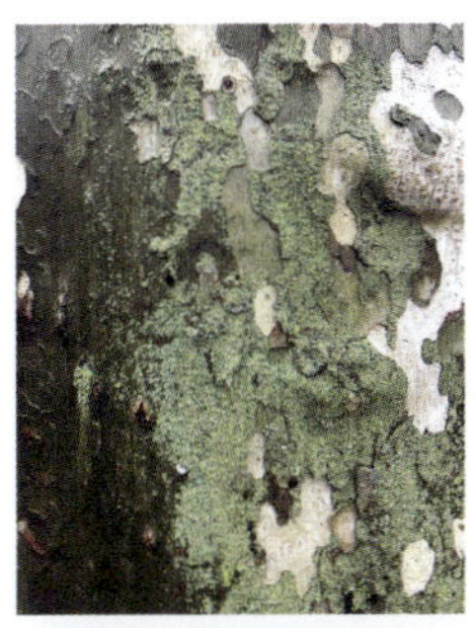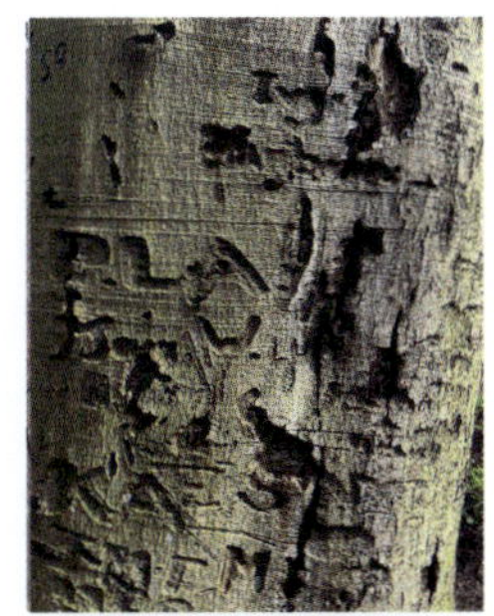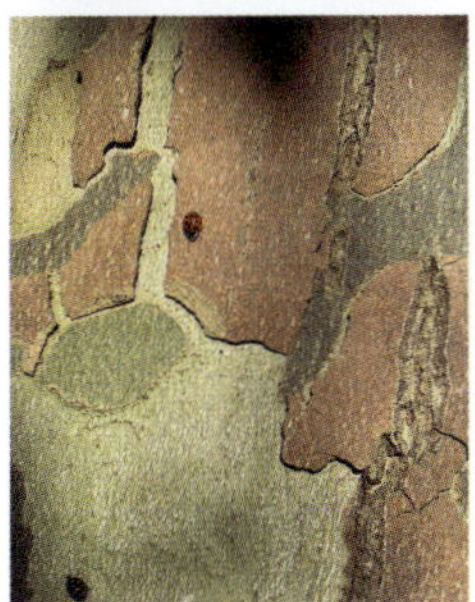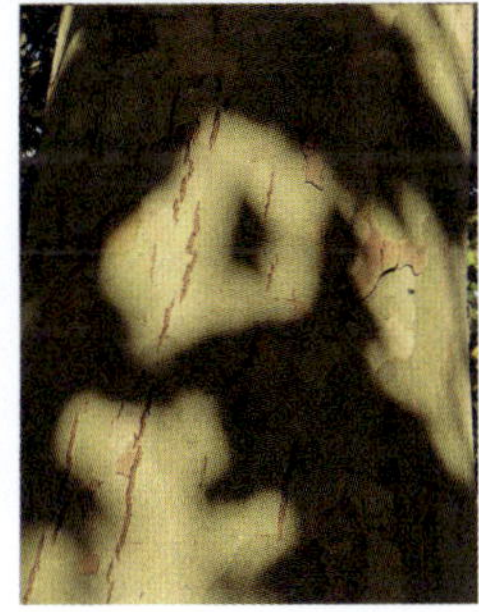

FINDING INSPIRATION IN TREES

Trees are an endless source of inspiration for me. Living in London, a city abundant with trees, gives me the privilege of seeing seasonal transformations during my daily walks. I have several trees that hold a special place in my heart, and I make it a point to regularly observe their evolving states. Natural elements can inspire reflection and creativity, whether watching clouds, gazing at rivers or observing trees.

Creative exercise

Identify a tree that intrigues you, noting its shape, colour and bark patterns. Describe these features vividly in your sketchbook. With a problem or idea in mind, revisit the bark's texture. Let the patterns you see offer fresh insights or solutions. This technique is popular in various practices, including CBT (cognitive behavioural therapy) and mindfulness.

Creative inspiration

Read *The Artist's Way* by Julia Cameron or *How to Do Nothing* by Jenny Odell.

SIMPLE BOOKS

HOW TO MAKE YOUR OWN BOOK

There are many ways to make a simple book to be used as a sketchbook, zine or notebook. Here are two of my favourites as they are so simple. On this page, see how you can make a booklet with one sheet of paper and one single cut. On the opposite page, I've shown you how to make a book with the simplest of bindings. No sewing required.

Creative exercise

Create your own zine. Start with a cover image, choose a theme and then try to fill the book with images, stories, quotes or found imagery related to the subject. Break the rules of what a book should look like by cutting up the pages, making holes or ripping pages.

Creative inspiration

The books of Bruno Munari and Keri Smith.

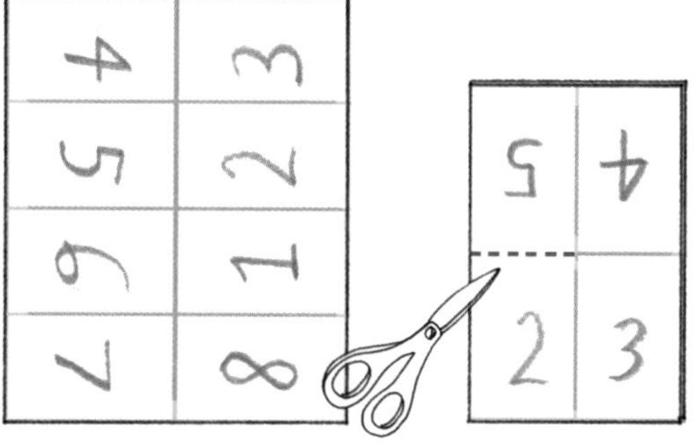

1. Fold a sheet of A4 paper into eighths. Open out again and pencil in the numbers shown above.

2. Fold in half and cut, as shown, starting from the folded edge.

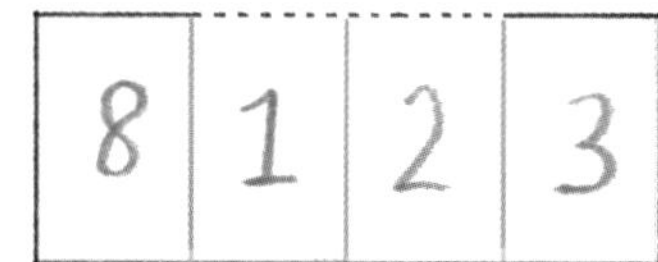

3. Open out again and fold lengthwise.

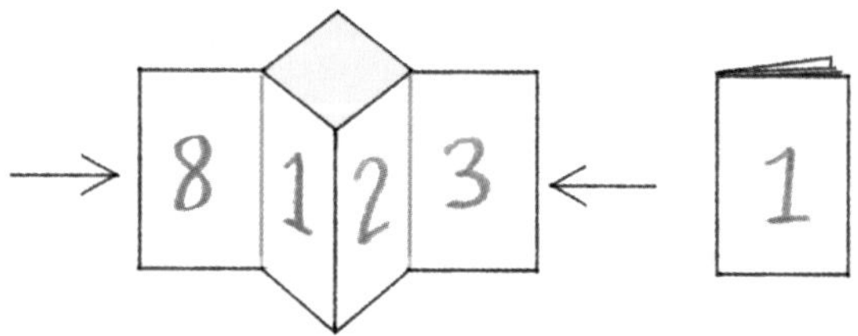

4. Push the two ends together and fold into a booklet.

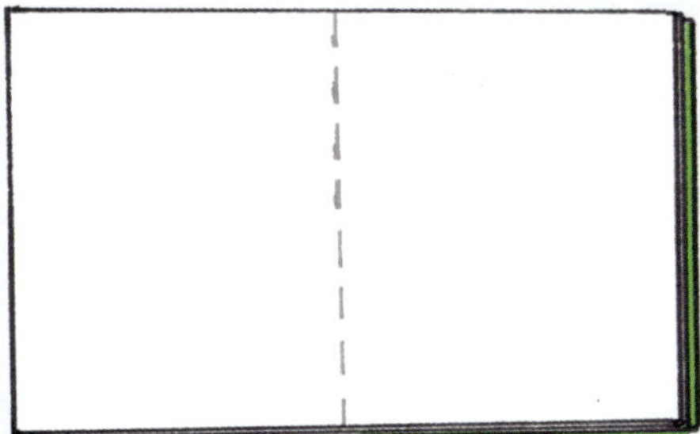
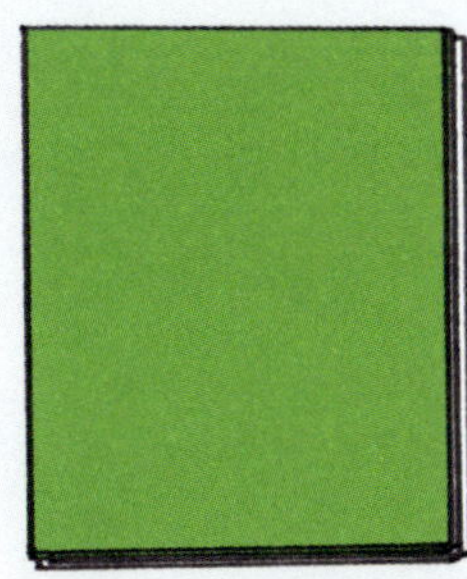

1. Start with a stack of paper approximately A4 size. Fold in half lengthwise. You can use all different kinds of recycled paper. Use a slightly thicker paper for the bottom of the stack.

2. Once the paper is folded over, press down hard to make a strong crease.

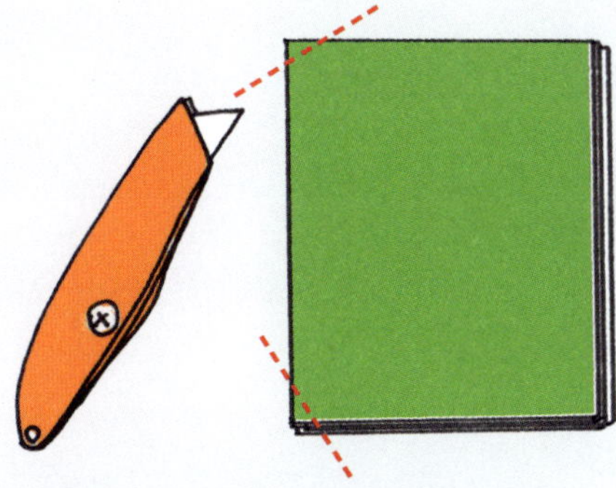
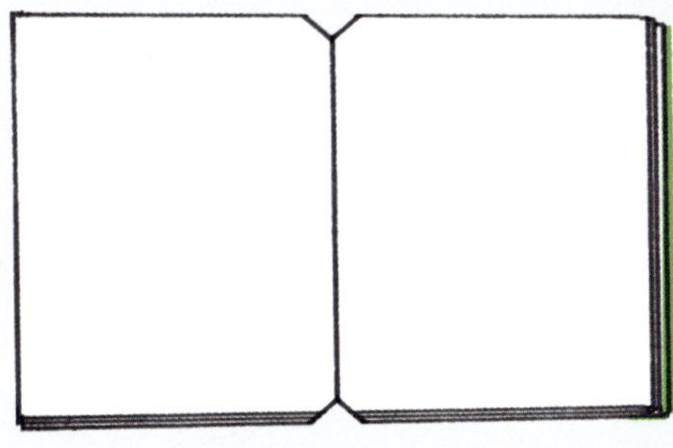

3. Using a strong cutting knife, cut two diagonals from the corners of the stack at the top and bottom of the folded side.

4. Open the stack of paper. It should look like this.

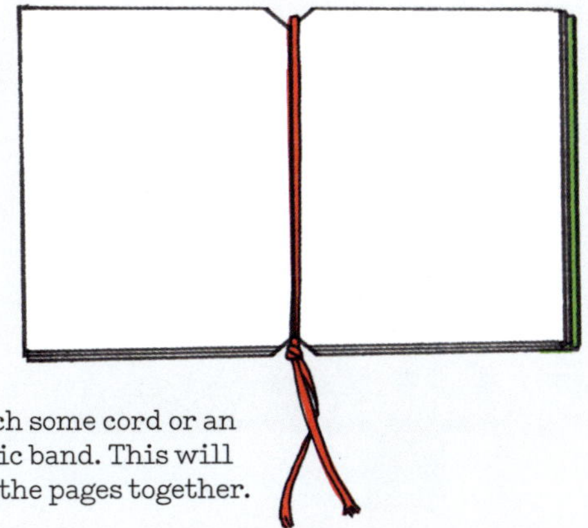
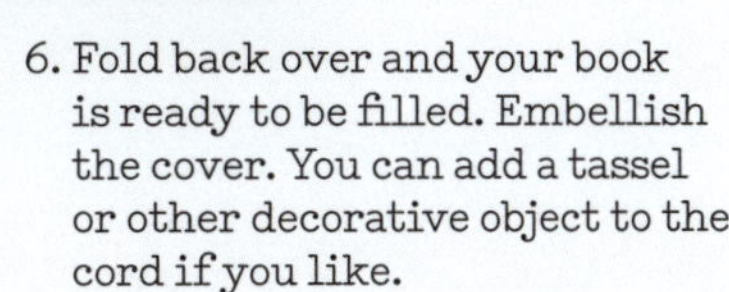

5. Attach some cord or an elastic band. This will hold the pages together.

6. Fold back over and your book is ready to be filled. Embellish the cover. You can add a tassel or other decorative object to the cord if you like.

A DIFFERENT VIEW

MAKE A VIEWFINDER

A viewfinder is a useful tool for artists and a playful device for anyone who wants to gain a new perspective on their surroundings. It helps you clear away the clutter and concentrate on the elements that matter. Making a viewfinder is easy and needs few materials. Cut a rectangle from strong paper or use two 'L' shapes taped together. The second option lets you easily change the size for different scenes.

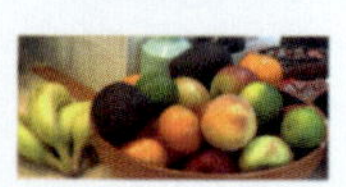

Creative exercise

Use your viewfinder to create quick sketches in your sketchbook, framing different scenes. You can focus on realism or abstraction. Try two options: one 'zoomed in' to focus on a smaller detail, and another 'zoomed out' to include more context.

Creative quickie

Try isolating just one type of element, like lines, shapes or textures, as you look through your viewfinder. Sketch or record what you see.

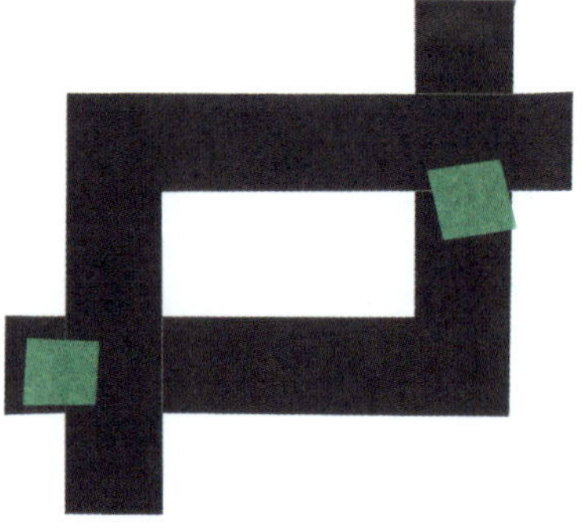

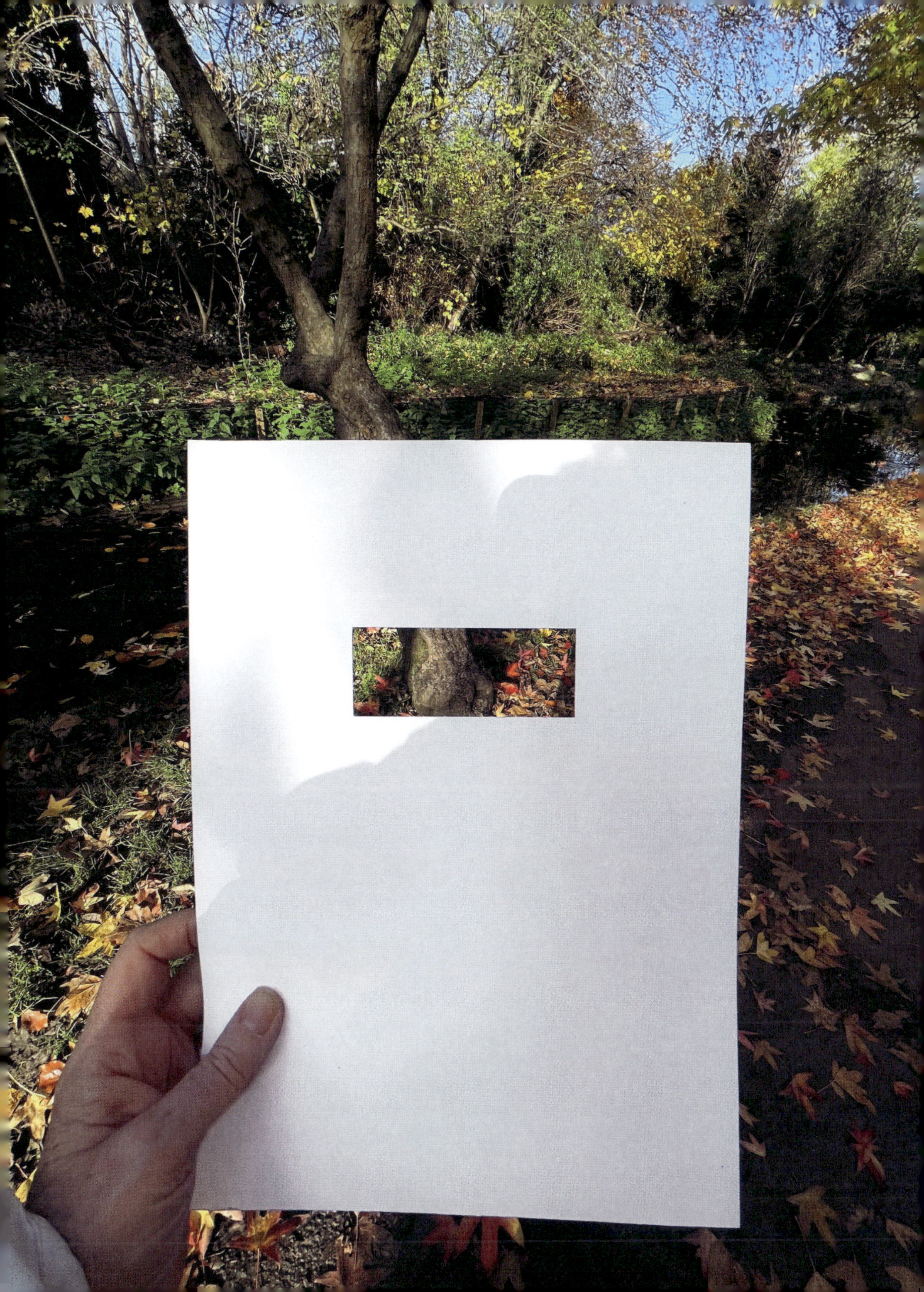

Do it FOR LOVE

The designer Milton Glaser said, 'Work for people you love'. It's not always possible to do things for love, but I find that when I do, what I create truly reflects that sentiment. If I'm struggling to start or complete an artwork, I imagine it's for someone I care about, someone I love or someone I deeply admire. Somehow, by shifting this perspective, I'm able to view the work more objectively and make some of the tougher decisions about what's working and what isn't.

PICK UP A PEBBLE

PAINTING ON PEBBLES OR STONES

I've always been fascinated by stones and pebbles, each one a miniature time capsule. My art on these stones leans towards graphic minimalism. Rather than pre-planning, I work instinctively, holding the stone in my hand for a while before starting. I sometimes use acrylic gouache for painting or, at other times, a dip pen and acrylic ink for detailed linework.

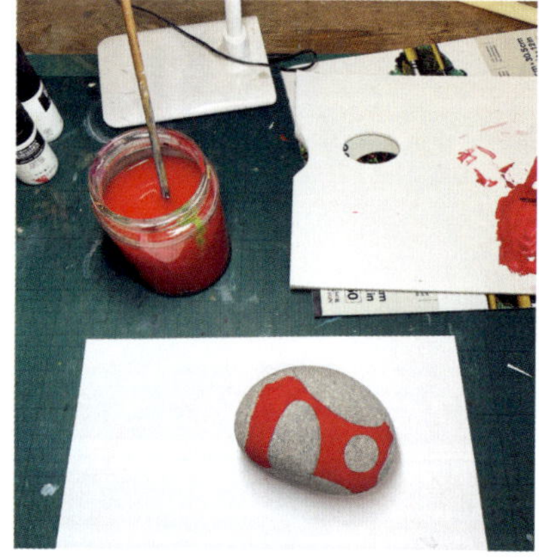

Creative exercise

Collect stones or pebbles where permitted, or find them at garden centres. Use masking tape to create shapes or lines. Paint, then remove the tape to reveal your art. As you grow more confident, try working freestyle and intuitively. Each pebble is unique, and your artwork will be too.

Creative quickie

Wander along a beach or riverbed and search for a specific type or colour of stone. This is a great exercise for focus and observation.

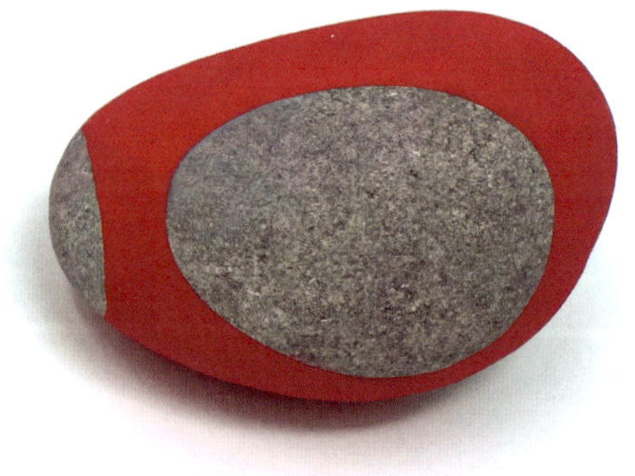

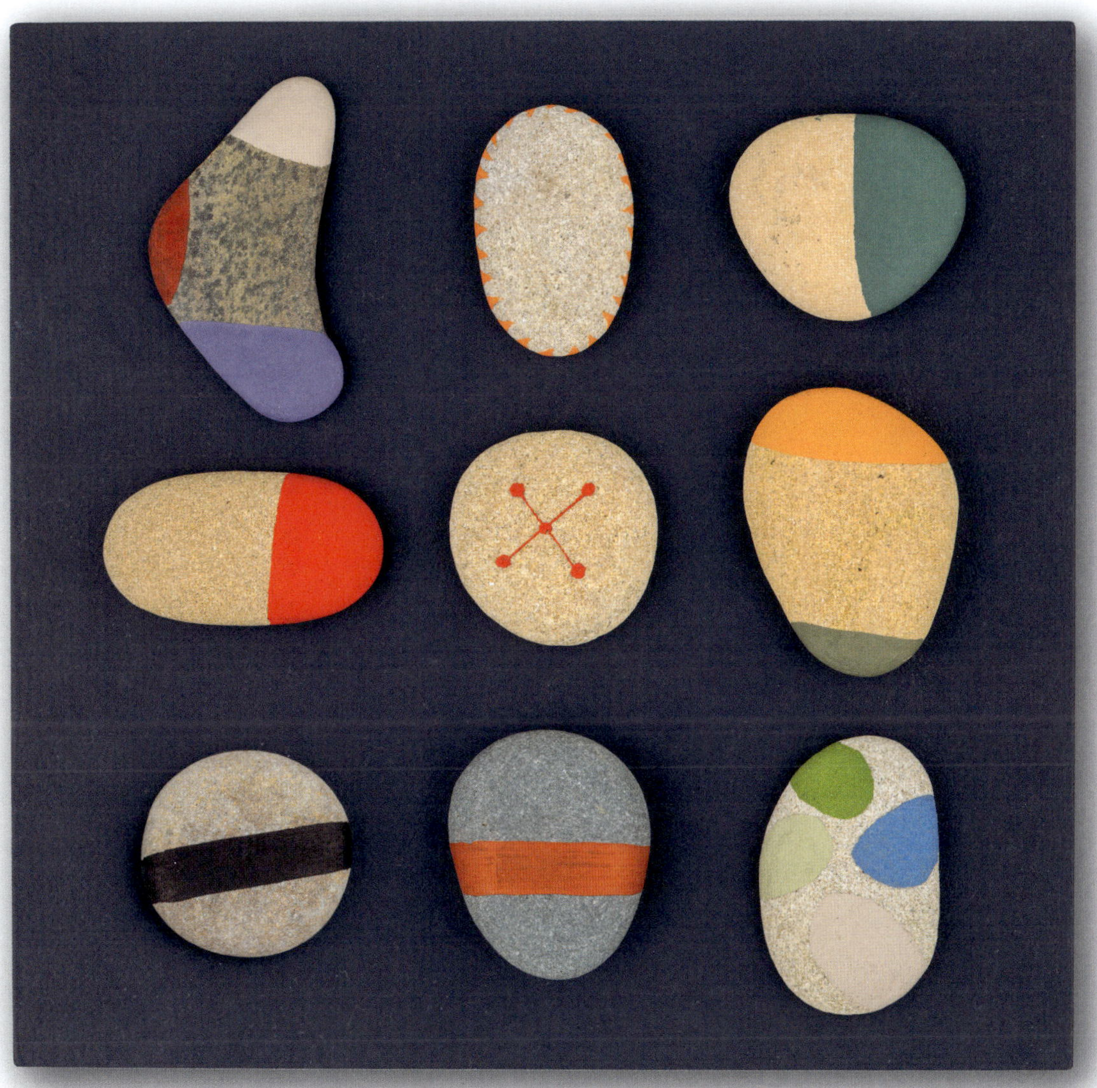

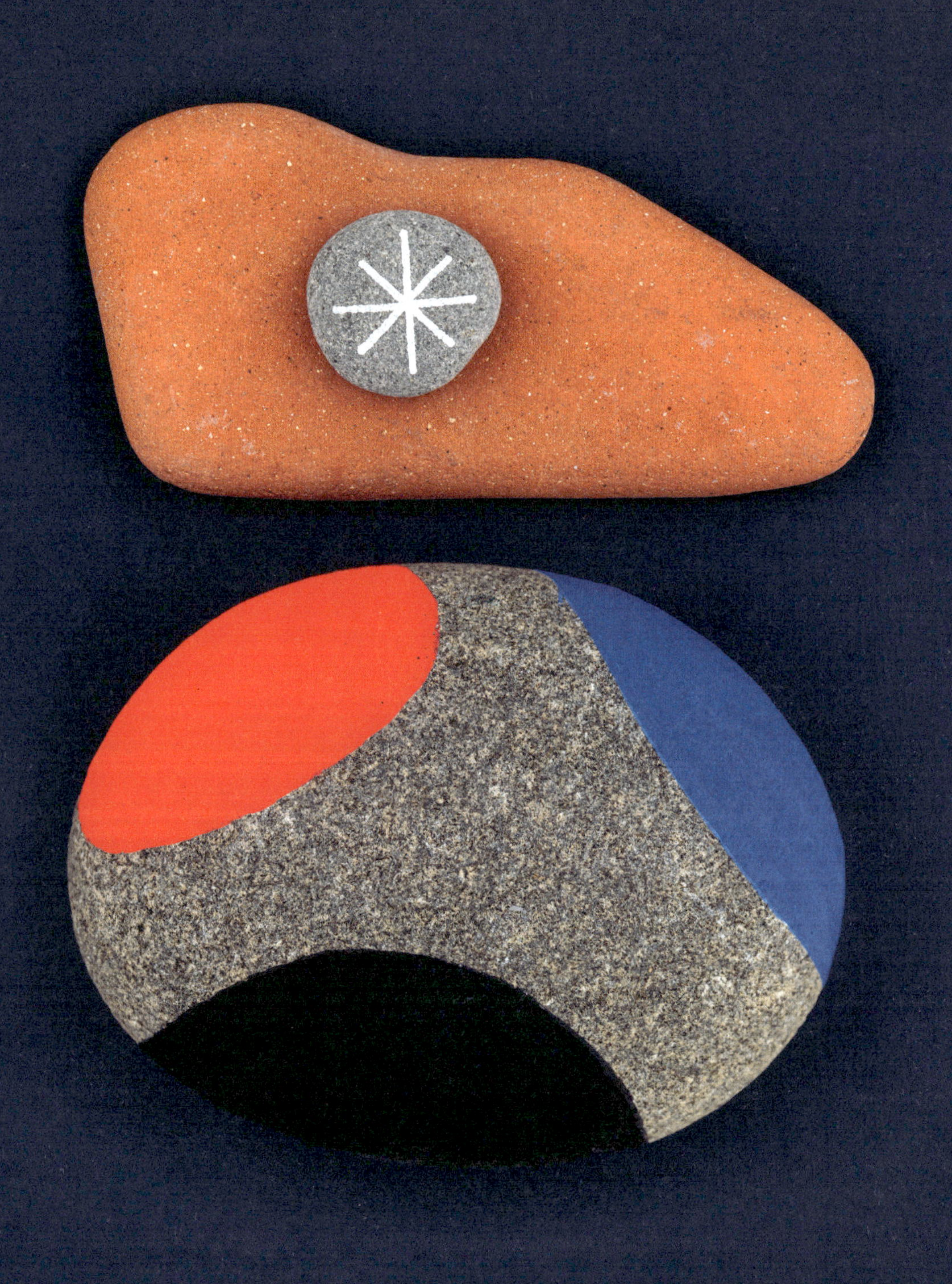

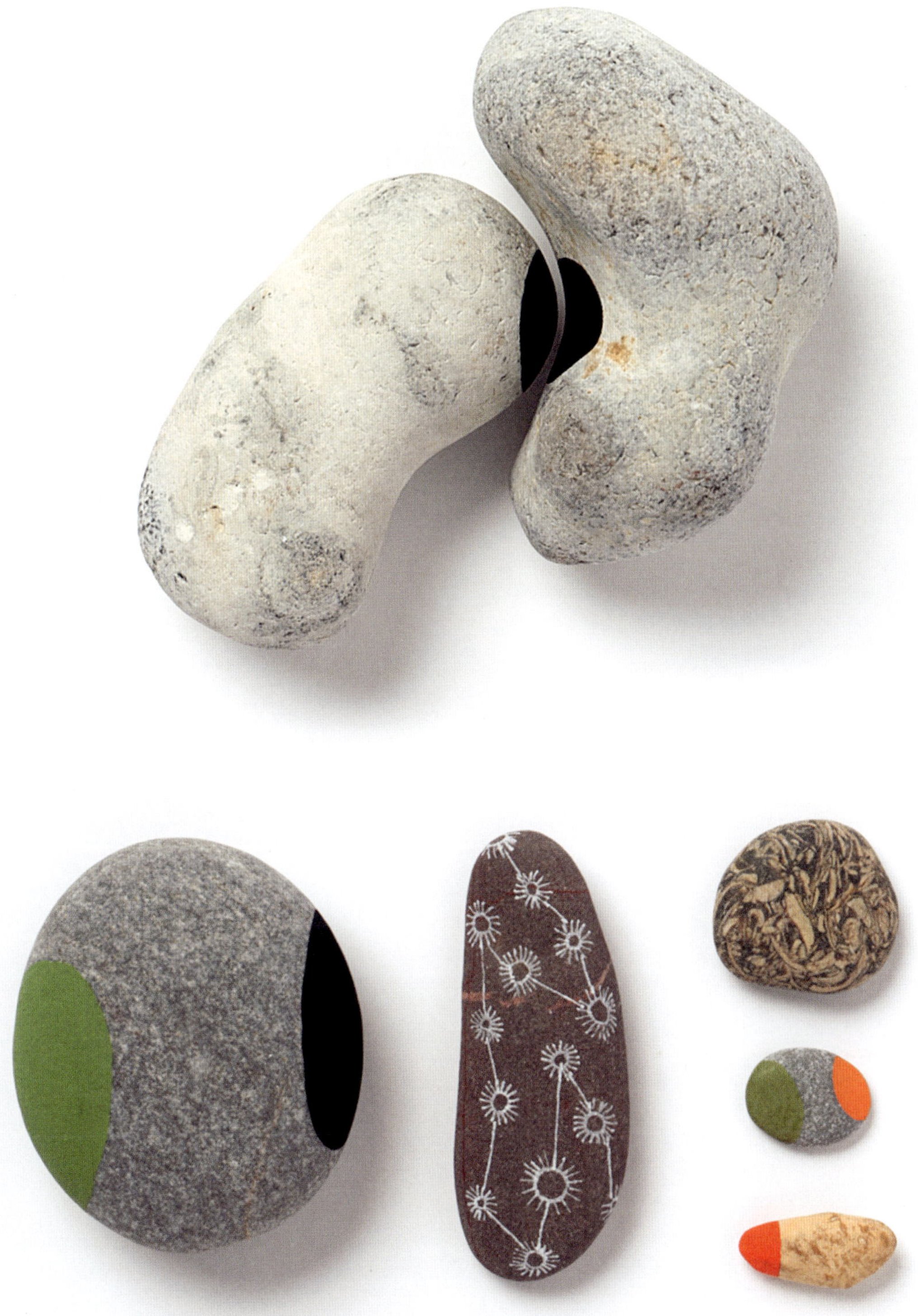

A CUP OF TEA

DRAWING ON CERAMICS

Personalize your own cup and saucer with drawings or lettering. Here I've drawn a diagram on how to make the perfect Scottish cup of tea. You will need to buy an oil-based ceramic paint pen that is non-toxic. They come in all different colours. You will also need a blank ceramic cup or plate. Follow the manufacturer's instructions – some may need to be baked in the oven for 30 minutes to cure.

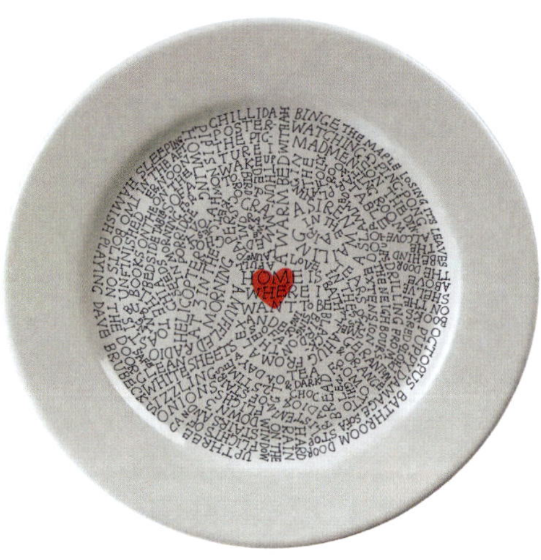

Creative exercise

I created a plate design inspired by the concept of 'home', featuring words of what home means to me. Make your own plate that captures your idea of home, where food often plays a big role.

Creative inspiration

The painted jelly moulds of painter Lubaina Himid.

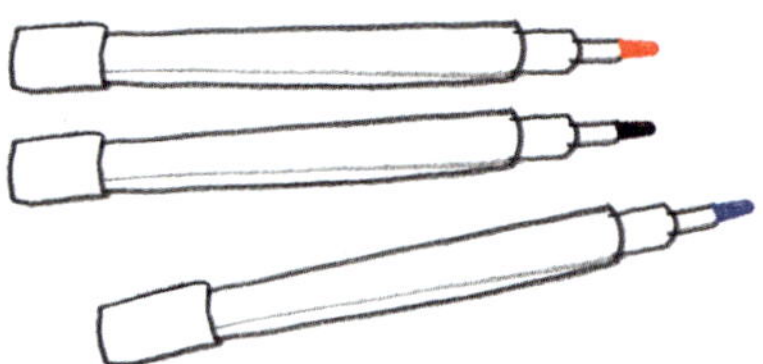

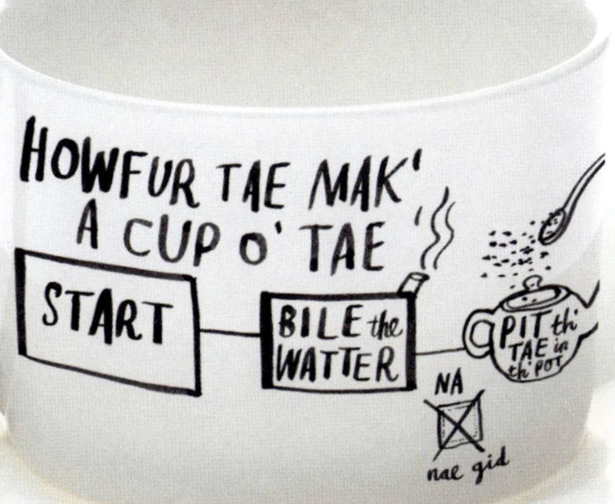

HOWFUR TAE MAK' A CUP O' TAE
START
BILE the WATTER
PIT th' TAE in th' POT
NA
nae gid

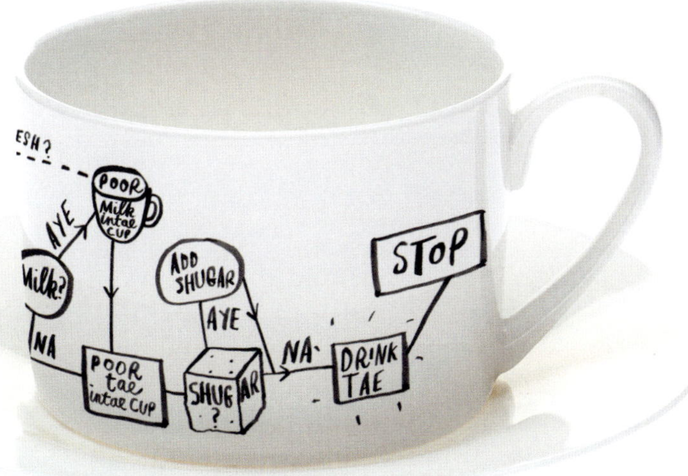

ESH?
POOR Milk intae CUP
AYE
Milk?
NA
POOR tae intae CUP
ADD SHUGAR
AYE
SHUGAR?
NA
DRINK TAE
STOP

REPEAT REPEAT

SIMPLE REPEAT PATTERN

While digital tools make it simple to create a repeat pattern template, there's a unique joy in making one by hand. Learning the manual method enriches your understanding of the creative process. After making your template, it's easy to scan it using a phone or scanner. From there, you can print it with your home printer or at a professional print shop. These repeat patterns can be used in textile design, wallpapers, stationery, ceramic tiles or digital backgrounds – to name only a few!

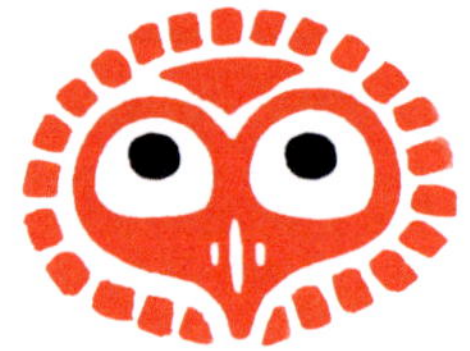
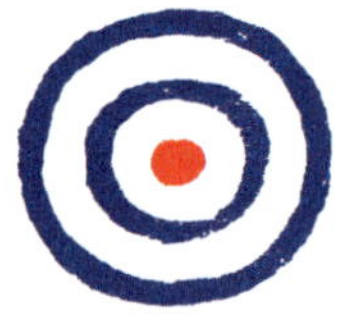

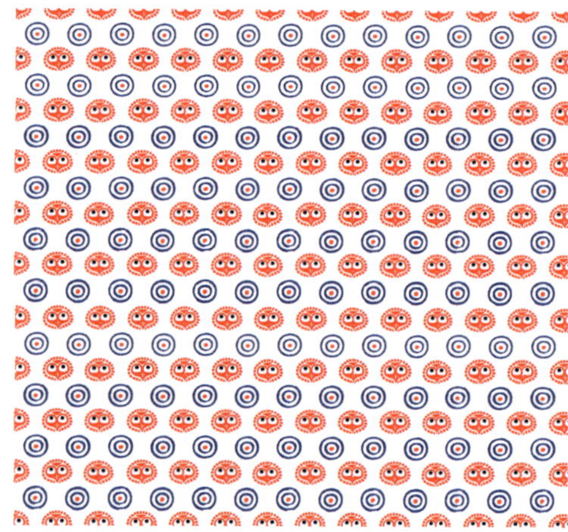

Creative exercise

Choose a theme or artist and use that as inspiration to make a design for a bespoke wrapping paper.

Creative inspiration

Look at the work of Anni Albers or research the ancient Persian and Indian paisley pattern.

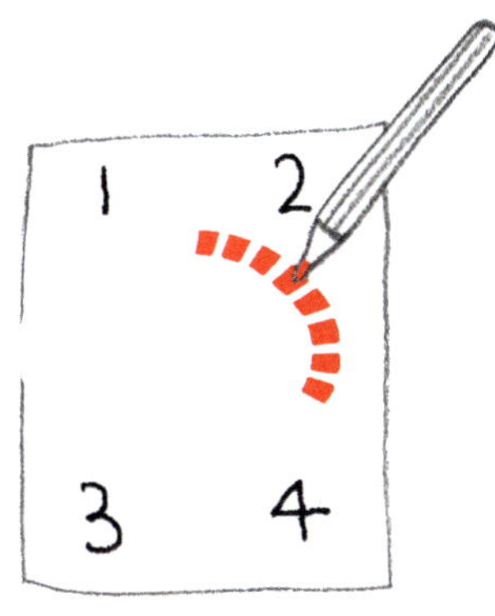

1. Number a sheet of paper in pencil, as shown, and draw your design in the middle.

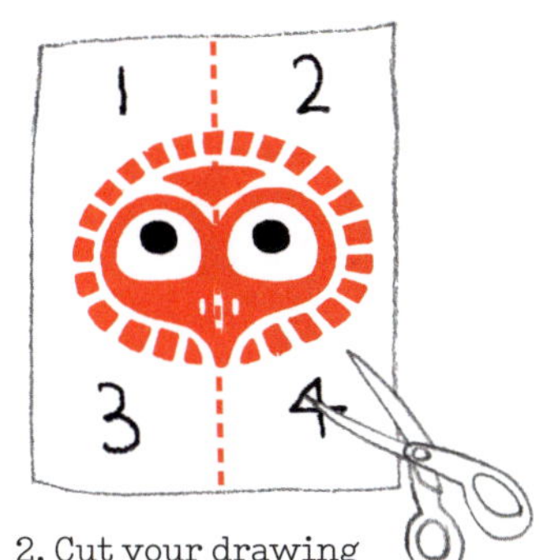

2. Cut your drawing in half vertically.

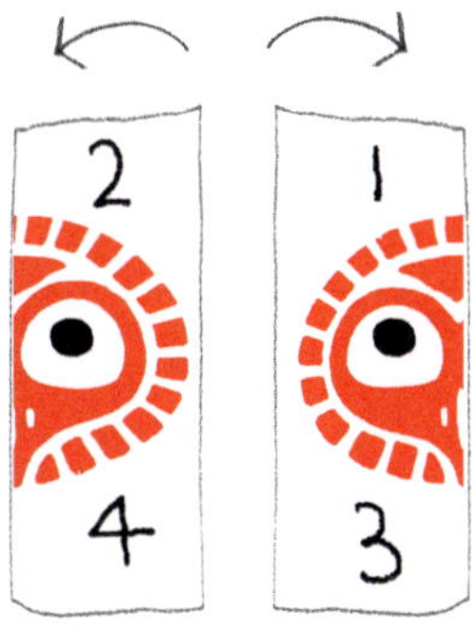

3. Swap the two halves over.

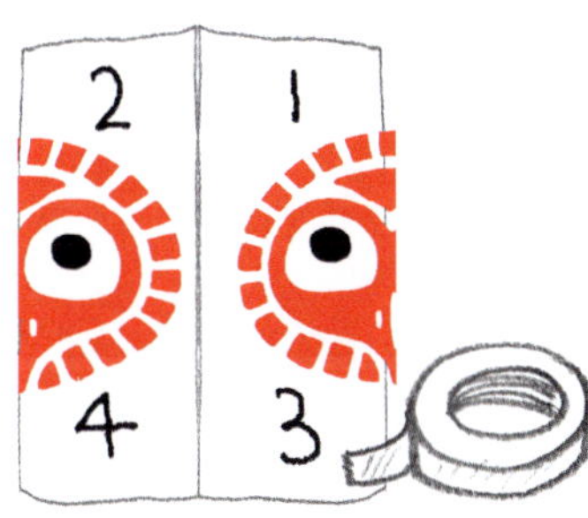

4. Tape them together.

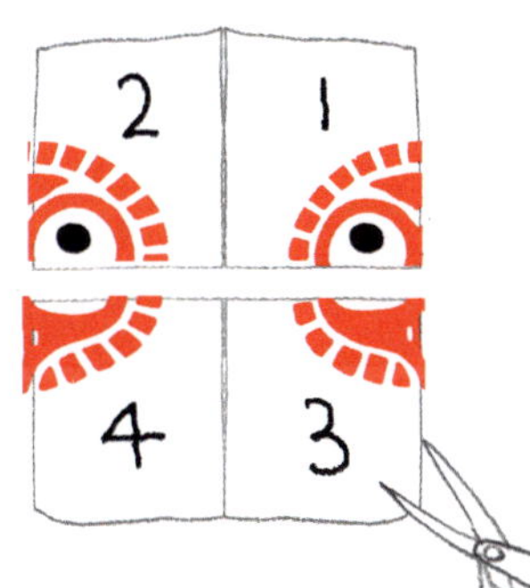

5. Now cut the drawing in half horizontally.

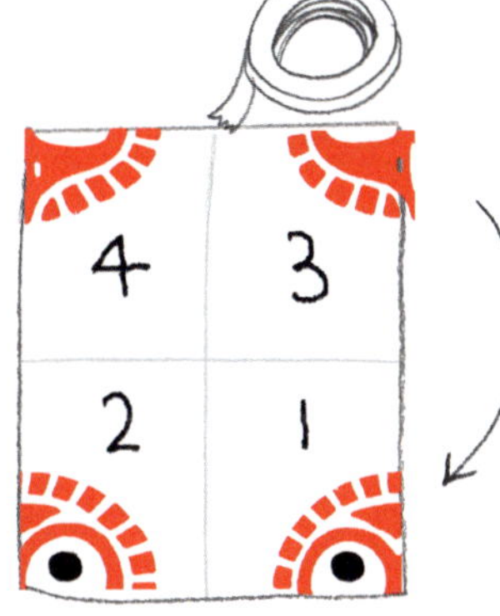

6. Swap over the top and bottom pieces and tape them together again.

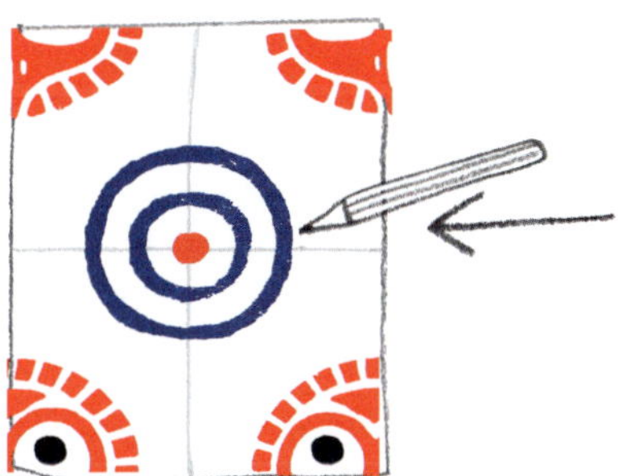

7. Draw a design in the middle of the paper. Rub out the guide numbers. This is your finished tile, ready for repeat printing.

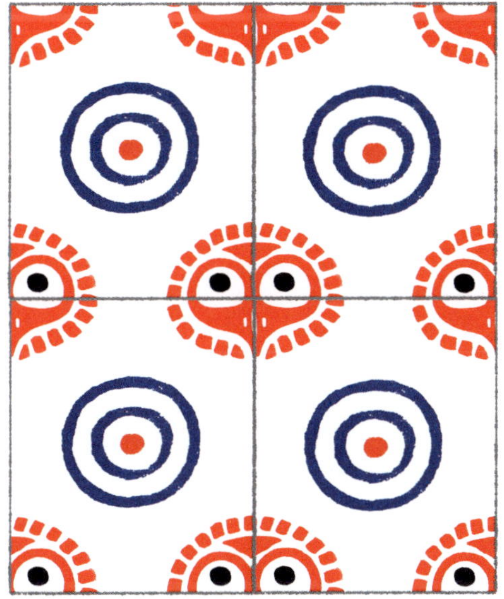

FLIP IT

DRAW WITH THE RIGHT SIDE OF YOUR BRAIN

Betty Edwards suggests turning a picture upside down before you try to draw it. This makes it harder for the brain to recognize familiar things like eyes or noses, instead allowing you to focus on simple shapes and lines. I've adapted this exercise from her book, *Drawing on the Right Side of the Brain*. Try drawing the figure on the opposite page without turning this book upside down. You'll be surprised by the results. Feel free to try it with other drawings or photographs as well.

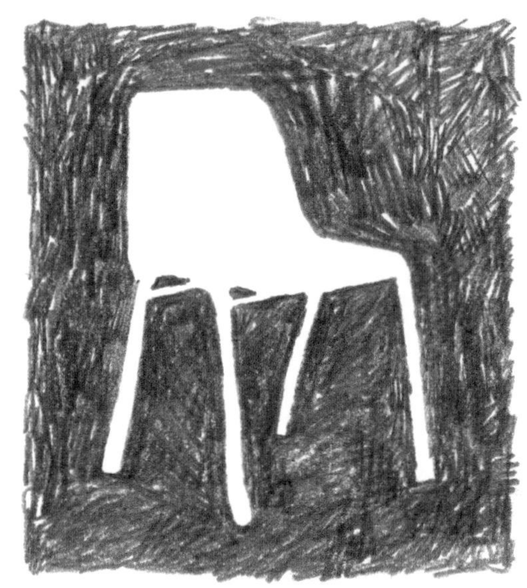

Creative exercise

Draw a chair, but instead of focusing on the chair itself, pay attention to the empty spaces around it. This will help you see the chair's shape more clearly and improve your drawing skills.

Creative inspiration

The work of Rachel Whiteread and Zarina Hashmi.

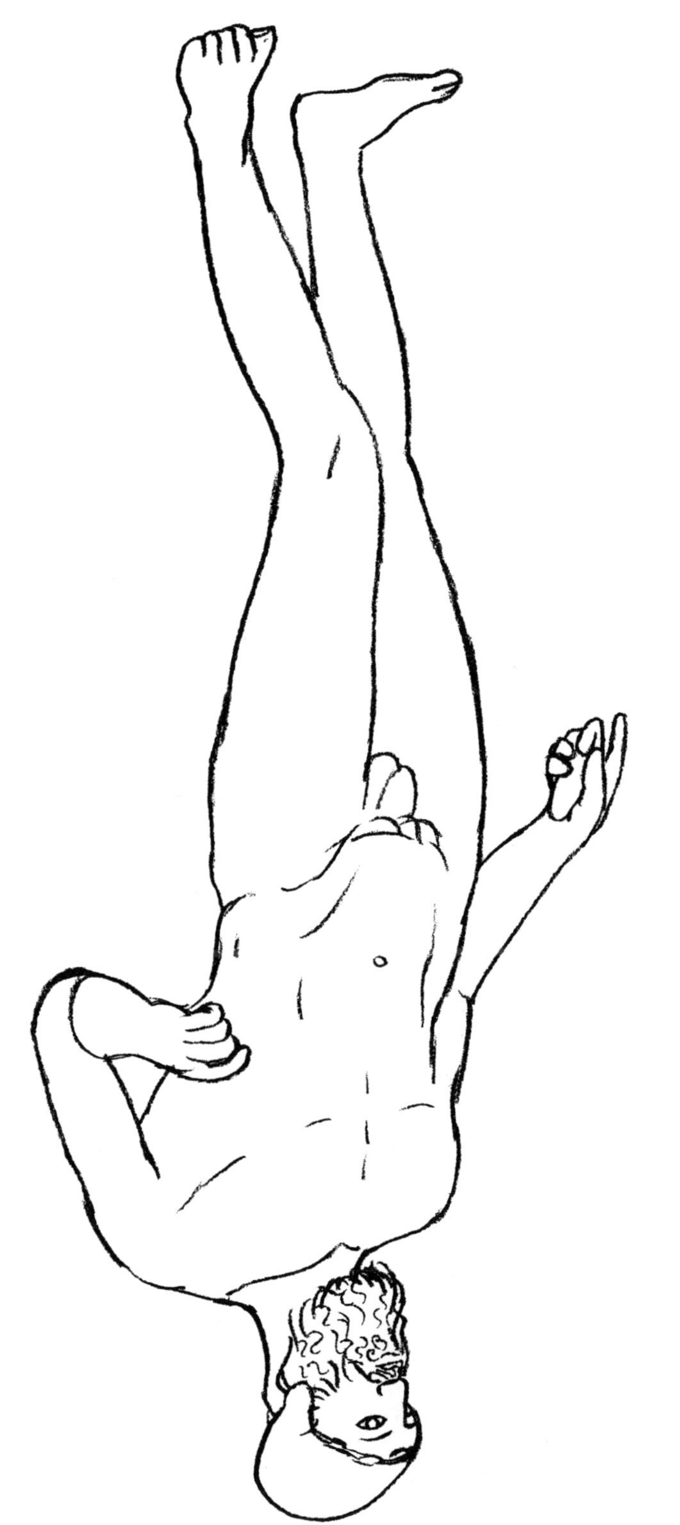

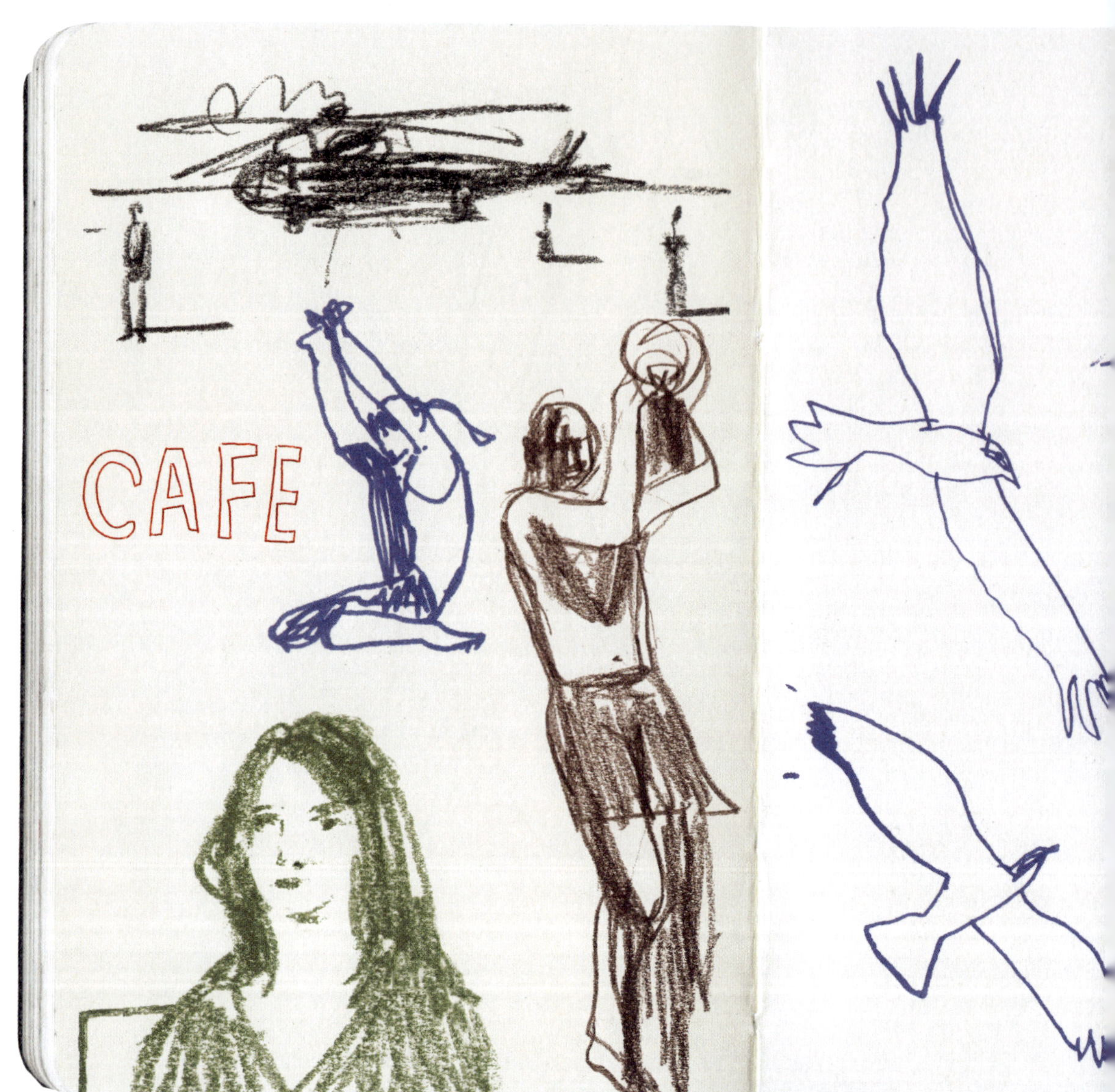
CAFE

TV SKETCHBOOK

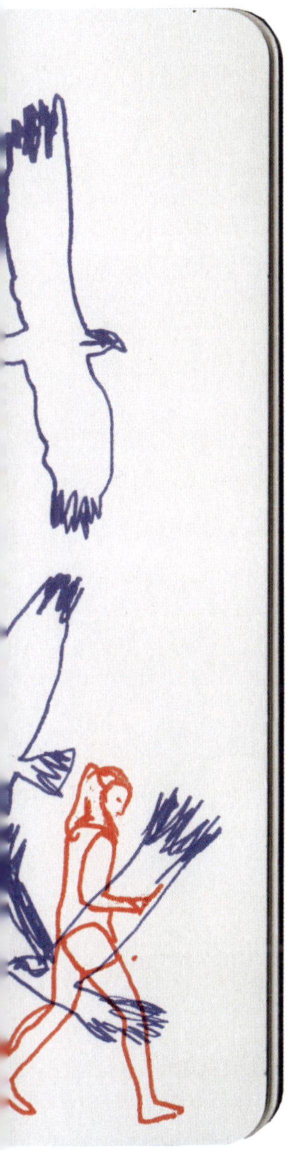

MEDIA MASH

Drawing from the television or computer can be great fun and really good for filling a sketchbook of ideas. All you need is a sketchbook, some coloured pens and pencils and a means to watch TV. Try to draw quickly and change the channel or stream often to build up a page of your sketchbook with random images and words.

Creative exercise

Using the same principle, write down all the words you can based on your observations. For example: hospital, dog, heatwave, cafe, man with pink wig, police car, etc. Write down lists, then use them to trigger ideas for short stories or visual artworks.

Creative inspiration

The sketchbooks of Serge Bloch and the multilayered work of Jean-Michel Basquiat and Kerry James Marshall.

SUN PRINT

PHOTOGRAPHIC PRINTS MADE FROM SUNLIGHT

A sun print is a user-friendly take on the traditional cyanotype, a photographic print made using UV light. When you expose the Sunprint paper to sunlight, the chemicals turn a deep, dark blue. Anything you place on the paper blocks the light, and the paper underneath stays white, giving you a negative image. You can buy a Sunprint kit from most craft stores. It's a great way to create stunning, evocative images, and really, anyone can do it.

Creative exercise

Gather a mix of objects like plants, keys, paper cut-outs, netting and feathers, and arrange them on your Sunprint paper. Expose to direct sunlight for ten minutes, remove the objects and rinse the paper. Let it dry to reveal a beautiful, evocative, blue and white image.

Creative inspiration

The cyanotypes of Anna Atkins, John Herschel, Robert Rauschenberg and Susan Weil.

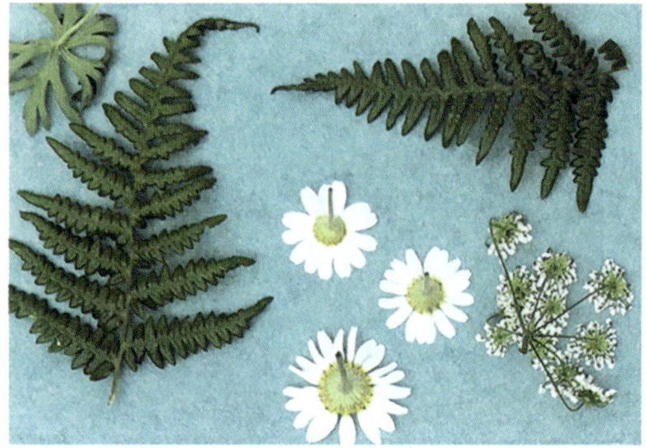

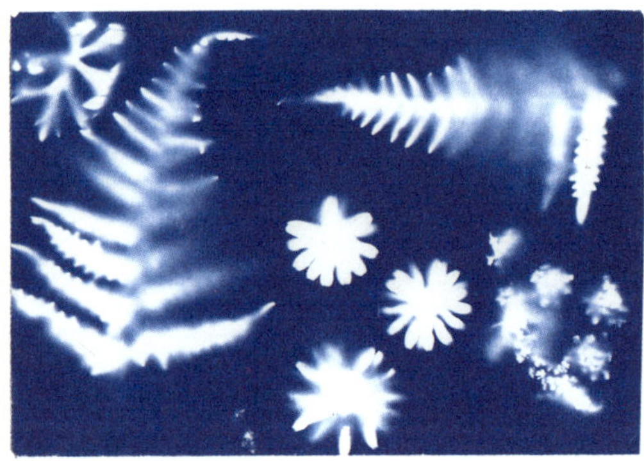

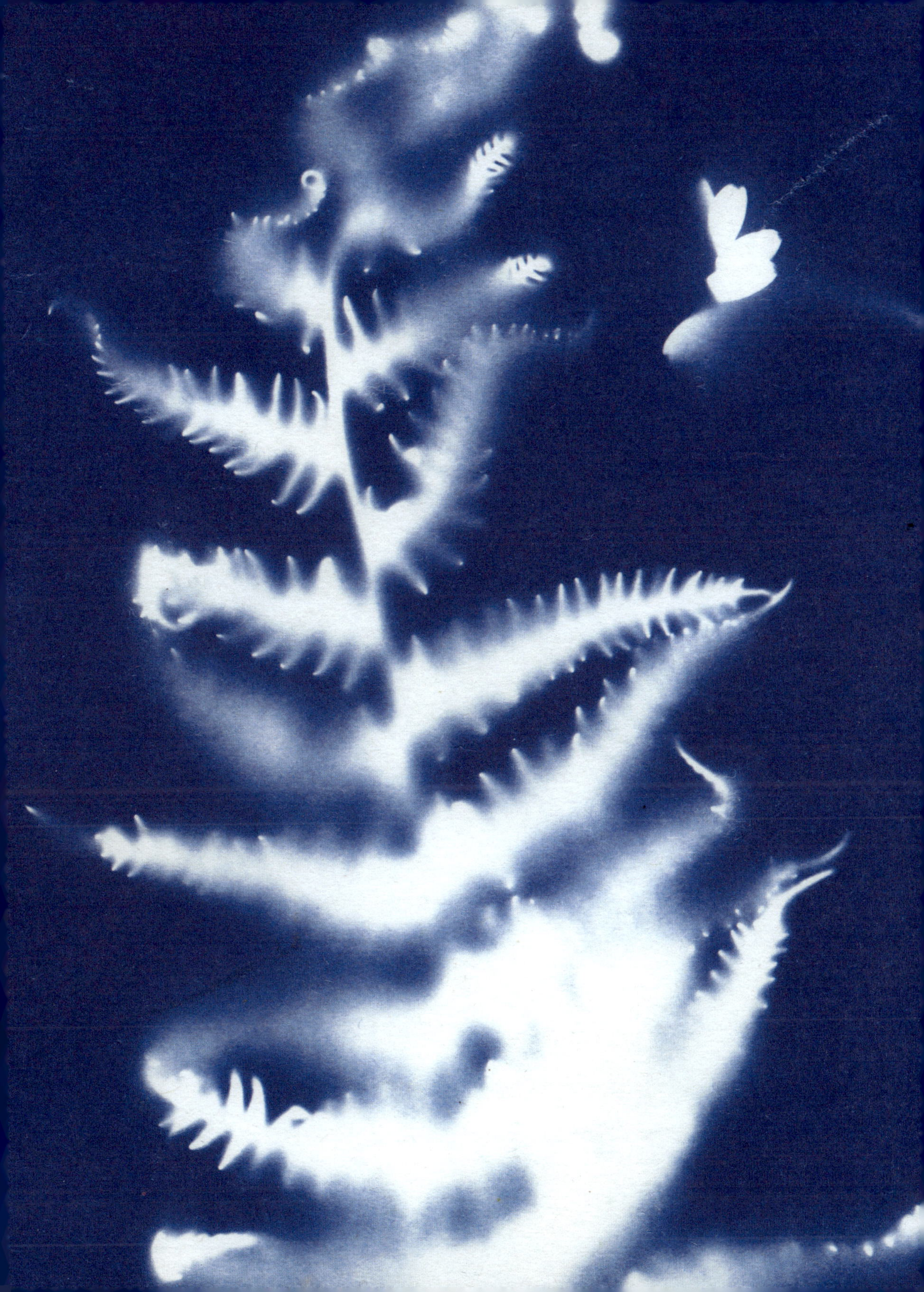

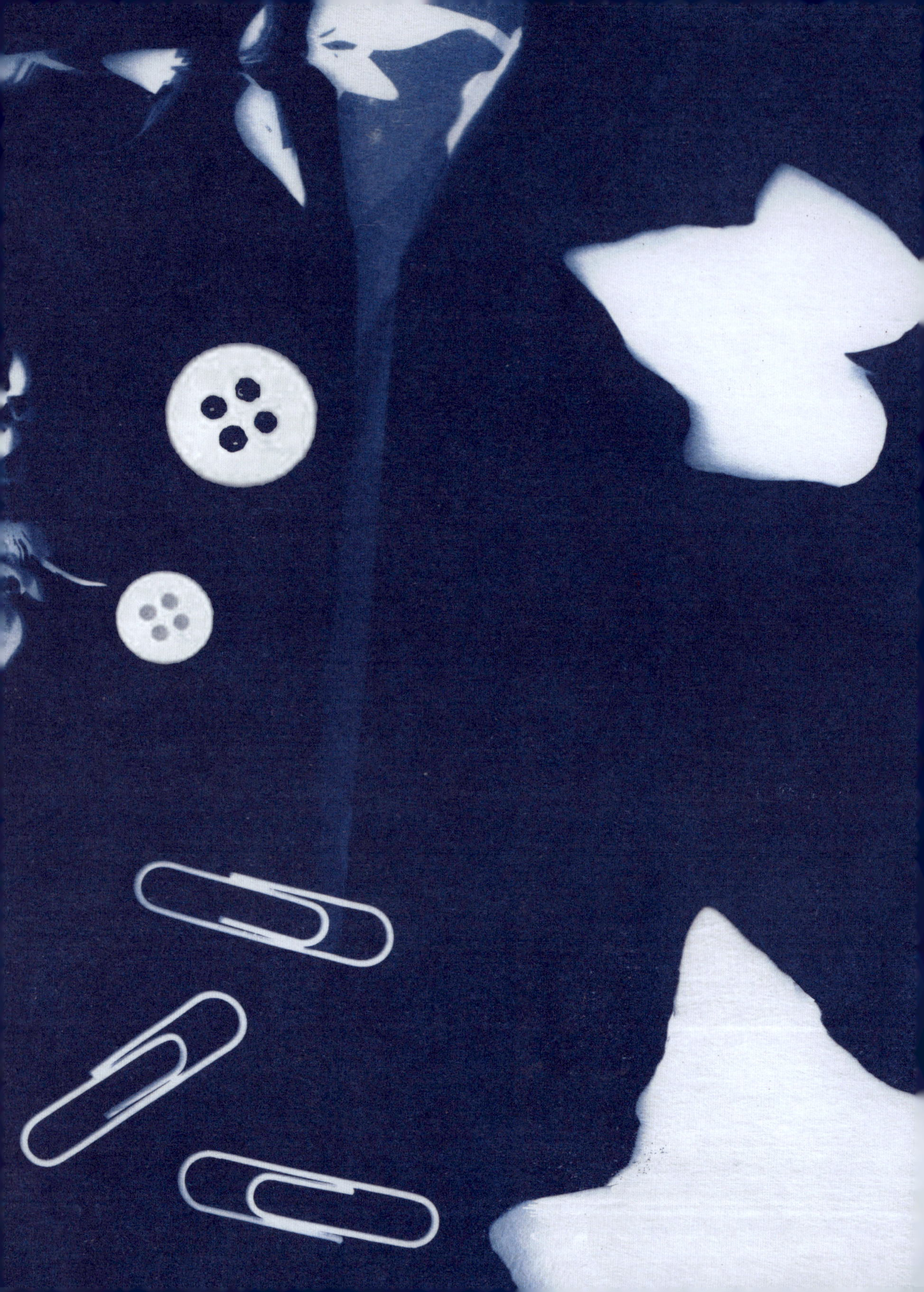

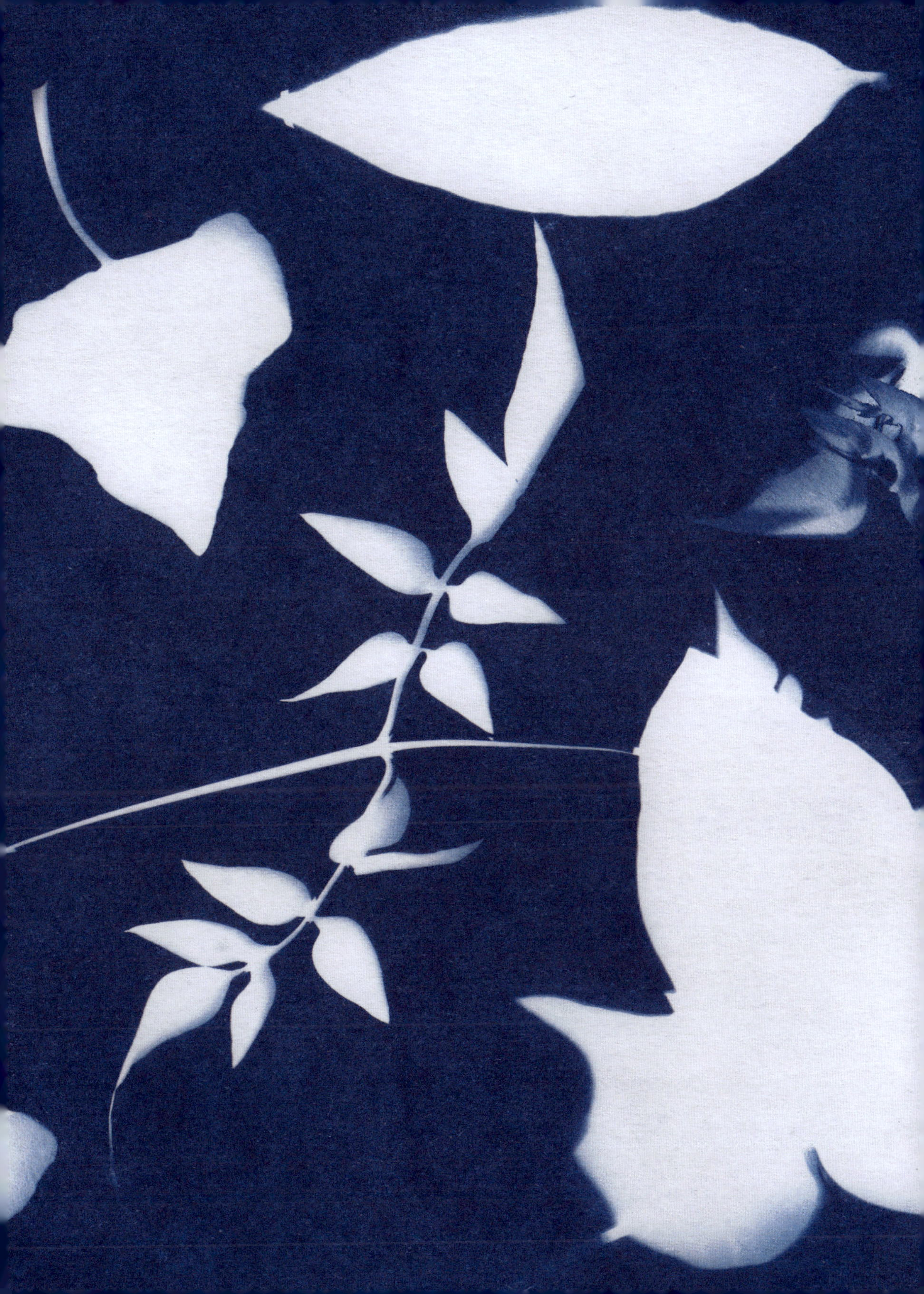

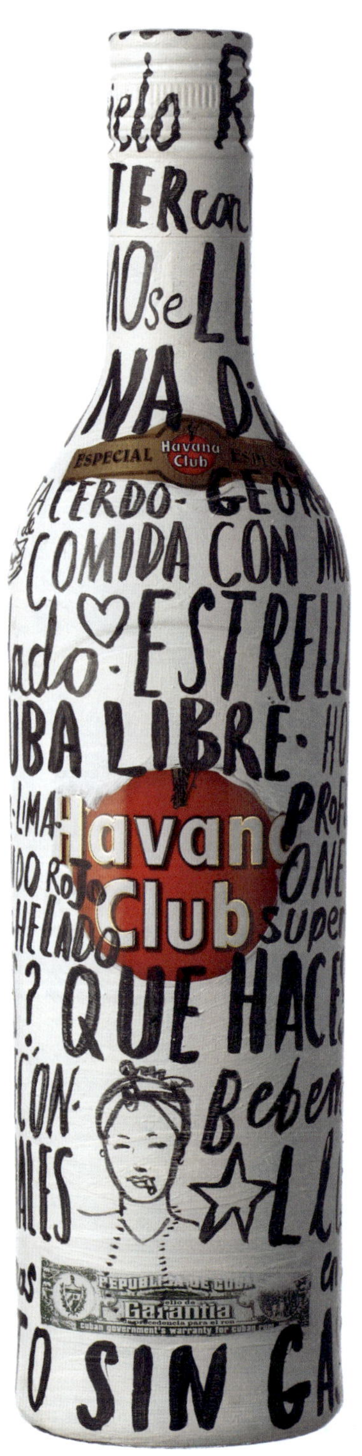

ESPECIAL Havana Club ESPECIAL
Havana Club
COMIDA CON M
ESTRELL
UBA LIBRE
QUE HACES
REPUBLICA DE CUBA
Garantia
Cuban government's warranty for cuban
SIN GA

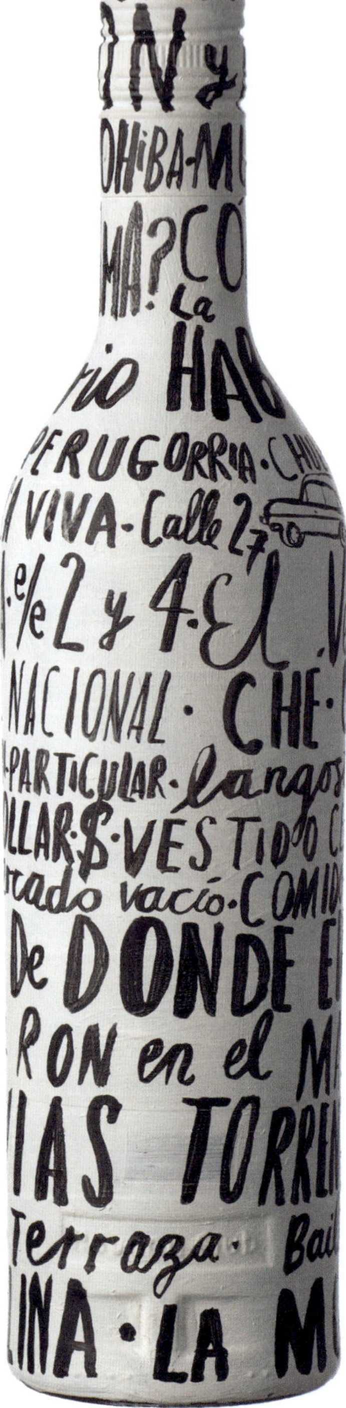

La HAB
VIVA · Calle 27
NACIONAL · CHÉ
PARTICULAR · langos
VESTIDO
vacío · COMID
De DONDE E
RON en el M
IAS TORRE
Terraza · Bai
INA · LA M

ART ON A BOTTLE

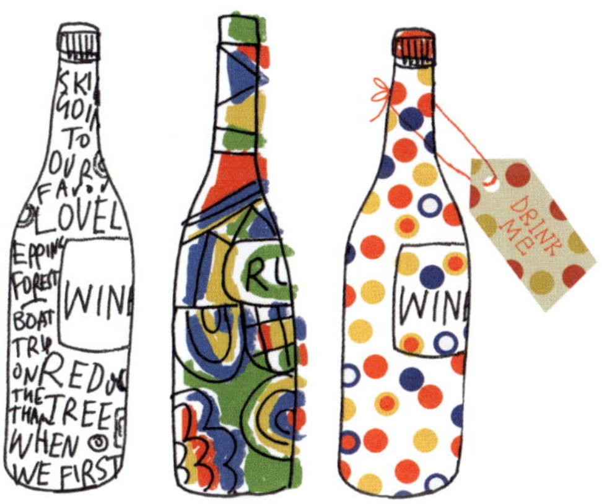

TURN OBJECTS INTO ART

I enjoy painting on reclaimed objects, from old jewellery boxes to bottles. This bottle was inspired by my trip to Cuba. It's coated in white acrylic and features lettering and drawings based on my travel experiences. I've customized similar bottles as gifts, tailoring the themes to the recipient; it makes a lovely, personal present. Acrylic paint pens work well on glass.

Creative exercise

Inscribe cherished memories or personal messages on a bottle for a friend. Create a complementary 'drink me' label for it too: punch a hole into a piece of stiff paper or card, decorate and attach it to the bottle with cord.

Creative inspiration

The work of Betye Saar and outsider artists like Howard Finster.

WILD WEEDS

LEAF PRINTING

I found revisiting this childhood activity to be incredibly rewarding. I spent many days sourcing leaf, weed and grass shapes. This, in itself, was a wonderful activity that brought me into the present moment. The leaves and flowers I've printed here have all been printed using good-quality coloured ink pads, which pick up more texture than paint. For small leaves or flowers, press them into the pad; for larger ones, use the pad to 'dab' the leaf. Using thin, smooth paper also helps; in fact, most of these were printed on inexpensive photocopy paper.

Creative exercise

Once you have printed lots of leaves and flowers, try printing some of them as a repeat pattern on a larger sheet of paper or collage them together.

Creative quickie

Collect the leaves without printing: the experience itself is worthwhile.

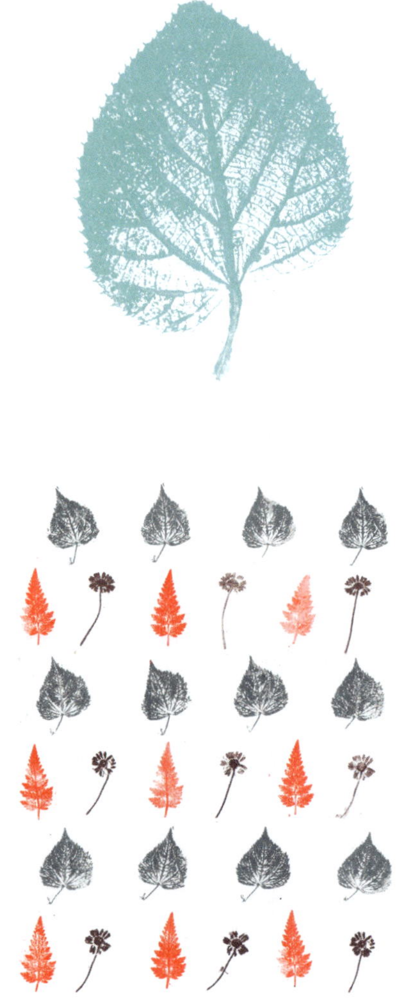

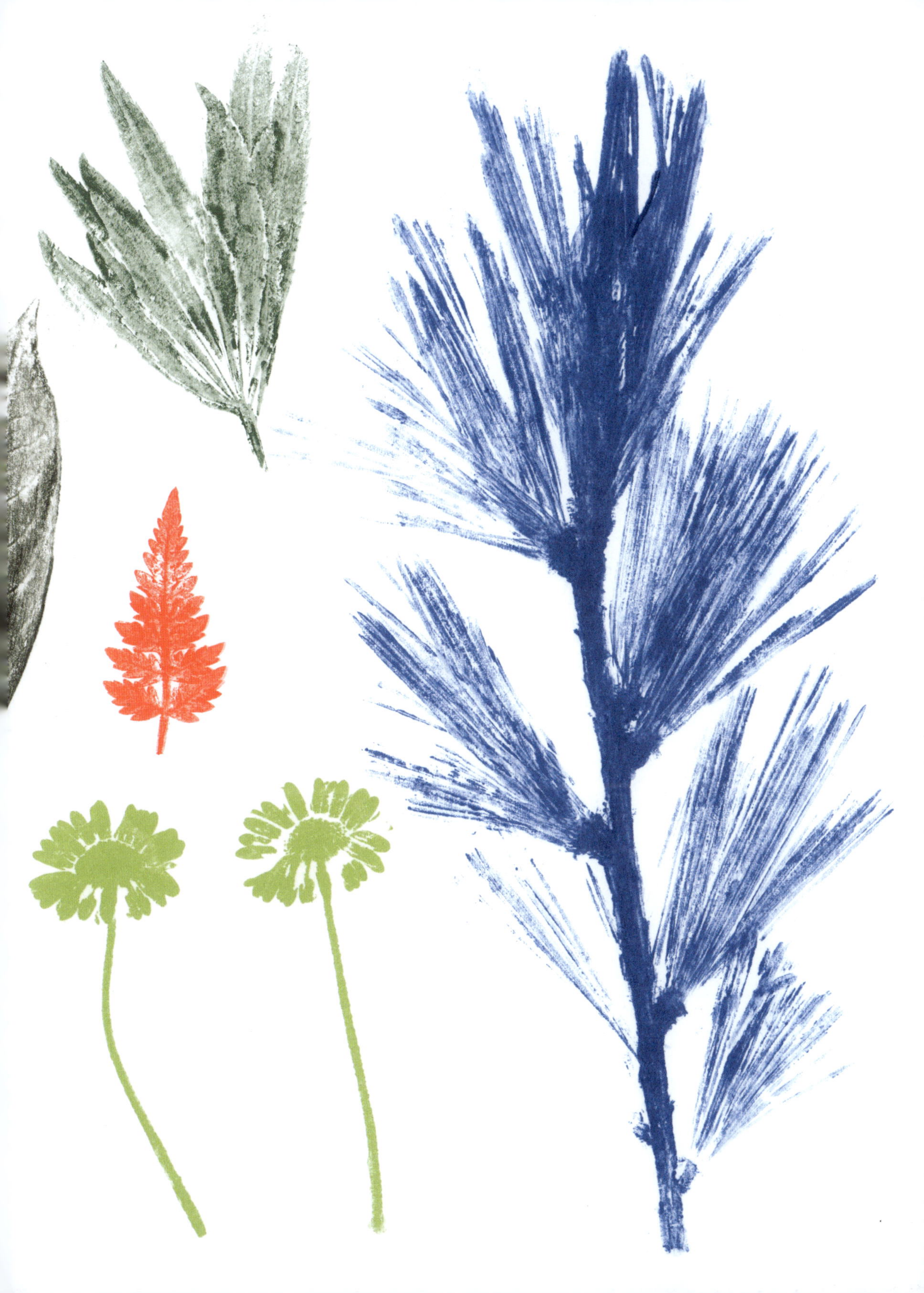

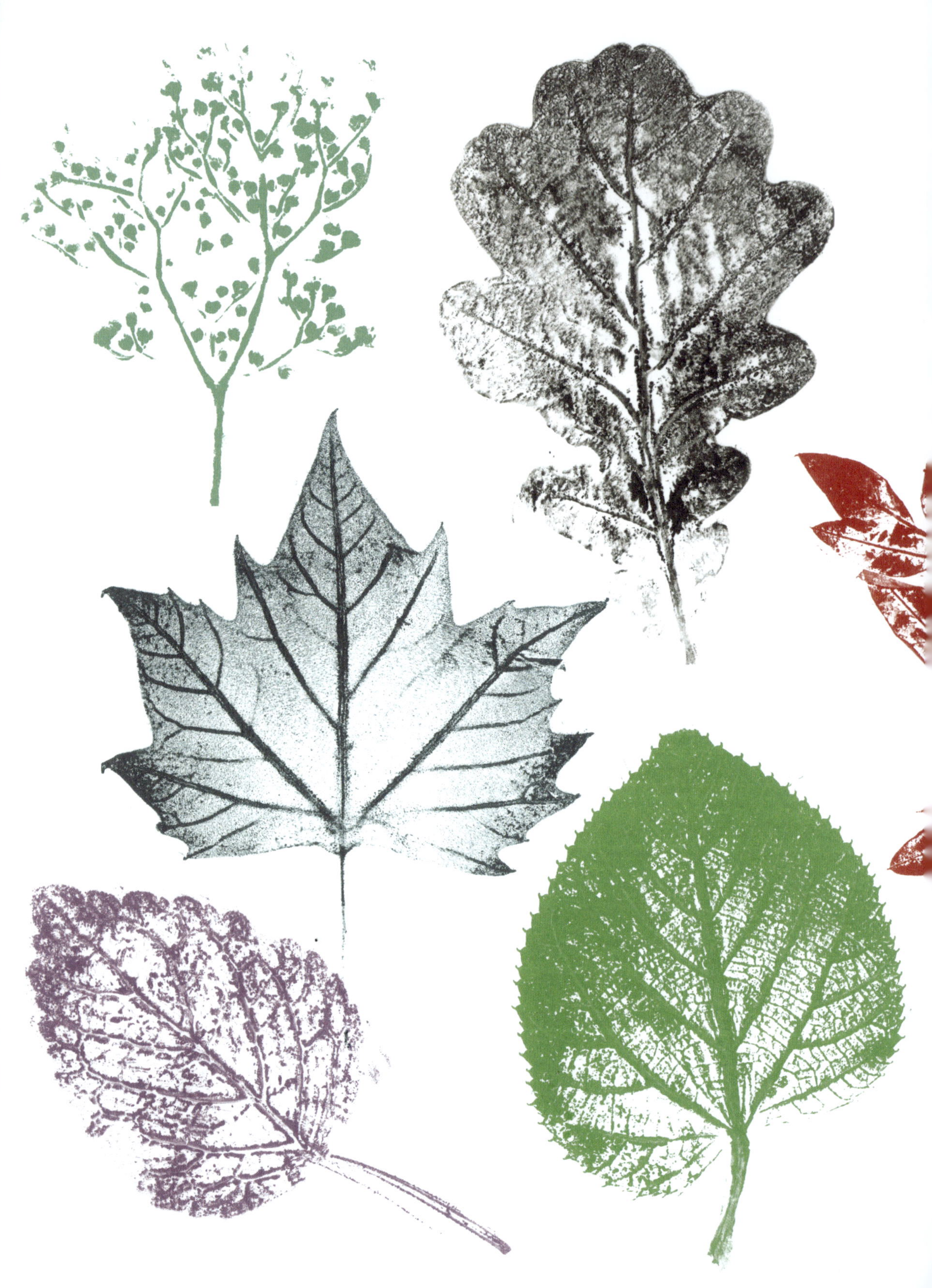

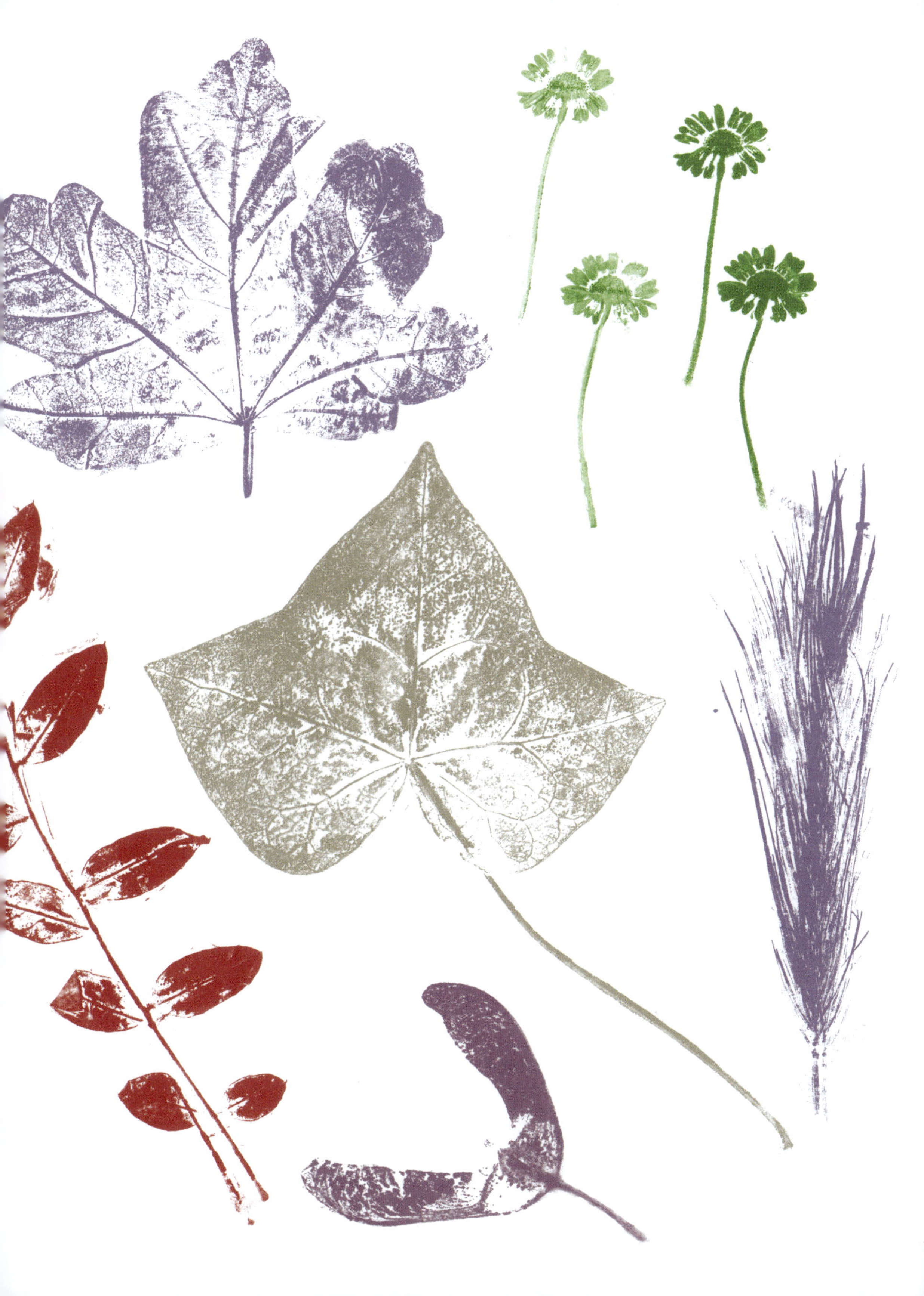

LISTEN UP

A SENSORY EXERCISE

We hear background noises every day but we rarely actually listen to them. Set aside 30 minutes of your day to fully concentrate on all the sounds around you. You can be out on a walk or sitting in a room. It doesn't matter if the sounds are unpleasant – a car engine roaring, someone shouting or an airplane overhead. The juxtaposition of this kind of noise with birdsong or the soft fall of rain becomes part of the day's symphony of sounds.

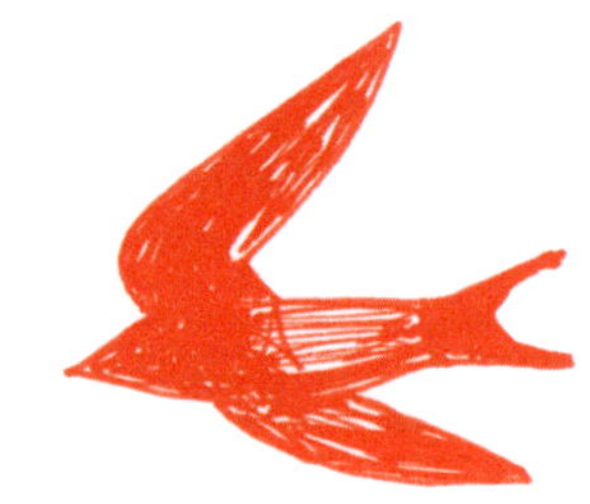

Creative exercise

Put on a song or soundtrack for around three minutes and don't do anything else while you concentrate fully on listening. Play it again and, this time with a pencil and paper, or your sketchbook, make some marks that you think relate to the sounds.

Creative inspiration

John Cage said, 'Everything we do is music.' Listen to his music.

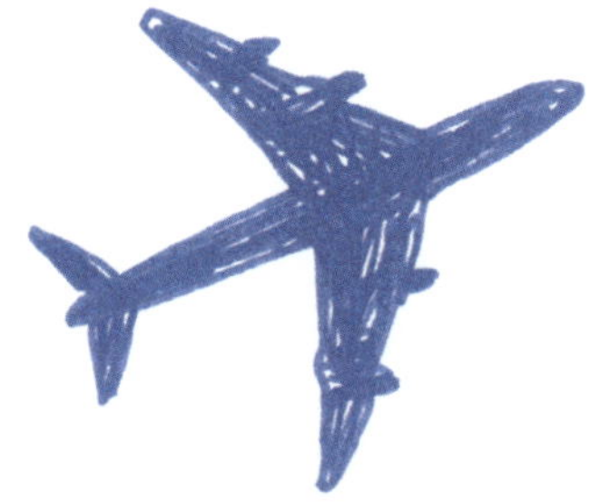

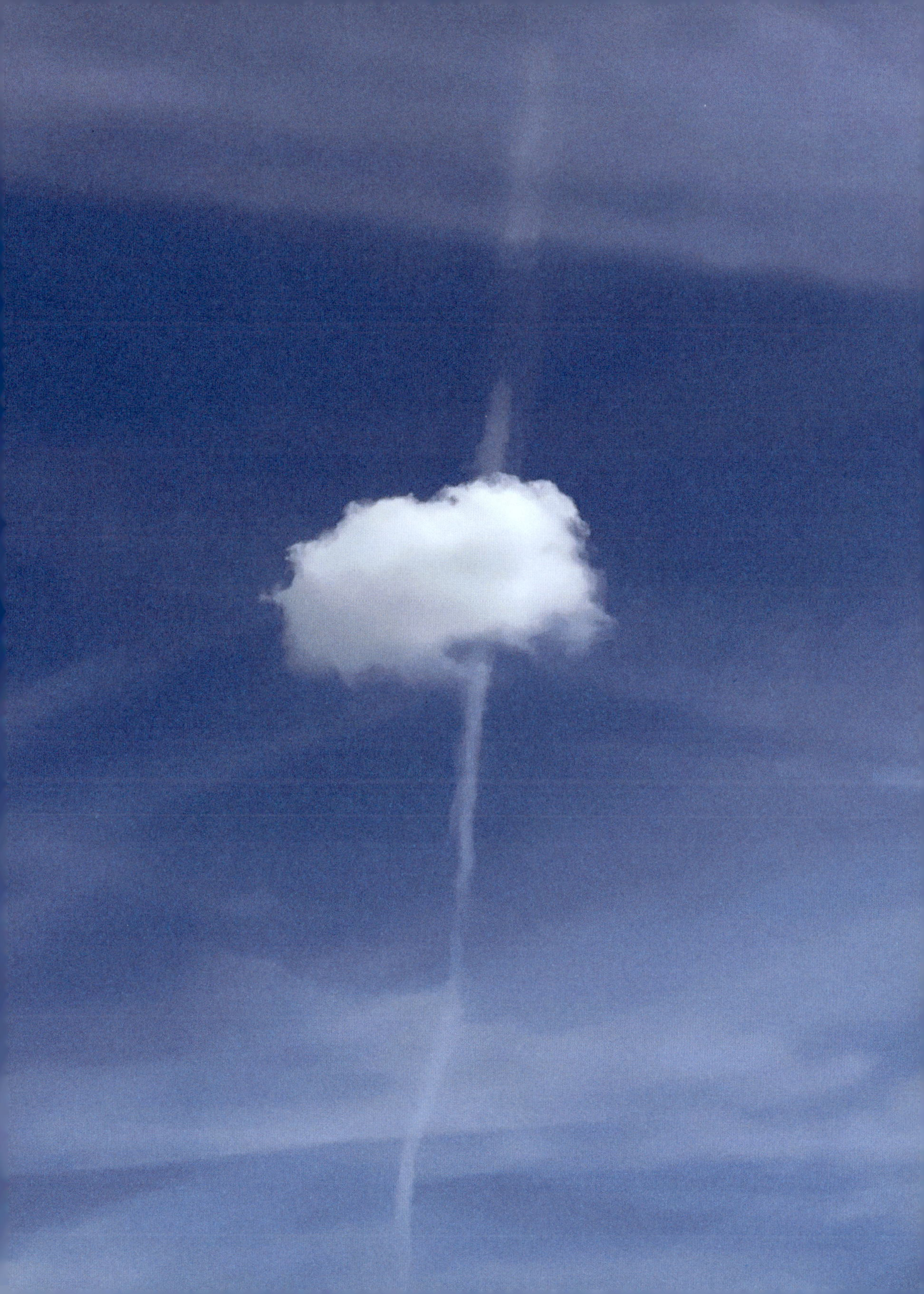

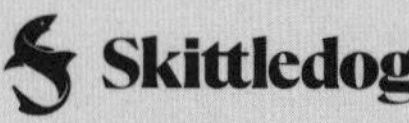

Skittledog

First published in the United Kingdom in 2024 by
Skittledog, an imprint of Thames & Hudson Ltd,
181A High Holborn, London WC1V 7QX

Make Every Day Creative © 2024 Thames & Hudson Ltd,
London

Text and illustrations © M. Deuchars Ltd 2024

All Rights Reserved. No part of this publication may
be reproduced or transmitted in any form or by any
means, electronic or mechanical, including photocopy,
recording or any other information storage and
retrieval system, without prior permission in writing
from the publisher.

British Library Cataloguing-in-Publication Data
A catalogue record for this book is available from
the British Library

ISBN 978-1-837-76015-2

Printed and bound in China by C&C Offset Printing
Co., Ltd.

Be the first to know about our new releases,
exclusive content and author events by visiting
skittledog.com
thamesandhudson.com
thamesandhudsonusa.com
thamesandhudson.com.au